Vocabulary Expansion I

Vocabulary Expansion I

Dorothy Rubin

Trenton State College

MACMILLAN PUBLISHING CO., INC.
New York

COLLIER MACMILLAN PUBLISHERS
London

Macmillan Publishing Co., Inc.
866 Third Avenue, New York, New York 10022

Collier Macmillan Canada, Ltd.

Printing: 1 2 3 4 5 6 7 8   Year: 2 3 4 5 6 7 8 9 0

With love to my understanding and supportive husband, Artie,
my delightful daughters, Carol and Sharon,
my precious granddaughter, Jennifer,
my dear brothers Herb and Jack,
and in memory of my dear mother, Clara.

PREFACE

Vocabulary development is an essential factor in reading comprehension. It is an important element in the successful completion of any academic curriculum and forms a standard component of academic achievement and aptitude tests. *Vocabulary Expansion I* and *Vocabulary Expansion II* provide a systematic, participatory approach to building and retaining a functional college-level vocabulary.

The two texts apply a number of sound psychological learning principles to vocabulary building. Words are presented in graduated levels of difficulty. The learning process in each lesson is stimulated by exercises and puzzles and reinforced by access to the solutions for self-evaluation of progress. Students' individual differences are accommodated not only in the self-contained chapters that permit each reader to work at his or her own pace, but also in the extra practice for those who need it and in the extension into more difficult words for those who are ready to absorb them.

Overlearning, the repetition of experience in different circumstances, shapes the instruction because it is essential to the retention of information. A word once introduced will usually recur in many subsequent exercises, for the later exercises build on what has been presented in earlier ones.

Although each book has a pedagogical structure, the structure is diffused among a variety of practices and drills, as well as in the crossword puzzles, word scrambles and squares, analogy activities, and cartoons. To heighten interest, more difficult words are presented in a more challenging approach. Extra practices appear in each chapter as a separate section labeled "Additional Practice Sets," in which a variety of alternative exercises cover words introduced in the chapter. Tests and scoring scales permit users of the book to determine their rate of achievement.

Vocabulary Expansion I emphasizes combining forms and words derived from them. (Combining forms are defined in both texts as word parts that join with a word or another word part to form a word or a new word.) A knowledge of combining forms is fundamental to the accurate use and construction of words as well as to the understanding of their meanings.

Vocabulary Expansion II presents words derived less obviously from combining forms. Although both books present words in context, Vocabulary Expansion II stresses the use and interpretation of context clues to learn word meanings.

The two volumes are derived in large part from a single precursor, *Gaining Word Power,* Macmillan, 1978. Because each is an expanded part of one whole, the two may be used consecutively in a comprehensive vocabulary building program; each, however, constitutes a self-contained unit that can be used independently in a conventional class or in a tutorial or self-instructional program.

ACKNOWLEDGMENTS

I would like to thank Anthony English for being the personification of a perfect editor. His valuable suggestions, creative editing, intelligent insights, and uncanny wit have made working with him an extreme pleasure and privilege. I would also like to thank John Travis for being such a patient, kind, considerate, and helpful production editor. In addition, I would like to express my appreciation to the administration of Trenton State College, and particularly to Dean Philip Olio and Dr. Barbara Harned, for their continued support.

CONTENTS

CHAPTER ONE[1]

This chapter discusses the organization of this book and how one can best go about improving one's vocabulary. Let us begin by considering the importance of vocabulary growth.

THE IMPORTANCE OF VOCABULARY GROWTH

A good vocabulary and good reading go hand in hand. Unless you know the meaning of words, you will have difficulty in understanding what is read. And the more you read, the more words you will add to your vocabulary. Read the following statement:

> The misanthrope was apathetic to the sufferings of those around him.

Do you understand it? Unless you know the meanings of *misanthrope* and *apathetic*, you are not able to read the statement. In order to *read*, you must know the *meanings* of words and the way words are used in sentences.

---

[1]It is very important that you read Chapter One. This chapter introduces you to *Vocabulary Expansion I*. It gives you the information you will need to use this book successfully.

Acquiring word meanings is an important reading skill. Because of its importance, this skill is being presented in a text by itself.

THE ORGANIZATION OF THIS BOOK

Vocabulary Expansion I deals with vocabulary building through *combining forms.* (The meaning of *combining forms* will be explained to you later on in this chapter.) The emphasis is on the *overlearning* of the combining forms so that they can help you to unlock the meanings of many words. (The term *overlearning* is explained later on.) Many words made up from combining forms are presented.

Answers for the exercises are provided at the end of each chapter.

HOW EXERCISES ARE PRESENTED

The exercises are presented in three steps. The steps are the same for all exercises:

Step I.   *Presentation of new combining forms and their meanings.*
    A. Learn new combining forms with their meanings.
    B. Cover the meanings of the combining forms, read the combining forms, and try to recall their meanings. Check the answers immediately.
    C. Cover the combining forms, read the meanings, and try to recall the combining forms. Check the answers immediately.
    D. Cover the meanings of the combining forms again, read the combining forms, and write their meanings in the space provided.

Step II. *Presentation of vocabulary derived[2] from combining forms.*
Learn words with their meanings and other information as you see the words used in sentences. The words are based on the combining forms learned in Step I. (See the following section.)

Step III. *Practice.*
Use the words in several different practices to ensure overlearning. After every three exercises, crossword puzzles, word scrambles, and analogies are provided for the given combining forms and words. A multiple-choice vocabulary test and a true/false vocabulary test are supplied for Step II words. Scoring scales are given so that you will know where you stand. If you score below a certain level, you are provided with additional practice sets. In these *additional practice sets,* you are directed to restudy only the combining forms and words

---

[2]*Derived* means "made up from."

you have missed. You are provided with different practice exercises to help you to learn the words you have missed.

HOW WORDS ARE PRESENTED

The combining forms and words presented are a base from which you can increase your vocabulary quickly and easily. Combining forms and words have been selected on the basis of how often they appear in novels, stories, poems, textbooks, and other nonfiction books, newspapers, and magazines. Words that are commonly used in college lectures are also included.

Words are presented with the following information to help your understanding of the word:

1. Correct spelling and plural (abbreviated *pl.*). Only irregular plurals are shown.

2. Division into syllables. For example: bi · ol · o · gy.

3. Pronunciation. The phonetic (pronunciation) spelling of the word may differ from the regular spelling to describe the pronunciation of the word. For example: **biology** (bī · ol′ o · jē) The syllabication and pronunciation aids are combined in one entry if the phonetic spelling of the word is similar to the regular spelling of the word. Otherwise, an extra entry is given following the syllabication entry. If a word is a one-syllable word, there is obviously no syllabication entry for the word.

4. Kind of word it is: *v.* for verb, *n.* for noun, *adj.* for adjective, *adv.* for adverb, and *prep.* for preposition.

5. Meaning of the word.[3]

6. Use of the word in a sentence. Only one sentence is given for each word even though the word may have more than one meaning.

Here is an example of the presentation of a word with an extra entry:

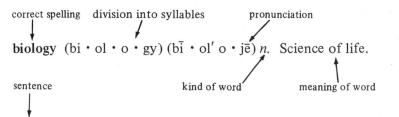

*Because I intend to be a doctor, I am taking a course in **biology** to learn about living things.*

---

[3]The meanings of the words are based on *Webster's Third New International Dictionary,* Unabridged; Funk & Wagnalls *Standard College Dictionary; Random House Dictionary of the English Language; The American Heritage Dictionary of the English Language; The World Book Dictionary;* and *Webster's New Twentieth Century Dictionary,* 2nd ed.

SPECIAL NOTES

A "Special Notes" section includes special information about words that might cause you unusual difficulty.

EXTRA WORD POWER

The combining forms presented in the "Extra Word Power" section are those often used with thousands of words. For this reason they are presented in a special boxed section. The "Extra Word Power" section will give additional help to your vocabulary growth.

ADDITIONAL WORDS

The "Additional Words" section presents some more difficult words. You can unlock their meanings by using combining forms and context clues. To help you still more, a practice activity is provided for these words.

UNDERSTANDING ANALOGIES

Analogy practice is presented after every three exercises. Analogies have to do with relationships. They are relationships between words or ideas. In order to make the best use of analogies or to supply the missing term in an analogy proportion, you must know not only the *meanings* of the words, but also the relationship of the words or ideas to one another. For example, "*doctor* is to *hospital* as *minister* is to _____ ." Yes, the answer is *church*. The relationship has to do with specialized persons and the places with which they are associated. Let's try another one: "*beautiful* is to *pretty* as ___ is to *decimate*." Although you know the meanings of *beautiful* and *pretty* and you can figure out that beautiful is more than pretty, you will not be able to arrive at the correct word to complete the analogy if you do not know the meaning of *decimate*. *Decimate* means "to reduce by one tenth" or "to destroy a considerable part of." Because the word that completes the analogy must express the relationship of more or greater than, the answer could be *eradicate* or *annihilate,* because these words mean "to destroy completely."

Some of the relationships that words may have to one another are similar meanings, opposite meanings, classification, going from particular to general, going from general to particular, degree of intensity, specialized labels, characteristics, cause-effect, effect-cause, function, whole-part, ratio, and many more. The preceding relationships do not have to be memorized. You will gain clues to these from the pairs making up the analogies; that is, the words express the relationship. For example: "*pretty* is to *beautiful*"—the relationship is degree of intensity; "*hot* is to *cold*"—the relationship is one of opposites; "*car* is to *vehicle*"—the relationship is classification.

4

PRONUNCIATION KEY

The pronunciation (the way a word sounds) of the words in this book is a simplified one based on the key presented on this page. In order to simplify pronunciation further, the author has given only long vowel markings and included only the primary accent mark (').

The accent mark (') is used to show which syllable in a word is stressed. This mark comes right after and slightly above the accented syllable. For example:

pilot (pī ′ lot)   **biology** (bī · ol′ o · jē)

In the preceding two words, the syllables *pi'* and *ol'* are sounded with more stress and are called the accented syllables. The dot (·) is used to separate syllables. Note that no dot is used between syllables when the syllable is accented. Also note that the *y* in *biology* has been changed to an *ē* and the *g* has been changed to a *j* to aid you in pronunciation.

The long vowel mark (–) also helps to indicate pronunciation. A vowel that has a long vowel mark sounds like its letter name.

A slash through a letter means that the sound it stands for is silent. For example:

bāk¢ nōt¢ āt¢ bō∤t

As an aid in pronunciation, the following key may be used:

Words ending in *tion, sion,* sound like *shun,* as in *nation.*

Words ending in *cian, tian,* and *sian* sound like *shin,* as in *Martian.*

Words ending in *cious* sound like *shus,* as in *delicious.*

Words having *ph* sound like *f* in *fat, foot,* as in *phone.*

Words ending in *ique* sound like *ēk* in *le∤k,* as in *critique, unique.*

Words ending in *le* preceded by a consonant sound like *ul* in *bull,* as in *bubble, candle.*

Words ending in *cial* sound like *shul,* as in *special.*

Words ending in *ce* sound like *s* in *safe, so,* as in *notice, sentence.*

Words beginning in *ce* or *ci* sound like *s* in *safe, so,* as in *cent, cease, citizen.*

Words ending in *c* sound like *k* in *like,* as in *picnic, traffic.*

Words beginning in *ca, cu,* or *co* sound like *k* in *kite,* as in *cat, cut, cot.*

Words beginning in *qu* sound like *kw* as in *queen, quick.*

Words ending in *ture* sound like *chur* as in *adventure.*

UNDERSTANDING THE TERM *OVERLEARNING*

Although you may have at one time or another met many of the vocabulary words presented in this book, you may not be able to read or use the words because you have not *overlearned* them. Throughout this book, the emphasis is on the overlearning of vocabulary. *Overlearning* is not bad like *overcooking* the roast. Overlearning will help you to hold on to information over a long period of time. To overlearn the material, concentrate on the words to be learned, memorize them, and do all the exercises. Overlearning will take place only if practice is continued even after you think you have learned the information. The additional practice you engage in after you think you have mastered the material is called *overlearning*. As practice is the key to overlearning, you will continue to meet in the practice sets of later exercises many words that you have learned earlier.

SUGGESTIONS ON HOW TO STUDY VOCABULARY

1. You should choose a time best for you so that you do not feel pressured.

2. You should try to find a place free of things that may disturb your studying.

3. You shouldn't try to do all the exercises in one sitting. Studies have shown that you will remember your material better if you space your studying over a period of time. The thing to do is to find and work at a pace that is good for you.

4. *Recall*, which refers to how much you remember, is very important in learning. Recall is used as part of the teaching method in this book. After the presentation of the word and its meaning(s), you should cover the meaning(s) to see if you can recall it (or them).

5. When the entire exercise is completed, go over the words you have learned. In addition, take a few minutes before a new exercise to *review* the previous exercise.

6. To make sure you remember the vocabulary words, try to use them daily in your written work or speech. In addition, see how many times you meet these words in your classroom lectures and readings.

© 1965 United Feature Syndicate, Inc.

6

INTRODUCTION TO COMBINING FORMS AND VOCABULARY
DERIVED FROM COMBINING FORMS

As a means of helping you to use combining forms to increase your vocabulary, some terms should be defined. There are a great number of words that combine with other words to form new words, for example, *grandfather* (*grand + father*) and *policeman* (*police + man*)—both compound words. Many words are combined with a letter or a group of letters—either at the beginning (prefix) or at the end (suffix) of the root word—to form a new, related word, for example, *replay* (*re + play*) and *played* (*play + ed*).

In the words *replay* and *played, play* is a root, *re* is a prefix, and *ed* is a suffix. A *root* is the smallest unit of a word that can exist and retain its basic meaning. It cannot be divided further. *Replay* is not a root word because it can be divided into *re* and *play*. *Play* is a root word because it cannot be divided further and still keep a meaning related to the root word.

Combining forms are usually defined as roots borrowed from another language that join together or that join with a prefix, a suffix, or both a prefix and .a suffix to form a word. Often the English combining forms are derived from Greek and Latin roots. Because the emphasis in this book is on the building of vocabulary meanings rather than on the naming of word parts, prefixes, suffixes, English roots, and combining forms will *all* be referred to as combining forms. *A combining form in this book is defined as any word part that can join with another word or word part to form a word or a new word.* Examples: *aqua + naut* = aquanaut (a word); *re + turn* = return (a new word); *aqua + duct* = aqueduct (a new word).

The exercises build on previously learned combining forms. Care is taken not to present those that are similar in appearance in the same exercise.

Knowledge of the most common combining forms is valuable in helping you to learn the meaning of an unfamiliar word. For example, knowing that *pseudo* means "false" helps you to "unlock" *pseudoscience*, which means "false science." Knowing that *bi* means "two" and *ped* means "foot" helps you to determine the meaning of *biped* as a two-footed animal.

As an indication of the power of knowing a few combining forms, it has been estimated that with the knowledge of thirty combining forms (which are included in this text), one can unlock the meanings of as many as 14,000 words. Obviously, familiarity with a mere thirty forms is the quickest way to learning the largest number of words. It is also a method that, once learned, helps you to unlock new words all through your life.

CHAPTER TWO

EXERCISE 1

Step I. Combining Forms

A. Directions: A list of combining forms with their meanings follows. Look at the combining forms and their meanings. Concentrate on learning each combining form and its meaning. Cover the meanings, read the combining forms, and state the meanings to yourself. Check to see if you are correct. Now cover the combining forms, read the meanings, and state the combining forms to yourself. Check to see if you are correct.

Combining Forms	*Meanings*
1. anni, annu, enni	year
2. aut, auto	self
3. bio	life
4. bi	two
5. graph	something written; machine

6. ology   the study of; the science of

7. ped,[1] pod   foot

B. Directions: Cover the preceding meanings. Write the meanings of the
following combining forms.

Combining Forms	Meanings
1. anni, annu, enni	_____
2. aut, auto	_____
3. bio	_____
4. bi	_____
5. graph	_____
6. ology	_____
7. ped, pod	_____

Step II. Words Derived[2] from Combining Forms

1. **biology** (bi · ol · o · gy) (bī · ol′ o · jē)[3] *n.* The science of life. ***Biology***
helps students to learn about living things.

2. **biography** (bi · og · ra · phy) (bī · og′ ra · fē) *n.* (*pl.* **phies**)[4] An account
of a person's life; a person's life story. *I learned all about the life of Martin
Luther King, Jr. when I read Coretta King's **biography** of him.*

3. **autobiography** (au · to · bi · og · ra · phy) (au · to · bī · og′ ra · fē) *n.* (*pl.*
phies) A person's life story written by himself or herself. *Helen Keller,
who was deaf, mute, and blind, gives an interesting account of her life in
her **autobiography**.*

4. **autograph** (au · to · graph) (au′ to · graf) *n.* Signature. *adj.* Written by a
person's own hand: *an **autograph** letter*; containing autographs: *an **autograph** album. v.* To write one's name on or in. *After I get the **autograph**
of a famous person, I compare that person's signature with other signatures
I have collected.*

---

[1]Only one meaning for the combining form *ped* is presented in Exercise 1. Another meaning will be
presented in a later exercise.

[2]*Derived* means "made up from."

[3]When you see two entries in parentheses following the word, the first refers to the syllabication of the
word, and the second refers to the phonetic spelling of the word.

[4]*Pl.* is the abbreviation for *plural*.

5. **annual** (an' n̶u · al) *adj.* Every year; yearly. *At the end of every year the stockholders receive their **annual** report concerning the company's progress.*

6. **anniversary** (an · ni · ver · sa · ry) (an · n̶i · ver' sa · rē) *n.* (*pl.* **ries**). The yearly return of a date marking an event or occurrence of some importance. *adj.* Returning or recurring each year. *On August 24 I always celebrate the **anniversary** of my marriage.*

7. **biannual** (bī · an ' n̶u · al) *adj.* Twice a year; (loosely) occurring every two years. *Our **biannual** block parties, which come twice a year, are lots of fun.*

8. **biennial** (bi · en · ni · al) (bī · en' n̶ē · al) *adj.* Once every two years; lasting for two years. *Our vacation is a **biennial** event because we can afford a vacation only every two years.*

9. **biweekly** (bi · week · ly) (bī · wē¢k ' lē) *adj.* Every two weeks; twice a week. *My **biweekly** paycheck is always gone at the end of two weeks.*

10. **bimonthly** (bi · month · ly) (bī · month' lē) *adj.* Every two months; twice a month. *I feel we should change our **bimonthly** meetings to monthly meetings because meeting every two months is not often enough.*

11. **bicycle** (bi · cy · cle) (bī' si · kul) *n.* A vehicle having two wheels. *You need good balance in order to be able to ride a **bicycle**.*

12. **biped** (bī ' ped) *n.* A two-footed animal. *Humans, who are **bipeds**, are not the only two-footed animals.*

13. **pedestrian** (pe · des · tri · an) (pe · des ' trē · an) *n.* One who goes on foot. ***Pedestrians** as well as motorists should obey traffic laws.*

Special Notes

Note that *biannual* almost always means "twice a year," but when *biannual* is used loosely, it can mean "every two years." *Biennial* means "every two years" or "lasting for two years." In botany, a biennial plant is one that lasts for two years.

Note that the meanings for *biweekly* and *bimonthly* may at times be almost the same, because *biweekly* can mean "every two weeks" and *bimonthly* can mean "twice a month." However, when a word has more than one meaning, *the sentence usually provides clues for the proper meaning.*

1. **bimonthly.** Once every two months; twice a month. *The theater group decided to stop giving **bimonthly** plays because two months did not give them enough time to practice.*

2. **biweekly**. Once every two weeks; twice a week. *The biweekly newspaper is very large because it comes out only every two weeks.*

Step III. Practice

A. Directions: Define the underlined word in each of the following sentences.

1. Our company holds its annual dinner dance in the spring; then, I see all the people I haven't seen all year. _____

2. To save energy, many students ride their bicycles to school. _____

3. At the first class meeting, our English instructor asked us to write our autobiographies. _____

4. The film's star was a car that tried to run down pedestrians, while the pedestrians were trying to cross the street. _____

5. The actress said that she knew that she had "arrived" when people began to stop her and ask for her autograph. _____

6. The author of biographies must have a special and continuing interest in his or her subjects. _____

7. It seems to be taking my nephew a long time to realize that he is not a four-footed animal but a biped, because he is still crawling on all fours. _____

8. The members of the club voted to meet once a month rather than bimonthly. _____

9. Biology has helped me have a better understanding of all living things. _____

10. The employees said that they would prefer to be paid every week rather than biweekly. _____

11. Inflation has dug such a hole in our monies that going out to eat may become a biennial event for us because it will probably take us two years to save enough money for such a luxury. _____

12. We celebrated my parent's twenty-fifth wedding anniversary last night. _____

13. The company I work for is not going to have biannual parties anymore because of the expense, so from now on there will only be one party a year. _____

STOP. Check answers at the end of Chapter Two (pp. 42–43).

B. Directions: Match each word with the *best* definition.

_____ 1. autobiography   a. a vehicle with two wheels

_____ 2. bimonthly   b. life story written by oneself

_____ 3. biweekly   c. one's signature

_____ 4. biology   d. twice a year

_____ 5. biannual   e. life story (written)

_____ 6. biography   f. a two-footed or two-legged animal

_____ 7. anniversary   g. the science or study of life

_____ 8. biennial   h. every two years

_____ 9. bicycle   i. one who goes on foot

_____ 10. autograph   j. once every two months; twice a month

_____ 11. biped   k. once a year

_____ 12. annual   l. yearly return of a date marking an event of some importance

_____ 13. pedestrian

    m. every two weeks; twice a week

STOP. Check answers at the end of Chapter Two (p. 43).

C. Directions: Use the combining forms that follow to build a word to fit the blank in the sentence.

Combining Forms

bi, anni, auto, bio, graph, ology, ped, pod.

1. January 24 is not a pleasant day for me because it is the _____ of my parent's divorce.

2. People say that I look like a famous movie star, but I never believed them until some people asked me to sign their _____ book.

3. The lecture part of my _____ course is fine, but I am having trouble with the lab part of it because I can't stand to take anything apart that had once been alive.

4. My mother convinced me to have _____ physical checkups rather than _____ ones because a lot of problems can arise and go unnoticed in a two-year period.

5. The famous doctor told the interviewer that he knew when he was still a child that he would someday write his _____, so he started keeping a diary at a very early age.

6. What other animals besides humans are _____ ?

7. Our English instructor asked us to choose a famous person and then to read two different _____ that had been written about that person and to compare them.

8. _____, as motorists, should obey safety rules.

9. The employees complained that their _____ checks weren't enough to cover their expenses because of the high inflation and that they wanted to be paid every week.

Stop. Check answers at the end of Chapter Two (p. 43).

Check answers at the end of Chapter Two (p. 43).

EXTRA WORD
POWER

> **ar, er, or.** One who; that which. Note the three different spellings. When *ar, er,* or *or* is found at the end of a word, the word concerns a person or thing. For example: *biographer*—a person who writes biographies; *killer*—one who kills; *player*—one who plays; *author*—one who writes; *beggar*—one who begs; *captor*—one who holds someone a prisoner; *prisoner*—one who is kept in prison. How many more words that end in *ar, er,* or *or* can you supply?

Additional Words Derived from Combining Forms

From your knowledge of combining forms, can you define the following words?

1. **graphology** (gra · phol · o · gy) (gra · fol′ o · jē) *n. Detectives sometimes use **graphology** to learn about the character of a suspect.*

   _____

2. **graphic** (graph · ic) (graf ′ ik) *adj. His description was so **graphic** that it left nothing to the imagination.*

   _____

3. **orthography** (or · thog · ra · phy) (or · thog′ ra · fē) *n.* (*pl.* **ies**) *Knowledge of the **orthography** of words helps in writing.*

   _____

14

4. **annuity** (an · nu · i · ty) (an̹ · nū′ i · tē) *n.* *He receives a sizable **annuity** each year from his investment.*

---

5. **bifocals** (bi · fo · cals) (bī · fō′ kulz) *n.* *(pl.)* *When my mother's eye doctor recommended **bifocals** for her, she felt that it was a sure sign that she was getting old.*

---

6. **bilateral** (bī · lat ′ er · al) *adj.* *The two nations began **bilateral** talks, hoping to conclude a peace treaty between them.*

---

7. **bilingual** (bi · lin · gual) (bī · ling′ gwal) *adj. n.* *A number of schools are providing **bilingual** programs for students who speak a language other than English.*

---

8. **binary** (bi · na · ry) (bī ′ na · rē) *adj. The **binary** system of numbers is used with digital computers.*

---

9. **biopsy** (bi · op · sy) (bī ′ op · sē) *n. In order to determine whether major surgery is necessary, the surgeon usually takes a **biopsy** of the organ in question.*

---

10. **podium** (po · di · um) (pō′ dē · um) *n. When the conductor took his position on the **podium**, all eyes were directed toward him.*

---

11. **pedestal** (ped ′ es · tal) *n. The newly acquired statue was placed on a special **pedestal** for all to view.*

---

12. **automatic** (au · to · mat · ic) (au ′ to · mat ′ ik) *adj. **Automatic** washers and dryers have helped to provide more leisure time for persons.*

---

13. **automaton** (au · tom ′ a · ton) *n. The goose-stepping soldiers in Hitler's army looked like **automatons**.*

---

14. **autonomous** (au · ton ′ o · møus) *adj. Because education is not mentioned in the Constitution, each state is **autonomous** in this area.*

STOP. Check answers at the end of Chapter Two (p. 43).

Practice for Additional Words Derived from Combining Forms

Directions: A list of definitions follows. Choose the word from the word list
that *best* fits the definition. Try to relate your definition to the
meanings of the combining forms.

Word List

*annuity, bifocals, bilateral, graphic, graphology, orthography, podium, pedestal,
binary, automatic, automaton, biopsy, bilingual, autonomous.*

1. Consisting of two parts   _____

2. The study of handwriting   _____

3. The cutting out of a piece of living tissue for examination   _____

4. Using two languages equally well   _____

5. Glasses with two-part lenses   _____

6. Self-governing   _____

7. Moving by itself   _____

8. Two-sided   _____

9. The art of correct spelling   _____

10. Yearly payment of money   _____

11. A base or bottom support   _____

12. A raised platform for an orchestra conductor   _____

13. Marked by realistic and vivid detail   _____

14. A person or animal acting in a mechanical way.   _____

STOP. Check answers at the end of Chapter Two (p. 43).

EXERCISE 2

Step I. Combining Forms

A. Directions: A list of combining forms with their meanings follows. Look
at the combining forms and their meanings. Concentrate on
learning each combining form and its meaning. Cover the
meanings, read the combining forms, and state the meanings to
yourself. Check to see if you are correct. Now cover the
combining forms, read the meanings, and state the combining forms to yourself. Check to see if you are correct.

Combining Forms	Meanings
1. tele	from a distance
2. scope	a means for seeing, watching, or viewing
3. geo	earth
4. meter	measure
5. micro	very small
6. scrib, scrip	write
7. phon, phono	sound

B. Directions: Cover the preceding **meanings**. Write the meanings of the following combining forms.

Combining Forms	Meanings
1. tele	_____
2. scope	_____
3. geo	_____
4. meter	_____
5. micro	_____
6. scrib, scrip	_____
7. phon, phono	_____

Step II. Words Derived from Combining Forms

1. **telegraph** (tel • e • graph) (tel′ e • graf) *n.* Instrument for sending a message in a code at a distance. *v.* To send a message from a distance. *The* **telegraph** *is not used as much today as it used to be because there are now faster and simpler ways to send messages from a distance.*

2. **telephone** (tel • e • phone) (tel′ e • fōn¢) *n.* Instrument that sends and receives sound, such as the spoken word, over distance. *v.* To send a message by telephone. *I use the* **telephone** *when my girl friend is away, and I want to hear the sound of her voice.*

3. **telescope** (tel • e • scope) (tel′ e • skōp¢) *n.* Instrument used to view distant objects. *Standing on the roof of the Empire State Building, he used the* **telescope** *to view the city.*

17

4. **microscope** (mi · cro · scope) (mī′ kro · skōpø) *n.* Instrument used to make very small things appear larger so that they can be seen. *The microscope has helped scientists to observe objects too small to be seen with the naked eye.*

5. **geometry** (ge · om · e · try) (jē · om′ e · trē) *n.* Branch of mathematics dealing with the measurement of points, lines, and planes, among other things. *An engineer uses his knowledge of geometry to measure the land for the building of new roads.*

6. **geography** (ge · og · ra · phy) (jē · og′ ra · fē) *n.* Study of the earth's surface and life. *In geography you learn about the earth's surface and about the plant and animal life there.*

7. **geology** (ge · ol · o · gy) (jē · ol′ o · jē) *n.* Study of the earth's physical history and makeup. *Geology helps people learn about the makeup of the earth, especially as revealed by rocks.*

8. **script** (skript) *n.* Writing that is cursive, printed, or engraved; a piece of writing; a written copy of a play for the use of actors. *The actors read from the script only for the first rehearsal, but after that they could not depend on any writing to help them.*

9. **scripture** (scrip · ture) (skrip′ chur) *n.* The books of the Old and New Testaments, or either of them; a text or passage from the Bible; the sacred writings of a religion. *Some lawyers quote from the Holy Scriptures because they feel a reference to the Bible will gain the jury's sympathy.*

10. **description** (de · scrip · tion) (de · skrip′ shun) *n.* An account that gives a picture of something in words. *Carol's description of the college was so graphic that I could actually picture it in my mind.*

Special Notes

1. Note that in the words *telescope* and *microscope* the meaning of the words includes the term *instrument*. A telescope is an instrument used to view distant objects. A microscope is an instrument used to make small objects appear larger so that they can be seen.

2. The word *script* can refer to typed or printed matter and also to a piece of writing, especially a written copy of a play or dramatic role for the use of actors. For example:
   a. *This sentence is in script.*
   b. *The researchers were looking for the original ancient script.*
   c. *The script for the new play was not ready.*

3. The term *Scripture* is used chiefly in the plural with the (and often Holy) and has a capital letter when it refers to the books of the Old and New Testaments or of either of them—in short, the Bible.

Step III. Practice

A. Directions: Use the combining forms that follow to build a word to fit the blank in the sentence.

Combining Forms

tele, scope, geo, meter, micro, scrib, scrip, phon, phono, graph, ology.

1. In the biology course, we mounted cells from the inside of our mouths on a slide and observed them under the _____ .

2. My friend intends to become a(n) _____ because he enjoys studying rock formations.

3. In a movie the murderer used a high-powered _____ to spy on his victims.

4. The _____ in the play called for the lead to be a popular, outgoing, attractive, and athletic individual—everything that the lead wasn't.

5. In the play *Inherit the Wind* both attorneys use quotes from _____ to try to prove their points.

6. When something good happens to me, I usually _____ my family and friends to tell them about it and to exchange other news with them.

7. Algebra and _____ are usually required mathematics courses for students planning to go to college.

8. Who would have thought that a course in _____ , which taught about the earth's surface, would help the shipwrecked persons when they were marooned on an unknown island far from civilization.

9. My mother has received only one _____ in her whole life, and that one did not bring very pleasant news.

10. When Jim gave us a(n) _____ of the cave, I started to tremble because I felt as though I had been there, yet that was impossible.

STOP. Check answers at the end of Chapter Two (p. 44).

B. Directions: A list of definitions follows. Choose a word from the word list that *best* fits the definition. There are more words in the list than you need.

Word List

telegraph, telephone, telescope, microscope, geology, biology, geography, geometry, biography, autobiography, Scripture, pedestrian, script, description, biographer.

1. Instrument used to view distant objects _____

2. Instrument used for sending coded messages _____

3. Branch of mathematics dealing with measurement _____

4. Study of the earth's physical history and makeup _____

5. A person who writes about the life of another _____

6. Printed matter; a piece of writing _____

7. Instrument that sends sound at a distance _____

8. Instrument used to make very small objects appear larger _____

9. Writings from the Bible _____

10. Study of the earth's surface _____

11. An account that gives a picture of something in words _____

12. A person who goes on foot _____

STOP. Check answers at the end of Chapter Two (p. 44).

C. Directions: Define the underlined word in each of the following sentences.

1. The honeymooners decided to give the news of their marriage in person rather than to <u>telegraph</u> it. _____

2. After the director read the <u>script</u> that called for so many peculiar characters, he developed a headache. _____

3. In <u>geometry</u> we learned that the shortest distance between two points is a straight line. _____

4. My brother who is majoring in <u>geology</u> told me that his instructor had found a rare stone that was worth a fortune. _____

5. My <u>telephone</u> bills are so high because I talk too long on the telephone, so I intend to use a timer for all my calls, and, when the timer buzzer rings, I intend to say "good-bye" and hang up. _____

20

6. Knowledge of <u>geography</u> helped Jim answer some questions on a quiz show. _____

7. The <u>description</u> that Jim gave was one that the victim had had in one of her recurring nightmares. _____

8. In the film a mad scientist, who is always looking at slides under a <u>microscope</u>, develops a monster plant. _____

9. On television there was a disabled private eye who spent all his time spying on other people by looking through a <u>telescope</u>. _____

10. In most motels and hotels you will find that each room is supplied with <u>Scripture</u>. _____

STOP. Check answers at the end of Chapter Two (p. 44).

EXTRA WORD
POWER

> **re.** Again; back. *Re* is found at the beginning of many words. For example: *rewrite*—to write again; *redo*—to do again; *recomb*—to comb again; *rerun*—to run again; *rework*—to work again; *repay*—to pay back; *return*—to go back. How many more words that begin with *re* can you supply?

Additional Words Derived from Combining Forms

From your knowledge of combining forms, can you define the following words?

1. **meter** (mē′ ter) *n. A **meter** is approximately 3.3 feet or 1.1 yards.*

_____

2. **telemeter** (te · lem′ e · ter) *n. The ground crew serving a space station uses a **telemeter** to learn what is happening in the space ship.*

_____

3. **micrometer** (mi · crom · e · ter) (mī · krom′ e · ter) *n. Technicians use a **micrometer** when measuring material because it helps them to be as accurate as possible.*

_____

4. **microbe** (mi · crobe) (mī′ krōbǝ) *n. Doctors determine through tests what **microbes** in our bodies are causing our diseases.*

_____

5. **microorganism** (mi · cro · or · gan · ism) (mī · krō · or′ gan · iz · um) *n.* *A virus is a **microorganism** that cannot be seen by the naked eye.*

6. **microphone** (mi · cro · phone) (mī′ kro · fōn¢) *n.* *The speaker used the **microphone** to make sure that the people in the rear of the large room could hear the speech.*

7. **microfilm** (mi · cro · film) (mī′ kro · film) *n.* *Many of the older copies of newspapers that I needed for my report were on **microfilm** in the library.*

8. **scribe** (skrīb¢) *n.* *In ancient times a **scribe** was held in very high esteem because not many persons were able to read or write then.*

9. **inscription** (in · scrip · tion) (in · skrip′ shun) *n.* *The **inscription** on the Statue of Liberty beckons all to our shores.*

10. **prescription** (pre · scrip · tion) (pre · skrip′ shun) *n.* *A patient may endanger his health because he fails to follow his doctor's **prescription.***

11. **transcript** (tran · script) (tran′ skript) *n.* *The lawyer asked for a **transcript** of a court case to review what had taken place during the trial.*

12. **geocentric** (ge · o · cen · tric) (jē · ō · sen′ trik) *adj.* *In ancient times man thought that the universe was **geocentric.***

13. **phonics** (phon · ics) (fon′ iks) *n.* *Children who are good in **phonics** are able to figure out many words independently.*

14. **phonetics** (pho · net · ics) (fo · net′ iks) *n.* *Many actors and actresses take courses in **phonetics** to learn how to pronounce words better.*

15. **stethoscope** (steth · o · scope) (steth′ o · skōp¢) *n.* *The doctor used the **stethoscope** to listen to his patient's heartbeat.*

STOP. Check answers at the end of Chapter Two (pp. 44–45).

Practice for Additional Words Derived from Combining Forms

Directions: Match the definition that *best* fits to the word.

_____ 1. telemeter

     a. a brief dedication in a book; something written or engraved on some surface

_____ 2. micrometer

     b. a writer

_____ 3. microorganism

     c. a very small living thing that cannot be seen with the naked eye

_____ 4. microbe

     d. study of the relationship of written symbols to sound symbols

_____ 5. microphone

     e. relating to the earth as the center

_____ 6. microfilm

     f. a copy of an original

_____ 7. transcript

     g. study of speech sounds

_____ 8. scribe

     h. A doctor's instrument used to hear heart, lungs, and so forth

_____ 9. prescription

     i. a device to magnify weak sounds

_____ 10. inscription

     j. an instrument used to measure distance

_____ 11. phonics

     k. film on which printed material is reduced in size

_____ 12. phonetics

     l. a doctor's written directions for medicine

_____ 13. geocentric

     m. an instrument that measures very small distances

_____ 14. stethoscope

     n. a very small living thing that cannot be seen with the naked eye

_____ 15. meter

     o. an instrument that measures the amount of something

STOP. Check answers at the end of Chapter Two (p. 45).

EXERCISE 3

Step I. Combining Forms

A. Directions: A list of combining forms with their meanings follows. Look at the combining forms and their meanings. Concentrate on learning each combining form and its meaning. Cover the meanings, read the combining forms, and state the meanings to yourself. Check to see if you are correct. Now cover the combining forms, read the meanings, and state the combining forms to yourself. Check to see if you are correct.

Combining Forms	Meanings
1. gram	something written or drawn; a record
2. uni	one
3. dic, dict	say; speak
4. contra	against; opposite
5. spect	see; view; observe
6. phob, phobo	fear

B. Directions: Cover the preceding meanings. Write the meanings of the following combining forms.

Combining Forms	Meanings
1. gram	_____
2. uni	_____
3. dic, dict	_____
4. contra	_____
5. spect	_____
6. phob, phobo	_____

Step II. Words Derived from Combining Forms

1. **telegram** (tel′ e · gram) *n.* Message sent from a distance. *A telegram is usually sent when the message is important.*

2. **uniform** (ū′ ni · form) *adj.* Being always the same; alike. *n.* A special form of clothing. *Persons in the armed forces wear uniforms that have been specially designed for them.*

3. **unique** (u · nique) (ū′ nēk) *adj.* Being the only one of its kind. *The ancient statue found in a cave was unique because there were no others like it.*

4. **union** (un · ion) (ūn′· yun) *n.* A joining; a putting together; something formed by joining. *A labor union is a group of people who have joined together because they have similar interests and purposes.*

5. **universe** (ū′ ni · versȩ) *n.* Everything that exists; all creation; all mankind. *With space exploration, man has made but a small probe into the vast unknown regions of the universe.*

6. **universal** (ū · ni · ver′ sal) *adj.* Applying to all. *It is very hard to give* **universal** *satisfaction to people because not everyone agrees on what is satisfactory.*

7. **unison** (ū′ ni · son) *n.* A harmonious agreement ; a saying of something together: **in unison.** *adv.* Precise and perfect agreement. *Choral groups speak* **in unison** *when they recite.*

8. **diction** (dic · tion) (dik′ shun) *n.* Manner of speaking; choice of words. *Mrs. Smith's* **diction** *is so precise that no one has any difficulty in understanding her speech.*

9. **dictation** (dic · ta · tion) (dik · tā′ shun) *n.* The act of speaking or reading aloud to someone who takes down the words. *On Monday Mr. Jones sometimes loses his voice because of the great amount of* **dictation** *he gives his secretary.*

10. **dictionary** (dic · tion · a · ry) (dik′ shun · a · rē) *n.* A book of alphabetically listed words in a language, giving information about their meanings, pronunciations, and so forth. *Whenever I don't know the pronunciation or meaning of a word, I look it up in the* **dictionary**.

11. **dictator** (dic · ta · tor) (dik′ tā · tor) *n.* A ruler who has absolute power; a ruler who has complete control and say. *Hitler was a* **dictator** *who had complete control over the German people.*

12. **contrary** (con · trar · y) (kon′ trar · ē) *adj.* Opposite. *We disagree because his opinion is* **contrary** *to ours.*

13. **contradiction** (con · tra · dic · tion) (kon · tra · dik′ shun) *n.* Something (such as a statement) consisting of opposing parts. *If I answer yes and no to the same statement, I am making a* **contradiction**.

14. **contrast** (con · trast) (kon′ trast) *n.* Difference between things; use of opposites for certain results. *The black chair against the white wall makes an interesting* **contrast**.

15. **spectacle** (spec · ta · cle) (spek′ ta · kul) *n.* Something showy that is seen by many (the public); an unwelcome or sad sight. *The drunken man made a terrible* **spectacle** *of himself for the crowd of people.*

16. **spectator** (spec · ta · tor) (spek′ tā · tor) *n.* An onlooker; one who views something, such as a spectacle. *There were many* **spectators** *at the fair who enjoyed looking at the sights.*

17. **spectacular** (spec · tac · u · lar) (spek · tak′ ū · lar) *adj.* Relating to something unusual, impressive, exciting, or unexpected. *The* **spectacular** *rescue of the child from the burning house was widely applauded.*

18. **phobia** (pho · bi · a) (fō′ bē · a) *n.* Extreme fear. *My friend, who has a* **phobia** *about cats, is afraid to be in the same room with one.*

Special Notes

1. The term *phobia* is usually used to refer to an extreme fear of something. For example: *The doctors tried to help the man to overcome his **phobia** about heights.*

2. The term *Union*, which begins with a capital letter, refers to the United States as a national unit or to any other nation that is a unit, such as the USSR.

3. The combining form *gram* means "something written; a record." However, *gram* is also a noun that refers to a measurement of weight in the metric system.

4. The plural of *spectacle* (spectacles) can also refer to eyeglasses.

Step III. Practice

A. Directions: A list of definitions follows. In the space provided, insert the letter for the word that *best* fits the definition.

___ 1. A saying of something together
    a. union   c. unison
    b. universe   d. uniform

___ 2. Refers to the Bible
    a. autobiography   c. autograph
    b. Scripture   d. script

___ 3. An extreme fear
    a. biology   c. phobia
    b. biped   d. pedestrian

___ 4. Being the same
    a. union   c. universe
    b. unique   d. uniform

___ 5. Applying to all
    a. unique   c. unison
    b. union   d. universal

___ 6. A joining together
    a. unique   c. universal
    b. union   d. uniform

___ 7. Something (such as a statement) consisting of opposing parts
    a. unique   c. contradiction
    b. unison   d. uniform

___ 8. The science of life
    a. geology   c. biography
    b. geography   d. biology

___ 9. Being unlike anything else
    a. phobic   c. telegraphic
    b. unique   d. contrasting

___10. Message from a distance
    a. telegraph   c. telescope
    b. telegram   d. autograph

___11. One who views something
    a. spectator   c. spectacular
    b. spectacle   d. script

___12.	Relating to something impressive	a. spectator	c. spectacular
		b. Scripture	d. spectacle
___13.	Something showy	a. spectacular	c. phobia
		b. spectator	d. spectacle
___14.	A ruler with complete control	a. dictation	c. autobiography
		b. diction	d. dictator
___15.	Manner of speaking	a. dictionary	c. diction
		b. dictation	d. dictator
___16.	The act of speaking to someone who takes it down	a. dictation	c. diction
		b. dictionary	d. dictator

STOP. Check answers at the end of Chapter Two (p. 45).

B. Directions: Twelve sentences follow. Define the underlined word.

1. It's a <u>contradiction</u> to be happy and unhappy at the same time.

_____

2. He is making a <u>spectacle</u> of himself by behaving that way in front of so many people.

_____

3. Although it is a statement <u>contrary</u> to the opinions of other people, I will stick to it.

_____

4. You have such a <u>unique</u> way of holding your tennis racket.

_____

5. If that is a <u>universal</u> belief, everyone should agree with it.

_____

6. Because I am still afraid to go in the water, my doctor has not cured me of my <u>phobia</u>.

_____

7. The color of your blouse makes a good <u>contrast</u> to your skirt.

_____

8. The <u>spectators</u> were not able to believe their eyes.

_____

9. The two feuding organizations decided to join together into one strong <u>union</u>.

_____

10. Although the trapped men seemed surely doomed, the firemen made a <u>spectacular</u> rescue at the last minute.

_____

11. John behaves like a <u>dictator</u> in class because he likes to have everyone do what he wants.

_____

12. Instructors' <u>diction</u> must be excellent if many students are to listen to their lectures.

_____

STOP. Check answers at the end of Chapter Two (p. 45).

EXTRA WORD
POWER

> **ion, sion, tion.** State of; act of; result of. Note the three spellings. When *ion, sion,* or *tion* is found at the end of a word, it means that the word is a noun. For example: *diction*—the act of speaking in a certain manner; *dictation*—the act of speaking to someone who takes it down; *question*—the act of asking; *description*—the act of describing.

Additional Words Derived from Combining Forms

From your knowledge of combining forms, can you define the following words?

1. **Dictaphone** (dic · ta · phone) (dik′ ta · fōn̸e) *n. Sometimes Mr. Jones used a **Dictaphone** to record his letters for his secretary.*

_____

2. **dictum** (dic · tum) (dik′ tum) *n. The union leaders impressed the strikers with their **dictum** of nonviolence.*

_____

3. **indictment** (in · dī¢t′ ment) *n. The jury felt that the prosecutor had enough evidence to warrant an **indictment** against the defendant.*

_____

4. **unilateral** (ū · ni · lat′ er · al) *adj. There is a tendency today in corporations toward consensus decisions by management rather than **unilateral** ones by individual executives.*

_____

5. **unify** (u · ni · fy) (ū′ ni · fī) *v. After the strike it was difficult to **unify** the different groups because there was still resentment against those who had crossed the picket lines.*

28

6. **acrophobia** (ac · ro · pho · bi · a) (ak · ro · fō′ bē · a) *n. You would not find a person with acrophobia at the top of the Empire State Building.*

_____

7. **hydrophobia** (hy · dro · pho · bi · a) (hī · dro · fō′ bē · a) *n. I know someone who developed hydrophobia after being thrown in the water as a child.*

_____

8. **claustrophobia** (claus · tro · pho · bi · a) (klaus · tro · fō′ bē · a) *n. How horrible to get stuck in an elevator when you have claustrophobia!*

_____

9. **grammar** (gram′ mar) *n. Studies have shown that a knowledge of grammar does not help students to speak or write better because grammar merely describes the way an individual speaks.*

_____

10. **speculate** (spec · u · late) (spek′ yu · lāte) *v. I do not like to speculate in the stock market because I like only sure things.*

_____

STOP. Check answers at the end of Chapter Two (pp. 45-46).

Practice for Additional Words Derived from Combining Forms

Directions: Match each word with the best definition.

_____	1. Dictaphone	a. a fear of heights
_____	2. dictum	b. that part of the study of language dealing with structure and word forms
_____	3. indictment	c. to think about from all sides; take part in any risky venture
_____	4. unilateral	d. a fear of closed-in places
_____	5. unify	e. a machine for recording speech
_____	6. acrophobia	f. a charge
_____	7. hydrophobia	g. form into one
_____	8. claustrophobia	h. an authoritative statement
_____	9. grammar	i. one-sided
_____	10. speculate	j. a fear of water

STOP. Check answers at the end of Chapter Two (p. 46).

CROSSWORD PUZZLE 1

Directions: The meanings of many of the combining forms from Exercises 1–3
follow. Your knowledge of these combining forms will help you to
solve this crossword puzzle. Note that *combining form* is abbreviated as *comb. f.*

Across

1. A word ending meaning "one who"
3. Past tense of the verb *have*
5. Comb. f. for *foot*
7. Comb. f. for *life*
9. Comb. f. for *from a distance*
11. Same as #1 Across
12. Third letter of the alphabet
13. Comb. f. for *something written*
16. Opposite of *night*

Down

1. You make this sound when you are surprised
2. To tap; strike
4. That which one owes
6. What you do when you stop breathing
8. Comb. f. for *the study of*
10. To make a mistake
12. You will do this to your lips

18. Sliced pork meat
20. Pronoun
21. Comb. f. for *a means for seeing*
23. A car you can hire to drive you somewhere
26. Opposite of *off*
27. Word meaning "on"; "near"; "by"
28. Comb. f. for *self*
30. Opposite of *out*
31. What you hang clothes on
34. Same as #1 Down

when they are too dry
14. An indefinite article
15. Comb. f. for *sound*
16. Comb. f. for *say*
17. Same as #14 Down
19. A pronoun
21. Nineteenth letter of the alphabet
22. Something to sleep on
24. Same as #14 Down
25. Money that is put up to release an arrested person from jail before his trial
27. Same as #14 Down
29. Comb. f. for *one*
32. Opposite of *yes*
33. A sound that means "What did you say?"

STOP.   Check answers at the end of Chapter Two (p. 46).

WORD SCRAMBLE 1

Directions: Word Scramble 1 is based on words from Exercises 1–3. The meanings are your clues to arranging the letters in correct order. Write the correct word in the blank.

Meanings

1. fmniuor   _____   being the same

2. ueqinu   _____   only one of its kind

3. hbaiop   _____   extreme fear

4. yclbeic   _____   two-wheeler

5. rpuotghaa   _____   signature

6. dseerniapt   _____   one who goes on foot; one who walks

7. iewbyelk   _____   every two weeks

8. elooygg   _____   study of the earth's physical history and makeup

9. oghuaaypoitbr   _____   life story written by oneself

31

10.	ebpid	_____	two-footed animal
11.	clesetepo	_____	instrument used for viewing distant objects
12.	crpits	_____	a piece of writing
13.	repicmoocs	_____	instrument used to make very small objects appear larger so that they can be seen
14.	luanvirse	_____	referring to all
15.	lunnaa	_____	yearly
16.	yoeghgrpa	_____	study of the earth's surface and life
17.	nitooctnricad	_____	something (such as a statement) consisting of opposite parts
18.	roptsacet	_____	one who views something
19.	blooyig	_____	the study of living things
20.	libeanni	_____	every two years

STOP. Check answers at the end of Chapter Two (p. 47).

ANALOGIES 1

Directions: Find the word from the following list that *best* completes each analogy. There are more words in the list than you need. The symbol : means "is to," and the symbol : : means "as."
Example: Brutal is to savage as viewer is to *spectator*.
Brutal: savage : : viewer : *spectator*.

Word List

autograph, spectacle, hydrophobia, podium, biped, annually, bifocals, orthography, biennial, biweekly, prescription, unique, automation, pedestrian, telescope, uniform, transcript, contrast, automatic, contradict, biography, indictment, unite, bicyclist, microbe, phobia, spectator, spectacular, automaton.

1. Riding : walking : : motorist : _____ .

2. Accessory : scarf : : instrument : _____ .

3. Height : acrophobia : : water : _____.

4. Hear : racket : : view : _____.

5. Solo : duet : : weekly : _____.

32

6. Snow : blizzard :: interesting :_____.

7. Groomed : disheveled :: common : _____.

8. Hamper : hinder :: same : _____.

9. Arrest : stop :: dais : _____.

10. Primary : first :: signature : _____ .

11. Automobile : vehicle :: robot : _____ .

12. Pretty : beautiful :: fear : _____ .

13. Smooth : wrinkled :: agree: _____ .

14. Dress : gown :: spectacles : _____.

15. Hate : detest :: join : _____ .

16. Structure : grammar :: spelling : _____ .

17. End : beginning :: original : _____ .

18. Advice : counsel :: charge : _____ .

19. One : two :: annual : _____.

20. Rule : law :: microorganism : _____ .

STOP. Check answers at the end of Chapter Two (p. 47).

MULTIPLE-CHOICE VOCABULARY TEST 1

Directions: This is a test on words in Exercises 1–3. Words are presented according to exercises. *Do all exercises before checking answers.* Underline the meaning that *best* fits the word.

Exercise 1

1. bicycle
   a. two-wheeler
   b. two-footed
   c. circles
   d. refers to time

2. biology
   a. study of earth
   b. study of people
   c. study of life
   d. science

3. biography
   a. life story written by oneself
   b. a science
   c. life story
   d. some writing

4. autograph
   a. life story
   b. a machine that writes
   c. some writing
   d. signature

5. annual
   a. money
   b. every year
   c. every two years
   d. twice a year

6. biennial

    a. every two years
    b. twice a year

    c. celebration of birthday
    d. once a year

7. autobiography

    a. life story
    b. life story written by oneself

    c. writing machine
    d. science of writing

8. anniversary

    a. refers to annual
    b. every two years

    c. yearly return of a date marking an important event
    d. a celebration

9. biannual

    a. lasting for two years
    b. yearly

    c. twice a year
    d. once a year

10. biweekly

    a. every two weeks
    b. once a week

    c. every four weeks
    d. two weeks every year

11. bimonthly

    a. every two months
    b. every month

    c. four times yearly
    d. two times yearly

12. biped

    a. feet
    b. two socks for feet

    c. two-footed animal
    d. two-footed human

13. pedestrian

    a. one who goes on foot
    b. a foot rest

    c. a foot doctor
    d. refers to two feet

Exercise 2

14. telescope

    a. an instrument used to view small objects
    b. an instrument used to see large objects

    c. an instrument used for viewing distant objects
    d. an instrument used to record sound

15. geology

    a. science of life
    b. study of the earth

    c. study of the earth's surface and life
    d. study of the earth's physical makeup

16. telegraph

    a. instrument used to see from a distance
    b. a machine used to send messages

    c. a machine that measures distance
    d. a message

17. microscope

    a. an instrument that makes things appear small
    b. an instrument used to make small objects appear larger

    c. an instrument that grows small things
    d. something small

18. telephone
   a. a sounding machine
   b. a recording machine
   c. an instrument that sends sound at a distance
   d. an instrument that measures sound at a distance

19. geography
   a. a branch of mathematics
   b. study of the earth
   c. study of the earth's physical makeup
   d. study of the earth's surface and life

20. geometry
   a. study of earth's physical makeup
   b. study of the earth's surface and life
   c. a branch of mathematics
   d. measurement

21. Scripture
   a. refers to any writings
   b. the Bible
   c. refers to a script
   d. refers only to the Old Testament

22. script
   a. a piece of writing
   b. a part in a play
   c. a writer
   d. the Bible

23. description
   a. an account that gives a picture of something in words
   b. some writing
   c. your signature
   d. a play script

Exercise 3

24. telegram
   a. a message sent from a distance
   b. a machine used to send a message
   c. something from a distance
   d. a record

25. phobia
   a. a disease
   b. refers to hate
   c. extreme fear
   d. refers to sound

26. uniform
   a. joining together
   b. clothing
   c. special form of clothing
   d. all

27. unique
   a. only one of its kind
   b. all
   c. the same
   d. joining together

28. union
   a. all
   b. refers to only one
   c. the act of putting together
   d. complete agreement

29. universal
   a. applying to none
   b. putting together
   c. applying to all
   d. only one of a kind

35

30. universe
   a. complete agreement
   b. similar
   c. everything that exists
   d. together

31. unison
   a. a saying of something together
   b. manner of speaking
   c. similar
   d. all

32. dictionary
   a. study of words
   b. a book on speech
   c. a book of alphabetically listed words in a language
   d. study of speaking

33. dictator
   a. ruler
   b. a ruler without power
   c. a person who speaks
   d. a ruler with absolute power

34. dictation
   a. act of speaking
   b. act of writing
   c. act of speaking to someone who takes down the words
   d. a ruler with absolute power

35. diction
   a. manner of speaking
   b. a ruler
   c. act of writing
   d. act of speaking to someone who takes down the words

36. contrary
   a. no agreement
   b. opposite
   c. use of opposites for effect
   d. against someone

37. contradiction
   a. something (such as a statement) consisting of opposing parts
   b. something not in complete agreement
   c. use of opposites for effect
   d. against

38. contrast
   a. difference between things
   b. against someone
   c. no agreement
   d. against everything

39. spectacle
   a. one who views something
   b. glasses
   c. something showy seen by the public
   d. a place to see things

40. spectator
   a. one who wears glasses
   b. one who views something
   c. a place for seeing
   d. something unusual

41. spectacular
    a. a person who sees things
    b. one who wears glasses
    c. a shameful sight
    d. refers to something unusual

TRUE/FALSE TEST 1

Directions: This is a true/false test on Exercises 1–3. Read each sentence carefully. Decide whether it is true or false. Put a *T* for *true* or an *F* for *false* in the blank. The number after the sentence tells you if the word is from Exercise 1, 2, or 3.

_____ 1. When something is done in <u>unison</u>, it is done together. 3

_____ 2. In <u>geology</u> class you learn about plants and animals. 2

_____ 3. When something is a <u>contradiction</u> of something else, it is in agreement with it. 3

_____ 4. A <u>biographer</u> would write your autobiography. 1

_____ 5. A <u>pedestrian</u> is one who goes on a bicycle. 1

_____ 6. When something is <u>unique</u>, it is the same for all persons. 3

_____ 7. If everyone were to agree, there would be a <u>universal</u> agreement. 3

_____ 8. If I receive interest <u>biennially</u>, I receive it twice a year. 1

_____ 9. Not all animals are <u>bipeds</u>. 1

_____ 10. The <u>telescope</u> helped me to get a better view of the one-celled animals. 2

_____ 11. If you had a <u>phobia</u> concerning water, you would fear going into deep water. 3

_____ 12. A <u>spectator</u> is one who watches others. 3

_____ 13. When something is <u>spectacular</u>, it is very exciting to observe. 3

_____ 14. *Scripture* refers to a play script. 2

_____ 15. When you give your <u>autograph</u>, you are giving your life story. 1

_____ 16. Any person who gives <u>dictation</u> is a dictator. 3

STOP. Check answers for both tests at the end of Chapter Two (p. 47).

SCORING OF TESTS

Multiple-Choice Vocabulary Test		True/False Test	
Number Wrong	*Score*	*Number Wrong*	*Score*
0–3	Excellent	0–1	Excellent
4–6	Good	2	Good
7–9	Weak	3–4	Weak
Above 9	Poor	Above 4	Poor
Score _____		Score _____	

1. If you scored in the excellent or good range on *both tests*, you are doing well. Go on to Chapter Three.

2. If you scored in the weak or poor range on either test, look below and follow directions for Additional Practice. Note that the words on the tests are arranged so that you can tell in which exercise to find them. This will help you if you need additional practice.

ADDITIONAL PRACTICE SETS

A. Directions: Write the words you missed on the tests from the three exercises in the space provided. Note that the tests are presented so that you can tell to which exercises the words belong.

Exercise 1 Words Missed

1. _____   6. _____

2. _____   7. _____

3. _____   8. _____

4. _____   9. _____

5. _____   10. _____

Exercise 2 Words Missed

1. _____   6. _____

2. _____   7. _____

3. _____   8. _____

4. _____   9. _____

5. _____   10. _____

Exercise 3 Words Missed

1. _____   6. _____

2. _____   7. _____

3. _____   8. _____

4. _____   9. _____

5. _____   10. _____

B. Directions: Restudy the words that you have written on p. 38 and this page. Study the combining forms from which those words are derived. Do Step I and Step II for those you missed. Note that Step I and Step II of the combining forms and vocabulary derived from these combining forms are on the following pages:

Exercise 1—pp. 9–12

Exercise 2—pp. 16–19

Exercise 3—pp. 23–26

C. Directions: Do Additional Practice 1 on this page and the next if you missed words from Exercise 1. Do Additional Practice 2 on pp. 40–41 if you missed words from Exercise 2. Do Additional Practice 3 on pp. 41–42 if you missed words from Exercise 3. Now go on to Chapter Three.

Additional Practice 1 for Exercise 1

A. Directions: The combining forms presented in Exercise 1 follow. Match the combining form with its meaning.

_____ 1. aut, auto   a. the study of or science of

_____ 2. bi   b. something written; machine

_____ 3. bio   c. self

_____ 4. graph   d. life

_____ 5. ology   e. foot

_____ 6. ped, pod   f. two

_____ 7. anni, annu, enni   g. year

STOP. Check answers at the end of Chapter Two (p. 48).

B. Directions: The words presented in Exercise 1 follow. Match the
word with its meaning.

_____ 1. bicycle   a. every two years

_____ 2. biology   b. yearly

_____ 3. biography   c. life story

_____ 4. autobiography   d. two-wheeler

_____ 5. autograph   e. one who goes on foot

_____ 6. bimonthly   f. signature

_____ 7. biweekly   g. yearly return of a date marking
                                             an event

_____ 8. pedestrian   h. two-footed animal

_____ 9. biped   i. every two weeks; twice a week

_____10. annual   j. every two months; twice a
                                             month

_____11. anniversary   k. life story written by oneself

_____12. biannual   l. twice a year

_____13. biennial   m. study or science of life

STOP. Check answers at the end of Chapter Two (p. 48).

Additional Practice 2 for Exercise 2

A. Directions: The combining forms presented in Exercise 2 follow.
Match the combining form with its meaning.

_____ 1. tele   a. a means for seeing, watching,
                                             or viewing

_____ 2. scope   b. sound

_____ 3. geo   c. very small

_____ 4. meter   d. earth

_____ 5. micro   e. write

_____ 6. scrib, scrip   f. measure

_____ 7. phon, phono   g. from a distance

STOP. Check answers at the end of Chapter Two (p. 48).

B. Directions: The words presented in Exercise 2 follow. Match the
word with its meaning.

_____ 1. telescope	a. instrument for sending a message in code at a distance
_____ 2. geology	b. a piece of writing
_____ 3. microscope	c. branch of mathematics dealing with the measurement of points, lines, and planes, among other things.
_____ 4. geography	d. study of the earth's surface and life
_____ 5. geometry	e. instrument that sends sound at a distance
_____ 6. telegraph	f. study of the earth's physical makeup
_____ 7. Scripture	g. instrument used to make very small objects appear larger so that they can be seen
_____ 8. telephone	h. instrument used for viewing distant objects
_____ 9. script	i. Bible
_____10. description	j. an account that gives a picture of something in writing

STOP. Check answers at the end of Chapter Two (p. 48).

Additional Practice 3 for Exercise 3

A. Directions: The combining forms presented in Exercise 3 follow.
Match the combining form with its meaning.

_____1. spect	a. against; opposite
_____2. uni	b. say; speak
_____3. phob, phobo	c. one
_____4. gram	d. fear
_____5. contra	e. something written or drawn; a record
_____6. dic, dict	f. see; view; observe

STOP. Check answers at the end of Chapter Two (p. 48).

B. Directions: The words presented in Exercise 3 follow. Match the
word with its meaning.

_____ 1. dictionary   a. manner of speaking

_____ 2. spectator   b. being the only one of its kind

_____ 3. telegram   c. the act of putting together

_____ 4. phobia   d. something (such as a statement) consisting of opposing parts

_____ 5. uniform   e. everything that exists

_____ 6. unique   f. applying to all

_____ 7. union   g. message sent from a distance

_____ 8. universe   h. being always the same

_____ 9. universal   i. extreme fear

_____ 10. unison   j. act of speaking to someone who takes down the words

_____ 11. contrary   k. a saying of something together

_____ 12. contradiction   l. book of alphabetically listed words in a language

_____ 13. contrast   m. one who views something

_____ 14. dictator   n. referring to something unusual; exciting

_____ 15. diction   o. opposite

_____ 16. dictation   p. difference between things

_____ 17. spectacle   q. something showy

_____ 18. spectacular   r. a ruler with absolute power

STOP. Check answers at the end of Chapter Two (p. 48).

ANSWERS: Chapter Two

Exercise 1 (pp. 9-16)

Practice A

(1) yearly, (2) two-wheelers, (3) own life stories, (4) walkers, (5) signature, (6) life stories, (7) two-footed animal, (8) every two months, (9) the study of life, (10) every two weeks, (11) every two years, (12) the yearly return of a date

marking an occurrence of some importance, (13) twice a year.

Practice B

(1) b, (2) j, (3) m, (4) g, (5) d, (6) e, (7) l, (8) h, (9) a, (10) c, (11) f, (12) k, (13) i

Practice C

(1) anniversary, (2) autograph, (3) biology, (4) annual, biennial, (5) autobiography, (6) bipeds, (7) biographies, (8) pedestrians, (9) biweekly.

Additional Words Derived from Combining Forms (pp. 14–15)

1. **graphology.** The study of handwriting, especially for character analysis.

2. **graphic.** Marked by realistic and vivid detail.

3. **orthography.** The part of language study that deals with correct spelling; the art of writing words with correct spelling.

4. **annuity.** An investment yielding a fixed sum of money, payable yearly, to continue for a given number of years or for life; a yearly payment of money.

5. **bifocals.** A pair of glasses with two-part lenses, with one part helping you see what is near and one part helping you see from a distance.

6. **bilateral.** Involving two sides.

7. **bilingual.** Having or using two languages equally well; a bilingual person.

8. **binary.** Made up of two parts; twofold; relating to base two.

9. **biopsy.** In medicine, the cutting out of a piece of living tissue for examination.

10. **podium.** A low wall serving as a foundation; a raised platform for the conductor of an orchestra; a dais.

11. **pedestal.** A base or bottom support; any foundation or support; to put or set on a pedestal; to regard with great admiration.

12. **automatic.** Moving by itself; performed without thinking about it.

13. **automaton.** Anything that can move or act by itself; a person or animal acting in an automatic or mechanical way.

14. **autonomous.** Self-governing; functioning independently of other parts.

Practice for Additional Words Derived from Combining Forms (p. 16)

(1) binary, (2) graphology, (3) biopsy, (4) bilingual, (5) bifocals, (6) autonomous, (7) automatic, (8) bilateral, (9) orthography, (10) annuity, (11) pedestal, (12) podium, (13) graphic, (14) automaton.

Practice A

(1) microscope, (2) geologist, (3) telescope, (4) script, (5) Scripture, (6) telephone, (7) geometry, (8) geography, (9) telegram, (10) description.

Practice B

(1) telescope, (2) telegraph, (3) geometry, (4) geology, (5) biographer, (6) script, (7) telephone, (8) microscope, (9) Scripture, (10) geography, (11) description, (12) pedestrian.

Practice C

(1) send a message from a distance, (2) a written copy of a play, (3) branch of mathematics dealing with the measurement of points, lines, and planes, among other things, (4) the study of the earth's physical history and makeup, (5) instrument that sends and receives sound, (6) study of the earth's surface and life, (7) account, (8) instrument used to make small things appear larger so that they can be seen, (9) instrument used to view distant objects, (10) the books of the Old and New Testaments.

Additional Words Derived from Combining Forms (pp. 21-22)

1. **meter.** In the metric system, a unit of length equal to approximately 39.37 inches; an instrument for measuring the amount of something (as water, gas, electricity); an instrument for measuring and recording distance, time, weight, speed, and so forth; a measure of verse.

2. **telemeter.** An instrument that measures distance; an instrument that sends information to a distant point.

3. **micrometer.** An instrument used to measure accurately very small distances, angles, and diameters.

4. **microbe.** A very small living thing, whether plant or animal; a microorganism.

5. **microorganism.** Any organism that is so small that it can be seen only under a microscope—protozoa, bacteria, viruses, and the like; a microbe.

6. **microphone.** A device that magnifies weak sounds (nontechnical definition used as shorthand for the entire sound amplification system); a device to convert sound waves to electrical waves (technical definition).

7. **microfilm.** Film on which documents, printed pages, and so forth, are photographed in a reduced size for storage convenience.

8. **scribe.** A writer, author; a public writer or secretary; in Scripture and Jewish history, a man of learning.

9. **inscription.** Something written or engraved (words, symbols) on some surface; a brief or informal dedication in a book to a friend.

10. **prescription.** A doctor's written directions for the preparation and use of medicine; an order; direction; rule.

11. **transcript.** A written or typewritten copy of an original; a copy or reproduction of any kind.

12. **geocentric.** Relating to the earth as the center.

13. **phonics.** Study of the relationship between letter symbols of a written language and the sounds they represent; a method used in teaching word recognition in reading.

14. **phonetics.** A study dealing with speech sounds and their production.

15. **stethoscope.** A hearing instrument used in examining the heart, lungs, and so on.

Practice for Additional Words Derived from Combining Forms (p. 23)

(1) j, (2) m, (3) c, n, (4) c, n, (5) i, (6) k, (7) f, (8) b, (9) 1, (10) a, (11) d, (12) g, (13) e, (14) h, (15) o.

Exercise 3 (pp. 23-29)

Practice A

(1) c, (2) b, (3) c, (4) d, (5) d, (6) b, (7) c, (8) d, (9) b, (10) b, (11) a, (12) c, (13) d, (14) d, (15) c, (16) a.

Practice B

(1) something consisting of opposites, (2) something showy, (3) opposite, (4) being the only one of its kind, (5) referring to all, (6) extreme fear, (7) use of opposites for certain results, (8) onlookers, (9) a joining, a putting together, (10) unusual, exciting, impressive, (11) a ruler who has absolute power, (12) manner of speaking.

Additional Words Derived from Combining Forms (pp. 28-29)

1. **Dictaphone.** A machine for recording and reproducing words spoken into its mouthpiece (differs from a tape recorder because it has controls that fit into use in transcription). *Dictaphone* is capitalized because it is a trademark.

2. **dictum.** An authoritative statement; a saying.

3. **indictment.** A charge; an accusation.

4. **unilateral.** Occurring on one side only; done by one only; one-sided.

5. **unify.** To make or form into one.

6. **acrophobia.** An abnormal fear of high places.

7. **hydrophobia.** An abnormal fear of water; an inability to swallow water when rabies is present.

8. **claustrophobia.** An abnormal fear of being confined, as in a room or a small place.

9. **grammar.** That part of the study of language that deals with the construction of words and word parts (morphology) and the way in which words are arranged relative to each other in utterances (syntax); the study or description of the way language is used.

10. **speculate.** To think about something by turning it in the mind and viewing it in all its aspects and relations; to take part in any risky business venture.

Practice for Additional Words Derived from Combining Forms (p. 29)

(1) e, (2) h, (3) f, (4) i, (5) g, (6) a, (7) j, (8) d, (9) b, (10) c.

Crossword Puzzle 1 (pp. 30–31)

Word Scramble 1 (pp. 31-32)

(1) uniform, (2) unique, (3) phobia, (4) bicycle, (5) autograph, (6) pedestrian, (7) biweekly, (8) geology, (9) autobiography, (10) biped, (11) telescope, (12) script, (13) microscope, (14) universal, (15) annual, (16) geography, (17) contradiction, (18) spectator, (19) biology, (20) biennial.

Analogies 1 (pp. 32-33)

(1) pedestrian, (2) telescope, (3) hydrophobia, (4) spectacle, (5) biweekly, (6) spectacular, (7) unique, (8) uniform, (9) podium, (10) autograph, (11) automaton, (12) phobia, (13) contradict, (14) bifocals, (15) unite, (16) orthography, (17) transcript, (18) indictment, (19) biennial, (20) microbe.

Multiple-Choice Vocabulary Test 1 (pp. 33-37)
Exercise 1

(1) a, (2) c, (3) c, (4) d, (5) b, (6) a, (7) b, (8) c, (9) c, (10) a, (11) a, (12) c,[5] (13) a.

Exercise 2

(14) c, (15) d, (16) b, (17) b, (18) c, (19) d, (20) c, (21) b, (22) a, (23) a.

Exercise 3

(24) a, (25) c, (26) c,[6] (27) a, (28) c, (29) c, (30) c, (31) a, (32) c, (33) d,[7] (34) c, (35) a, (36) b, (37) a,[8] (38) a, (39) c, (40) b, (41) d.

True/False Test 1 (p. 37)

(1) T, (2) F, (3) F, (4) F, (5) F, (6) F, (7) T, (8) F, (9) T, (10) F, (11) T, (12) T, (13) T, (14) F, (15) F, (16) F.

STOP. Turn to page 38 for the scoring of the tests.

---

[5]*Two-footed animal* is a better answer than *two-footed human* because there are animals other than humans who are bipeds.

[6]*Special form of clothing* is a better answer than *clothing* because clothing refers to all that you wear. Not all clothing is a uniform; a uniform is a special form of clothing.

[7]*A ruler with absolute power* is a better answer than *a ruler* because not all rulers are dictators.

[8]A contradiction refers to something, such as *two statements about the same thing that are complete opposites.* It is not the use of opposites for effect.

Additional Practice 1

A. (1) c, (2) f, (3) d, (4) b, (5) a, (6) e, (7) g.
B. (1) d, (2) m, (3) c, (4) k, (5) f, (6) j, (7) i, (8) e, (9) h, (10) b, (11) g, (12) l, (13) a.

Additional Practice 2

A. (1) g, (2) a, (3) d, (4) f, (5) c, (6) e, (7) b.
B. (1) h, (2) f, (3) g, (4) d, (5) c, (6) a, (7) i, (8) e, (9) b, (10) j.

Additional Practice 3

A. (1) f, (2) c, (3) d, (4) e, (5) a, (6) b.
B. (1) l, (2) m, (3) g, (4) i, (5) h, (6) b, (7) c, (8) e, (9) f, (10) k, (11) o, (12) d, (13) p, (14) r, (15) a, (16) j, (17) q, (18) n.

CHAPTER THREE

EXERCISE 4

Step I. Combining Forms

A. Directions: A list of combining forms with their meanings follows. Look at the combining forms and their meanings. Concentrate on learning each combining form and its meaning. Cover the meanings, read the combining forms, and state the meanings to yourself. Check to see if you are correct. Now cover the combining forms, read the meanings, and state the combining forms to yourself. Check to see if you are correct.

Combining Forms	Meanings
1. cent, centi	hundred; hundredth part
2. dec, deca	ten
3. milli	thousand; thousandth part
4. port	carry
5. cred	believe

B. Directions: Cover the preceding meanings. Write the meanings of the following combining forms.

Combining Forms	Meanings
1. cent, centi	_____
2. dec, deca	_____
3. milli	_____
4. port	_____
5. cred	_____

Step II. Words Derived from Combining Forms

1. **century** (cen · tu · ry) (sen′ chu · rē) *n. (pl.* **ies**) Period of one hundred years. *A man who is 110 years old has lived more than a whole century.*

2. **centennial** (cen · ten · ni · al) (sen · ten′ n̶ē · al) *adj.* Pertaining to a period of one hundred years; lasting one hundred years. *n.* A one-hundredth anniversary. *The centennial celebration for the United States took place in 1876.*

3. **bicentennial** (bi · cen · ten · ni · al) (bī · sen · ten′ n̶ē · al) *adj.* Pertaining to or in honor of a two-hundredth anniversary; consisting of or lasting two hundred years; occurring once in two hundred years. *n.* A two-hundredth anniversary. *The United States celebrated its bicentennial in 1976.*

4. **million** (mil · lion) (mil′ yun) *n.* One thousand thousands (1,000,000); a very large or indefinitely large number. *adj.* Being one million in number; very many; one thousand thousands. *A million years equals ten thousand centuries.*

5. **millennium** (mil · len · ni · um) (mil · len′ n̶ē · um) *n. (pl.* **niums, nia**) Period of one thousand years; a one-thousandth anniversary; a period of great happiness (the millennium). *When the millennium arrives, there will be great happiness on earth.*

6. **decade** (dec · ade) (dek′ ād¢) *n.* Period of ten years. *I can't believe that ten years have passed and that it's already a decade since I last saw my married brother.*

7. **credible** (cred · i · ble) (kred′ i · bul) *adj.* Believable. *I doubt if anyone will believe you because that is not a credible story.*

8. **credit** (cred · it) (kred′ it) *n.* Belief in something; trust; faith; good name; a recognition by name of a contribution to a performance; something that adds to a person's reputation; in an account, the balance in one's favor, an amount of goods or money a person receives and pays for in the future; a

50

unit of academic study. *v.* To supply something on credit to. *Because of his strong financial position, he can receive as much **credit** as he needs from the bank.*

9. **credential** (cre · den · tial) (kre · den′ shul) *n.* Something that entitles one to credit or confidence; something that makes others believe in a person; a document such as a degree, diploma, or certificate; *pl.* **credentials**: testimonials entitling a person to credit or to exercise official power. *His **credentials** for the job were so good that everyone felt he would do the work very well.*

10. **incredible** (in · cred · ible) (in · kred′ i · bul) *adj.* Not believable. *It is not believable that you could have gotten yourself into such an **incredible** situation.*

11. **porter** (port′ er) *n.* A person who carries things; one who is employed to carry baggage at a hotel or transportation terminal. *At the airport, I always tip the **porter** who carries my luggage.*

12. **reporter** (rē · port′ er) *n.* A person who gathers information and writes reports for newspapers, magazines, and so on. *I have always wanted to be a **reporter** because I like to gather information and write reports.*

13. **port** (port) *n.* Place to or from which ships carry things; place where ships may wait. *When a ship comes to **port**, its cargo is usually unloaded immediately.*

14. **export** (ex · port) (ek · sport′) *v.* To carry away; to transport or send something to another country. *n.* Something that is exported. *The United States **exports** wheat to many nations.*

15. **import** (im · port′) *v.* To carry in; bring in goods from another country. *n.* Something that is imported. *The United States **imports** coffee from South America.*

16. **portable** (port · a · ble) (port′ a · bul) *adj.* Can be carried; easily or conveniently transported. ***Portable** goods are those that you can easily take from one place to another.*

Special Notes

1. The combining form *centi* meaning "hundredth part" is used chiefly in terms belonging to the metric system (*centimeter*).
2. The combining form *deci* means "tenth part."
3. The combining form *kilo* means "thousand."

Step III. Practice

A. Directions: Underline the word that *best* fits the meaning given for each group of words.

1. A hundredth anniversary
   - a. century
   - b. centennial
   - c. bicentennial
   - d. decade

2. A period of ten years
   - a. centennial
   - b. century
   - c. million
   - d. decade

3. Believable
   - a. credit
   - b. credential
   - c. credible
   - d. incredible

4. Place where ships wait
   - a. port
   - b. porter
   - c. import
   - d. deport

5. A person who gathers information for newspapers
   - a. port
   - b. import
   - c. deport
   - d. reporter

6. A document such as a degree or diploma
   - a. credit
   - b. credential
   - c. credible
   - d. incredible

7. Period of one hundred years
   - a. decade
   - b. century
   - c. bicentennial
   - d. millennium

8. Someone who carries things
   - a. reporter
   - b. port
   - c. porter
   - d. import

9. One thousand thousands
   - a. millennium
   - b. centennial
   - c. bicentennial
   - d. million

10. Period of a thousand years
    - a. century
    - b. millennium
    - c. million
    - d. bicentennial

11. Not believable
    - a. credit
    - b. credential
    - c. incredible
    - d. credible

12. Can be carried
    - a. porter
    - b. import
    - c. deport
    - d. portable

13. Two-hundredth anniversary
    - a. bicentennial
    - b. millennium
    - c. centennial
    - d. century

14. Bring in goods from another country
    - a. import
    - b. export
    - c. portable
    - d. porter

15. Balance in one's favor
    - a. credential
    - b. credit
    - c. credible
    - d. incredible

16. To carry or send something to another country or region
    - a. port
    - b. import
    - c. reporter
    - d. export

STOP. Check answers at the end of Chapter Three (p. 80).

B. Directions: A few paragraphs with missing words follow. Fill in the blanks with the word that *best* fits. Words may be used more than once.

Word List

million, credential, reporter, decade, incredible, portable, port, export, import, credible, credit.

    As a 1_____ for a large newspaper, I am always looking for a good story. Approximately nine and one-half years ago, almost a whole 2_____ ago, a lot of drugs were stolen right under the noses of the police. Only persons with proper 3_____ s were allowed to deal with the drugs. It just did not seem possible that the drugs could be stolen. It seemed 4_____. The amount of money involved was said to be thousands of thousands of dollars, over a(n) 5_____ dollars.

    Recently, 6_____ for this 7_____ robbery was given to insiders who had proper police 8_____ s. The inform- er's story about the robbery is a(n) 9_____ one, and everyone seems to believe it. It seems that persons with 10_____ s were able to get into the place where the drugs were stored. They were able to place the drugs on a 11_____ table and calmly walk out with them. They replaced the drugs with a mixture of sugar and salt. The robbers than took the drugs to 12_____ , where they had a ship waiting for them. The drugs were 13_____ ed to another country. When things quiet- ed down, the drugs were 14_____ ed to the United States and sold for 15_____ s of dollars.

STOP. Check answers at the end of Chapter Three (p. 80).

EXTRA WORD POWER

> **able, ible.** Can do; able. When *able* or *ible* is found at the end of a word, the word is an adjective mean- ing "able" or "can do." For example: *portable*— able to be carried; *incredible*—not able to be believed; *credible*—able to be believed; *manageable*—able to be managed; *laughable*—able to be laughed at; *enjoyable*— able to be enjoyed. How many more *able* or *ible* words can you think of?

Additional Words Derived from Combining Forms

From your knowledge of combining forms, can you define the following words?

1. **decimal** (dec • i • mal) (des′ i • mal) *adj. n. Most of the world's currency uses the **decimal** system, which divides the prime unit of money (such as dollars) into tenths or hundredths.*

2. **decimate** (dec · i · mate) (des′ i · māt¢) *v. If you have to lose a battle, it is better to be decimated than obliterated because in the former case, nine tenths of your troops will survive.*

3. **decameter** (dec · a · me · ter) (dek′ a · mē · ter) *n. Because the United States is converting to the metric system, persons should become familiar with such terms as decameter.*

4. **decimeter** (dec · i · me · ter) (des′ i · mē · ter) *n. A decimeter is approximately 4 inches, so that it would take about 3 decimeters to equal 1 foot.*

5. **millimeter** (mil′ li · mē · ter) *n. Microorganisms are even smaller than a millimeter.*

6. **centimeter** (cen · ti · me · ter) (sen′ ti · mē · ter) *n. I measured the distance in centimeters because I needed to know it to the nearest hundredth of a meter.*

7. **kilometer** (ki · lo · me · ter) (kil′ om · e · ter) *n. There are approximately 1.6 kilometers to a mile.*

8. **centipede** (cent · i · pede) (sent′ i · pēd¢) *n. The centipede crawled along on its many feet.*

9. **creed** (krē¢d) *n. The creed "All men are created equal" is found in our Constitution.*

10. **accreditation** (ac · cred · i · ta · tion) (aḱ · kred · i · tā′ shun) *n. If a college does not have the proper accreditation, students might have difficulty in getting jobs or getting into graduate schools.*

11. **creditor** (cred · i · tor) (kred′ it · or) *n. Savings and loan associations are more likely to be large creditors to the public through home purchase loans than are commercial banks.*

12. **deportment** (dē · port′ ment) *n.* *Because his **deportment** has always been above question, everyone is confused by his present behavior.*

STOP. Check answers at the end of Chapter Three (p. 81).

Practice for Additional Words Derived from Combining Forms

Directions: Match each word with the *best* definition.

_____ 1. decimal	a. statement of belief
_____ 2. decimate	b. one to whom something is due
_____ 3. decameter	c. conduct
_____ 4. millimeter	d. 1/100 of a meter
_____ 5. centimeter	e. wormlike animal with many legs
_____ 6. centipede	f. 1/1,000 of a meter
_____ 7. accreditation	g. to destroy one tenth of; to destroy but not completely
_____ 8. creed	h. ten meters
_____ 9. creditor	i. numbered by ten
_____10. deportment	j. a giving authority to
_____11. decimeter	k. 1,000 meters
_____12. kilometer	l. 1/10 of a meter

STOP. Check answers at the end of Chapter Three (p. 81).

EXERCISE 5

Step I. Combining Forms

A. Directions: A list of combining forms with their meanings follows. Look at the combining forms and their meanings. Concentrate on learning each combining form and its meaning. Cover the meanings, read the combining forms, and state the meanings to yourself. Check to see if you are correct. Now cover the combining forms, read the meanings, and state the combining forms to yourself. Check to see if you are correct.

Combining Forms	Meanings
1. agog, agogue	leading; directing; inciting
2. arch	rule; chief
3. ali	other
4. dem, demo	people
5. mon, mono	one
6. theo	God

B. Directions: Cover the preceding meanings. Write the meanings of the following combining forms.

Combining Forms	Meanings
1. agog, agogue	_____
2. arch	_____
3. ali	_____
4. dem, demo	_____
5. mon, mono	_____
6. theo	_____

Step II. Words Derived from Combining Forms

1. **monarchy** (mon · ar · chy) (mon′ ar · kē) *n.* A government or state headed by a single person, who is usually a king, queen, or emperor; called absolute (or despotic) when there is no limitation on the monarch's power and constitutional (or limited) when there is such limitation. *Although England is a **monarchy**, the king or queen does not exercise any power at all.*

2. **autocracy** (au · toc · ra · cy) (au · tok′ ra · sē) *n.* A form of government in which one person possesses unlimited power. *In any **autocracy** the head of government has absolute control of the country.*

3. **autocrat** (au · to · crat) (au′ to · krat) *n.* A ruler who has absolute control of a country. *The head of government who has absolute control in an autocracy is called an **autocrat**.*

4. **anarchy** (an · ar · chy) (an′ ar · kē) *n.* No rule; disorder; the absence of government; chaos. *In the West, years ago, **anarchy** existed in many towns because there were no laws.*

56

5. **atheist** (ā' thē · ist) *n.* One who does not believe in the existence of God. *An atheist does not believe in the existence of God.*

6. **theocracy** (the · oc · ra · cy) (thē · ok' ra · sē) *n.* Government by a religious group. *A country ruled by clergy (persons allowed to preach the gospel) would be called a theocracy.*

7. **theology** (the · ol · o · gy) (thē · ol' o · jē) *n.* The study of religion. *Mininsters, priests, and rabbis must take courses in theology to learn about religion.*

8. **democracy** (de · moc · ra · cy) (de · mok' ra · sē) *n.* A form of government in which there is rule by the people either directly or through elected representatives. *In a democracy the people, through their voting power, have a say in who the leaders of the government will be.*

9. **demagogue** (dem' a · gogᵫ) *n.* A person who stirs up the emotions of people in order to become a leader and achieve selfish ends. *A demagogue is usually a highly persuasive speaker who plays on the emotions of the crowds for his own ends.*

10. **alias** (a · li · as) (ā' lē · as) *n.* (*pl.* **ses**) Another name taken by a person, often a criminal. *A person who uses an alias doesn't want others to know what his real name is.*

11. **alien** (al · ien) (ā' lē · un) *n.* A foreigner; a person from another country. *adj.* Foreign. *If aliens in the United States neglect to register as aliens, they may be deported to their country of origin.*

12. **alienate** (al · ien · ate) (āl' yun · ātᵫ) *v.* To make others unfriendly to one; to estrange (to remove or keep at a distance). *The politicians try not to alienate any voters.*

Special Notes

1. The word *demagogue* is a little more difficult to define even though you know the meanings of the combining forms. A *demagogue* is a person who stirs the emotions of people to become a leader and gain selfish ends. A *demagogue* appeals usually to popular passion, especially by making extravagant promises or charges. This word is used to refer to leaders who use people for their own ends. *Hitler is probably the most hated demagogue of the twentieth century.*

2. The word *autocrat* means "a ruler in absolute control." An *autocrat* does not have to be a king or a queen. The word *autocracy* means "government by an autocrat." A *monarchy,* which is rule by a monarch, be it a king, queen, or emperor, does not have to be an autocracy; that is, a country

can have a king or a queen, but the king or queen does not necessarily have absolute control of the government.

3. When the combining form *arch* is the final element of a word, it means "rule." When *arch* is used at the beginning of a word (such as *archbishop, archfiend*), it means "chief."

Step III. Practice

A. Directions: The words presented in Exercise 5 follow. Match the word with its meaning. Put the letter of the meaning in the space before the word.

Words	*Meanings*
_____ 1. theocracy	a. a person who stirs emotions of people in order to become a leader and achieve selfish ends
_____ 2. theology	b. a ruler in absolute control
_____ 3. atheist	c. to make others unfriendly to one
_____ 4. alien	d. another name, usually used by criminals
_____ 5. alienate	e. one who does not believe in God
_____ 6. monarchy	f. a government headed by a king, queen, or emperor
_____ 7. autocrat	g. the study of religion
_____ 8. anarchy	h. a foreigner
_____ 9. democracy	i. the absence of government
_____10. autocracy	j. a form of government in which one person possesses unlimited power
_____11. demagogue	
_____12. alias	
	k. government of a state by a religious group
	l. a form of government in which there is rule by the people

STOP. Check answers at the end of Chapter Three (p. 81).

B. Directions: A number of sentences with missing words follows. Underline
the word that *best* fits the sentence. Two choices are given
for each sentence.

1. When there are no laws or government, a state of (autocracy, anarchy)
    usually exists.

2. Huey Long, a former governor of Louisiana, was known to be a(n) (auto-
    crat, demagogue) because he was able to stir persons' emotions to achieve
    his own selfish ends.

3. In a (monarchy, democracy) there is rule by the people directly or through
    elected representatives.

4. A monarchy that is also a(n) (theocracy, autocracy) is one in which the
    ruler has supreme and unlimited power.

5. A country that is headed by a king, a queen, or an emperor is called an
    absolute (democracy, monarchy) when there are no limitations on the
    ruler's powers.

6. A person who does not believe in the existence of God is called an (atheist,
    anarchist).

7. An (atheist, autocrat) is a ruler who has absolute power in his or her govern-
    ment.

8. John used an (autograph, alias) when he didn't want people at the hotel to
    recognize his famous name.

9. Every year (autocrats, aliens) living in the United States must register as
    citizens of another country.

10. I never (alienate, describe) anyone on purpose because I don't like to have
    enemies.

11. In a(n) (autocracy, theocracy) God is recognized as the ruler.

STOP. Check answers at the end of Chapter Three (p. 81).

> **a.** Without; not. *A* is used in front of some words and means "without" or "not." For example: *an-archy*—without rule; *atheist*—one who is without belief in God; *amoral*—without morals; without being able to tell right from wrong. *Those that bombed many buildings filled with people are **amoral** because they do not know right from wrong.* The people in this sentence are *amoral.* An amoral person does not have a sense of right or wrong. However, an *immoral* person does know the difference between right and wrong, but he or she chooses to do wrong.

Additional Words Derived from Combining Forms

From your knowledge of combining forms, can you define the following words?

1. **apodal** (ap′ o · dal) *adj. The snake is an **apodal** animal.*

   _____

2. **demography** (de · mog · ra · phy) (de · mog′ ra · fē) *n. Demographers study the **demography** of a population to determine the trends of vital statistics.*

   _____

3. **archetype** (ar · che · type) (ar′ ke · tīpe) *n. The architect showed an **archetype** of the building to the interested spectators.*

   _____

4. **monotone** (mon′ o · tōne) *n. v. When a lecturer speaks in a **monotone**, listeners have difficulty paying attention to what is being said.*

   _____

5. **monotonous** (mo · not′ o · nous) *adj. Doing the same things over and over again is very **monotonous.***

   _____

6. **monorail** (mon′ o · rāil) *n. When you ride on the **monorail** at Walt Disney World, everything on the ground appears to be so small.*

   _____

7. **monophobia** (mon · o · pho · bi · a) (mon · o · fō′ bē · a) *n. I can't imagine a person who is suffering from **monophobia** living alone in the mountains.*

   _____

8. **monoglot** (mon' o · glot) *n. adj. There are probably more **monoglots** in the United States than in Europe because Europe does not have a single dominant language.*

9. **monopoly** (mo · nop · o · ly) (mo · nop' o · lē) *n. (pl. ies). Because the company had a **monopoly** on the grain market, they were able to charge whatever they wanted for grain.*

10. **oligarchy** (ol · i · gar · chy) (ol' i · gar · kē) *n. (pl. ies). **Oligarchy**, as a form of government, usually fails because each of the rulers generally competes with the others to try to gain more power for himself.*

STOP. Check answers at the end of Chapter Three (pp. 81–82).

Practice for Additional Words Derived from Combining Forms

Directions: Match each word with the *best* definition.

_____ 1. apodal

_____ 2. demography

_____ 3. archetype

_____ 4. monophobia

_____ 5. monoglot

_____ 6. monorail

_____ 7. monotone

_____ 8. monotonous

_____ 9. monopoly

_____10. oligarchy

a. cars suspended from a single rail

b. a form of government in which there is rule by a few

c. dull; changeless

d. speech not having any change in pitch

e. being without feet

f. the exclusive control of something

g. the first of its kind; model

h. study of populations

i. the fear of being alone

j. a person who knows only one language

STOP. Check answers at the end of Chapter Three (p. 82).

EXERCISE 6

Step I. Combining Forms

A. Directions: A list of combining forms with their meanings follows. Look at the combining forms and their meanings. Concentrate on learning each combining form and its meaning. Cover the meanings, read the combining forms, and state the meanings to yourself. Check to see if you are correct. Now cover the combining forms, read the meanings, and state the combining forms to yourself. Check to see if you are correct.

Combining Forms   *Meanings*

1. mis, miso[1]   hate; wrong

2. poly   many

3. gamy   marriage

4. hom, homo[1]   same; man; human

5. gen, geno   race; kind; descent

6. anthrop, anthropo   man; human; mankind

7. leg, legis, lex   law

B. Directions: Cover the preceding meanings. Write the meanings of the following combining forms.

Combining Forms   *Meanings*

1. mis, miso   _____

2. poly   _____

3. gamy   _____

4. hom, homo   _____

5. gen, geno   _____

6. anthrop, anthropo   _____

7. leg, legis, lex   _____

---

[1]When words combine with *mis* in this exercise, *mis* means "hate." When words combine with *homo* in this exercise, *homo* means "same." You will meet words with the other meanings for *mis* and *homo* in a later exercise.

1. **monogamy** (mo • nog • a • my) (mo • nog′ a • mē) *n.* Marriage to one spouse at one time. *In the United States, **monogamy** is practiced, so you can be married to only one spouse (husband or wife) at one time.*

2. **bigamy** (big • a • my) (big′ a • mē) *n.* Marriage to two spouses at the same time. *Because **bigamy** is not allowed in the United States, you will not find many persons who are married to two spouses at the same time.*

3. **polygamy** (po • lyg • a • my) (po • lig′ a • mē) *n.* Marriage to many spouses at the same time. *Because **polygamy** is allowed in some Middle Eastern countries, you will find some persons with many spouses in such countries.*

4. **anthropology** (an • thro • pol • o • gy) (an • thro • pol′ ŏ • jē) *n.* The study of mankind; the study of the cultures and customs of people. *In **anthropology** we studied about a tribe of people who had an entirely different way of life from ours.*

5. **misanthrope** (mis′ an • thrōpė) *n.* Hater of mankind. *Although Jim does not like women, he is not a **misanthrope** because he doesn't hate all people.*

6. **legal** (lē′ gal) *adj.* Referring to law; lawful. *Although the business deal was **legal**, it did not sound lawful to me.*

7. **legislature** (leg • is • la • ture) (lej′ is • lā • chur) *n.* Body of persons responsible for lawmaking. *The **legislature** is the body of persons given the power to write laws for a state or nation.*

8. **homosexual** (ho • mo • sex • u • al) (hō • mo • sek′ shū • al) *adj.* Referring to the same sex or to sexual desire for those of the same sex. *n.* A homosexual individual. *A **homosexual** is one who prefers a relationship with an individual of the same sex.*

9. **homograph** (hom • o • graph) (hom′ o • graf) *n.* A word spelled the same way as another but having a different meaning. *The verb saw and the noun saw are **homographs**.*

10. **homogeneous** (ho • mo • ge • ne • ous) (hō • mo • jē′ nē • ɸus) *adj.* Being the same throughout; being uniform. *It is difficult to have a **homogeneous** group of students because students are not all the same.*

11. **general** (gen • er • al) (jen′ er • al) *adj.* Referring to all. *n.* In the U.S. Army and Air Force, an officer of the same rank as an admiral in the U.S. Navy. *The statement "All men are equal" is a **general** statement.*

12. **generic** (ge • ner • ic) (je • ner′ ik) *adj.* Referring to all in a group or class. *When one uses the term man in the **generic** sense, one is referring to both males and females.*

Special Notes

1. A *homograph* is a word written the same way as another but having a different meaning. *General* and *general* are two words in this exercise that are *homographs* because they are spelled alike but have different meanings.

2. The term *generic* means "general," "referring to all in a group or class." Persons use the word *generic* in order to make their statements more clear. For example: *I am speaking in the **generic** sense when I use the word* mankind *because* mankind *refers to both males and females.* When the word *chairman* is used, it is used in the *generic* sense; that is, a person can be chairman and be either a man or a woman. Today the word *chairperson* is used more often because it is more general.

Step III. Practice

A. Directions: A number of sentences with missing words follows. Choose the word that *best* fits the sentence. Put the word in the blank. There are more words in the list than you need.

Word List

monogamy, alien, alienate, homogeneous, generic, anthropologist, biology, geology, autocracy, atheist, centennial, bicentennial, anthropology, homograph, misogamist, misanthrope, legal, legislature, homosexual, bigamy, decade, incredible, century.

1. Because I am interested in learning about other cultures and the way man lives, I studied _____ in college.

2. The term *man* in sentence 1 is used in the _____ sense because it refers to both men and women.

3. In the year 1976 America celebrated its _____.

4. It is not _____ to practice _____ in the United States.

5. In the United States _____ is practiced because it's not legal to have more than one spouse.

6. The terms *spring* meaning "season" and *spring* meaning "to leap" are _____ s.

7. A person who hates people would be called a(n) _____.

8. We will be entering another _____ in the year 2000.

9. The _____ has voted more rights for women.

64

10. Margaret Mead, who studied about other people around the world, is known as a famous _____.

11. Margaret Mead has written about the customs of other people, and these may appear _____ to people in the Western world.

STOP. Check answers at the end of Chapter Three (p. 82).

B. Directions: A list of definitions follows. Choose the word that *best* fits the definition. Try to relate your definition to the meanings of the combining forms. All the words are used.

Word List

misanthrope, monogamy, bigamy, decade, anthropology, anthropologist, legal, legislature, homosexual, century, bicentennial, homogeneous, polygamist, homograph, generic, centennial.

1. hater of mankind _____
2. one who is married to many spouses at the same time _____
3. hundredth anniversary _____
4. being of the same kind _____
5. lawful _____
6. a period of one hundred years _____
7. word spelled the same as another but having a different meaning _____
8. every two hundred years _____
9. referring to a relationship with the same sex _____
10. the study of mankind or different cultures _____
11. marriage to one spouse at one time _____
12. referring to all in a group or class _____
13. marriage to two spouses at the same time _____
14. one who studies different cultures _____
15. body of persons responsible for lawmaking _____
16. a period of ten years _____

STOP. Check the answers at the end of Chapter Three (p. 82).

ist. One who. When *ist* is found at the end of a noun, it means "one who" and changes the word to a certain type of person. For example, let's add *ist* to a number of words you have met: *geologist*—one who is in the field of geology; *biologist*—one who is in the field of biology; *anthropologist*—one who is in the field of anthropology; *theologist*—one who is in the field of theology; *bigamist*—one who is married to two spouses at the same time; *polygamist*—one who is married to many spouses at the same time; *monogamist*—one who believes in or practices monogamy; *anarchist*—one who believes that there should be no government. How many more words with *ist* can you add to this list?

Additional Words Derived from Combining Forms

From your knowledge of combining forms, can you define the following words?

1. **polyglot** (pol · y · glot) (pol′ ē · glot) *n. adj. It's helpful for ambassadors to be **polyglots**.*

   _____

2. **polygon** (pol · y · gon) (pol′ ē · gon) *n. In geometry I always had difficulty solving problems involving **polygons** because they have so many angles.*

   _____

3. **podiatrist** (po · dī′ a · trist) *n. After I went on a ten-mile hike, my feet hurt so much that I needed to visit a **podiatrist**.*

   _____

4. **bisexual** (bi · sex · u · al) (bī · sek′ shū · al) *adj. n. Because some plants are **bisexual**, they can fertilize themselves to reproduce the next generation.*

   _____

5. **misogamist** (mi · sog′ a · mist) *n. Although Jim has never married, I do not think he is a **misogamist**.*

   _____

6. **anthropomorphic** (an · thro · po · mor · phic) (an · thro · pō · mor′ fik) *adj. In Walt Disney films, all of the animals have **anthropomorphic** characteristics*

   _____

7. **anthropoid** (an' thro · poid) *n. adj. The gorilla, orangutan, and chimpanzee are **anthropoids**.*

_____

8. **genealogy** (ge · ne · al · o · gy) (jē · nē · al' o · jē) *n. (pl.* **ies**) *Mrs. Smith went to England to acquire certain documents that would help her in tracing the **genealogy** of her family.*

_____

9. **genus** (ge · nus) (jē' nus) *n. (pl.* **genera**) (jen' er · a) *In biology, when plants or animals are classified according to common characteristics, the name of the **genus** begins with a capital letter.*

_____

10. **generate** (gen · er · ate) (jen' er · āt¢) *v. Every animal **generates** its own species or kind.*

_____

STOP. Check answers at the end of Chapter Three (pp. 82–83).

Practice for Additional Words Derived from Combining Forms

Directions: Match each word with the *best* definition.

_____ 1. polyglot	a.	hater of marriage
_____ 2. polygon	b.	resembling or suggesting an ape
_____ 3. podiatrist	c.	speaking many languages
_____ 4. bisexual	d.	class, kind, or group marked by common characteristics
_____ 5. misogamist	e.	to produce
_____ 6. anthropomorphic	f.	foot doctor
_____ 7. anthropoid	g.	described in human terms
_____ 8. genealogy	h.	study of one's descent
_____ 9. genus	i.	a many-sided plane figure
_____ 10. generate	j.	of both sexes

STOP. Check answers at the end of Chapter Three (p. 83).

CROSSWORD PUZZLE 2

Directions: The meanings of many of the combining forms from Exercises 4–6 follow. Your knowledge of these combining forms will help you to solve this crossword puzzle. Note that *combining form* is abbreviated as *comb. f.*

Across

1. A small word that refers to a position
3. A small word that means "in the same manner"
5. Comb. f. for *ten*
8. A monkey
9. A musical syllable
10. In poker, the stake put up before dealing the cards
11. Comb f. for *kind* or *species*
13. Same as #9 Across
15. Refers to yourself
16. Part of a shoe
18. Comb. f. for *mankind*
24. Same as #8 Across

Down

1. Abbreviation for *advertisement*
2. Comb. f. for *from a distance*
3. Abbreviation for *apartment*
4. Meaning of *spect*
6. A container
7. Comb. f. for *without*
8. An indefinite article
10. Same as #7 Down
11. Word meaning *class; kind; group*
12. Fifteenth letter of the alphabet
13. Supporting yourself against something
14. A high mountain
15. An informal way of referring to mother

26. Twenty-first letter of the alphabet
27. Comb. f. for *one*
28. Opposite of *men*
30. Same as #7 Down
31. A piece of wood that supports a sign
33. Opposite of *gain*
34. Refers to a kind of metal
37. Sound made to quiet someone
38. Comb. f. for *marriage*
41. Twentieth letter of the alphabet
42. Opposite of *yes*
43. Meaning of *uni* and *mono*

16. Comb. f. for *man; same*
17. Fifth letter of the alphabet
19. Refers to an explosive
20. A greeting
21. Eighteenth letter of the alphabet
22. Sound made when you are hurt
23. Comb. f. for *many*
25. What you do when you are hungry
26. Opposite of *down* (pl.)
29. The ending of *highest*
32. An exclamation of surprise
35. Opposite of *out*
36. A negative answer
38. Opposite of *stop*
39. Same as #8 Down
40. Same as #15 Across

STOP. Check answers at the end of Chapter Three (p. 83).

WORD SCRAMBLE 2

Directions: Word Scramble 2 is based on words from Exercises 4–6. The meanings are your clues to arranging the letters in correct order. Write the correct word in the blank.

Meanings

1. onllmii _____ one thousand thousands

2. eecrildb _____ believable

3. nucteyr _____ period of one hundred years

4. eddace _____ period of ten years

5. primto _____ to bring goods in from another country

6. leraiedtcn _____ something that gives someone authority

7. bropelat _____ able to be carried

8. yrcmnoah _____ government headed by a king, queen, or emperor

9. aanychr _____ no rule

10. seiahtt _____ one who does not believe in God

11. cttuoaar _____ absolute ruler

12. nalei _____ a foreigner

13. ooelytgh _____ the study of religion

14. saail _____ another name

15. ooohalgyntrp _____ the study of mankind

16. llgea _____ lawful

17. reengla _____ a high-ranking officer in the army

18. ooguhsoenem _____ being of same kind

19. namgoyom _____ marriage to one at one time

20. magyib _____ marriage to two spouses at one time

STOP. Check answers at the end of Chapter Three (p. 84).

ANALOGIES 2

Directions: Find the word from the following list that *best* completes each analogy. There are more words in the list than you need.

Word List

physician, polyglot, polygon, cent, deca, podiatrist, anthropoid, milli, century, decade, anthropology, million, export, anarchy, millennium, penny, archetype, arch, autocracy, bigamy, alienate, alias, credential, decimate, decimal, alien, decameter, centimeter, millimeter, credit, incredible, atheist, reporter, creditor.

1. Scientist : biologist : : doctor :_____.

2. Mono : poly :: monoglot :_____.

3. Millimeter : centimeter :: meter : _____ .

4. Vehicle : automobile :: writer :_____.

5. Pepper : spice : : hexagon :_____.

6. Milli : cent : : cent : _____ .

7. Pedestal : base : : foreigner : _____ .

8. Two : binary : : ten : _____ .

9. Democracy : autocracy : : import : _____ .

10. None : universal :: credible :_____.

11. Decade : century : : century :_____.

70

20. anarchy
   a. without belief in God
   b. no rule
   c. absolute rule
   d. rule by one

21. atheist
   a. one who believes in no rule
   b. one who believes in absolute rule
   c. one who believes in rule by a religious group
   d. one who does not believe in God

22. theocracy
   a. belief in God
   b. rule by a religious group
   c. the study of religion
   d. absolute rule

23. theology
   a. rule by a religious group
   b. belief in God
   c. absolute rule
   d. the study of religion

24. democracy
   a. absolute rule
   b. leader who influences persons for his own purposes
   c. rule by the people
   d. the study of people

25. demagogue
   a. ruler of people
   b. rule by the people
   c. leader who influences persons for his own purposes
   d. leader of people

26. alias
   a. a foreigner
   b. unfriendly
   c. another name
   d. turns people away

27. alien
   a. another name
   b. a foreigner
   c. turns people away
   d. unfriendly

28. alienate
   a. make others unfriendly
   b. a foreigner
   c. another name
   d. makes friends

Exercise 6

29. monogamy
   a. hater of marriage
   b. no belief in marriage
   c. marriage to one spouse at one time
   d. the study of marriage

30. bigamy
   a. something not lawful
   b. marriage to two spouses at the same time
   c. having been married twice
   d. marriage to one spouse at one time

31. polygamy
   a. marriage to many spouses at one time
   b. many marriages
   c. something not legal
   d. the study of many marriages

32. misanthrope	a. hater of marriage b. married to a man	c. hater of mankind d. the study of mankind
33. anthropology	a. marriage to men b. the study of mankind	c. a science d. hater of mankind
34. legal	a. person responsible for law b. body of persons responsible for lawmaking	c. lawful d. a person who defends others
35. legislature	a. lawful b. person responsible for laws	c. body of persons responsible for lawmaking d. persons who defend others
36. homosexual	a. same kind b. referring to man	c. one who prefers relationships with the same sex d. one who prefers relationships with the opposite sex
37. homogeneous	a. being of the same kind b. the same sex	c. referring to man d. one who prefers relationships with the same sex
38. homograph	a. the study of man b. the study of graphs	c. the same word d. a word spelled the same as another but having a different meaning
39. general	a. referring to the same b. referring to all	c. referring to a group of people d. referring to kinds of people
40. generic	a. referring to all in a group or class b. referring to people	c. referring to a group d. referring to generals in the army

TRUE/FALSE TEST 2

Directions: This is a true/false test on Exercises 4–6. Read each sentence carefully. Decide whether it is true or false. Put a *T* for *true* or an *F* for *false* in the blank. The number after the sentence tells you if the word is from Exercise 4, 5, or 6.

_____ 1. One who hates mankind is called a <u>misanthrope</u>. 6

_____ 2. A <u>misogamist</u> must also be a <u>misanthrope</u>. 6

_____ 3. Ten hundred thousand equals one <u>million</u>. 4

74

_____ 4. Ten decades do not equal a century. 4

_____ 5. An anthropologist is interested in studying ants. 6

_____ 6. An atheist believes in God. 5

_____ 7. A bachelor must be a misogamist. 6

_____ 8. When you import something, you send it out of the country. 4

_____ 9. A centennial celebration takes place every one thousand years. 4

_____10. If you have a good credit rating, you have a good financial reputation. 4

_____11. Your credentials are what you have that makes persons believe you can do a certain job. 4

_____12. An autocrat is a ruler in a democracy. 5

_____13. An anarchist is one who believes in no government. 5, 6

_____14. An anarchist must be an atheist. 5, 6

_____15. A demagogue uses people for his or her own selfish ends. 5

_____16. An alien is someone who enters another country not legally. 5, 6

_____17. When you use an alias, you are using your given name. 5

_____18. Saw (the past tense of to see) and saw (something that you cut with) are examples of homographs. 6

_____19. Persons with homogeneous tastes are persons who must like men. 6

_____20. In the word mankind, "man" is used in the generic sense because it refers to both men and women. 6

_____21. Someone who commits bigamy may be jailed because this is not legal in the United States. 6

_____22. The legislature is responsible for making laws for the state or federal government. 6

STOP. Check answers for both tests at the end of Chapter Three (p. 84).

SCORING OF TESTS

Multiple-Choice Vocabulary Test		True/False Test	
Number Wrong	_Score_	_Number Wrong_	_Score_
0–3	Excellent	0–1	Excellent
4–6	Good	2–3	Good
7–9	Weak	4–5	Weak
Above 9	Poor	Above 5	Poor
Score _____		Score _____	

1. If you scored in the excellent or good range on *both tests*, you are doing well. Go on to Chapter Four.

2. If you scored in the weak or poor range on either test, look below and follow directions for Additional Practice. Note that the words on the test are arranged so that you can tell in which exercise to find them. This will help you if you need additional practice.

ADDITIONAL PRACTICE SETS

A. Directions: Write the words you missed on the tests from the three exercises in the space provided. Note that the tests are presented so that you can tell to which exercises the words belong.

Exercise 4 Words Missed

1. _____   6. _____

2. _____   7. _____

3. _____   8. _____

4. _____   9. _____

5. _____   10. _____

Exercise 5 Words Missed

1. _____   6. _____

2. _____   7. _____

3. _____   8. _____

4. _____   9. _____

5. _____   10. _____

Exercise 6 Words Missed

1. _____   6. _____

2. _____   7. _____

3. _____   8. _____

4. _____   9. _____

5. _____   10. _____

B. Directions: Restudy the words that you have written down on this page. Study the combining forms from which those words are derived. Do Step I and Step II for those you missed. Note that Step I and Step II of the combining forms and vocabulary derived from these combining forms are on the following pages:

Exercise 4—pp. 49–51

Exercise 5—pp. 55–58

Exercise 6—pp. 62–64

C. Directions: Do Additional Practice 1 on this page and the next if you missed words from Exercise 4. Do Additional Practice 2 on pp. 78–79 if you missed words from Exercise 5. Do Additional Practice 3 on pp. 79–80 if you missed words from Exercise 6. Now go on to Chapter Four.

Additional Practice 1 for Exercise 4

A. Directions: The combining forms presented in Exercise 4 follow. Match the combining form with its meaning.

_____ 1. cent, centi   a. carry

_____ 2. dec, deca   b. hundred; hundredth part

_____ 3. milli   c. believe

_____ 4. port   d. thousand; thousandth part

_____ 5. cred   e. ten

STOP. Check answers at the end of Chapter Three (p. 85).

B. Directions: Sentences containing the meanings of vocabulary presented in Exercise 4 follow. Choose the word that *best* fits the meaning of the word or phrase underlined in the sentence.

Word List

century, centennial, bicentennial, million, millennium, decade, credible, credits, credentials, incredible, porter, reporter, port, export, imports, portable.

_____ 1. It is <u>not believable</u> that you are able to do all that.

_____ 2. In <u>a period of one hundred years</u> many changes have taken place in the United States.

_____ 3. What do you call <u>the place where a ship waits?</u>

_____ 4. <u>The one-hundredth anniversary</u> of the first spaceship's landing on the moon will be in 2069.

_____ 5. When complete peace comes to earth, a period of great happiness will exist.

_____ 6. That is a believable statement.

_____ 7. How many academic units have you earned toward your degree?

_____ 8. One thousand thousands is a large number.

_____ 9. The man's college degree, as well as his work experiences, helped him to get the job.

_____ 10. The person who carried my baggage was very strong.

_____ 11. My television set is on a table that can be moved very easily to any part of the room.

_____ 12. She is a person who gathers information and writes articles for the magazine.

_____ 13. When will you take the goods out of the country?

_____ 14. The year 1976 was the two-hundredth anniversary of the United States.

_____ 15. Every year the United States brings into the country many goods made by foreign countries.

_____ 16. In a ten-year period clothing styles may change from one extreme to another.

STOP. Check answers at the end of Chapter Three (p. 85).

Additional Practice 2 for Exercise 5

A. Directions: The combining forms presented in Exercise 5 follow. Match the combining form with its meaning.

_____ 1. agog, agogue   a. rule; chief

_____ 2, arch   b. other

_____ 3. ali   c. God

_____ 4. dem, demo   d. leading, directing; inciting

_____ 5. mon, mono   e. people

_____ 6. theo   f. one

STOP. Check answers at the end of Chapter Three (p. 85).

B. Directions: A number of sentences with missing words follows. Fill in the blank with the word that *best* fits.

Word List

monarchy, autocracy, autocrat, anarchy, atheist, theocracy, theology, democracy, demagogue, alias, alien, alienate.

1. You will _____ a lot of people by the way you are acting.

2. As I did not want to be recognized when I traveled, I wore a disguise and used a(n)_____ .

3. A(n) _____ is a person who belongs to another country.

4. In a(n)_____ a king or queen may be at the head of government but not necessarily have any power.

5. A(n) _____ has absolute power in his country.

6. I would not like to live in a(n) _____ because one does not have any freedom to disagree with the ruler.

7. In our_____ all persons over eighteen have the right to vote and the government is ruled by the people through elected representatives.

8. In a state of_____ there is confusion because there are no laws.

9. A(n) _____ would not be a churchgoer because he or she does not believe in the existence of God.

10. _____ does not exist any more, as it did in the Middle Ages, when the Church ruled a large part of Europe.

11. Persons who study_____ are interested in religion.

12. Hitler is a good example of a(n)_____ because he could stir persons' emotions and get them to do what he wanted.

STOP. Check answers at the end of Chapter Three (p. 85).

Additional Practice 3 for Exercise 6

A. Directions: The combining forms presented in Exercise 6 follow. Match the combining form with its meaning.

_____ 1. mis, miso	a. law
_____ 2. poly	b. many
_____ 3. gamy	c. kind; race, descent
_____ 4. hom, homo	d. marriage
_____ 5. gen, geno	e. hate; wrong
_____ 6. anthrop, anthropo	f. man; human; mankind
_____ 7. leg, legis, lex	g. same; man; human

STOP. Check answers at the end of Chapter Three (p. 85).

B. Directions: The words presented in Exercise 6 follow. Match the word with its meaning.

_____ 1. hater of mankind

_____ 2. a high-ranking office in the army; referring to all

_____ 3. marriage to many spouses at the same time

_____ 4. marriage to one spouse at one time

_____ 5. marriage to two spouses at the same time

_____ 6. referring to all in a group or class

_____ 7. being of the same kind

_____ 8. lawful

_____ 9. body of persons who make laws

_____ 10. referring to sexual desire for the same sex

_____ 11. the study of mankind

_____ 12. a word spelled in the same way as another but having a different meaning

a. homograph

b. bigamy

c. monogamy

d. legislature

e. legal

f. homogeneous

g. misanthrope

h. homosexual

i. generic

j. anthropology

k. general

l. polygamy

STOP. Check answers at the end of Chapter Three (p. 85).

ANSWERS: Chapter Three

Exercise 4 (pp. 49-55)

Practice A

(1) b, (2) d, (3) c, (4) a, (5) d, (6) b, (7) b, (8) c, (9) d, (10) b, (11) c, (12) d, (13) a, (14) a, (15) b, (16) d.

Practice B

(1) reporter, (2) decade, (3) credential, (4) incredible, (5) million, (6) credit, (7) incredible, (8) credential, (9) credible, (10) credential, (11) portable, (12) port, (13) export, (14) import, (15) million.

Additional Words Derived from Combining Forms (pp. 53-55)

1. **decimal.** Numbered by tens; based on 10; pertaining to tenths or the number 10; a decimal fraction.

2. **decimate.** To take or destroy a tenth part of; to destroy but not completely; to destroy a great number or proportion of.

3. **decameter.** In the metric system, a measure of length containing 10 meters, equal to 393.70 inches or 32. 81 feet.

4. **decimeter.** In the metric system, a unit of length equal to 1/10 meter.

5. **millimeter.** In the metric system, a unit of length equal to 1/1,000 meter (0.03937 inch).

6. **centimeter.** In the metric system, a unit of measure equal to 1/100 meter (0.3937 inch).

7. **kilometer.** In the metric system, a unit of length equal to 1,000 meters.

8. **centipede.** Wormlike animal with many legs.

9. **creed.** A statement of religious belief; a statement of belief, principles.

10. **accreditation.** The act of bringing into favor; a vouching for; a giving authority to.

11. **creditor.** One to whom a sum of money or other thing is due.

12. **deportment.** The manner of conducting or carrying oneself; behavior; conduct.

Practice for Additional Words Derived from Combining Forms (p. 55)

(1) i, (2) g, (3) h, (4) f, (5) d, (6) e, (7) j, (8) a, (9) b, (10) c, (11) l, (12) k.

Exercise 5 (pp. 55-61)

Practice A

(1) k, (2) g, (3) e, (4) h, (5) c, (6) f, (7) b, (8) i, (9) l, (10) j, (11) a, (12) d.

Practice B

(1) anarchy, (2) demagogue, (3) democracy, (4) autocracy, (5) monarchy, (6) atheist, (7) autocrat, (8) alias, (9) aliens, (10) alienate, (11) theocracy.

Additional Words Derived from Combining Forms (pp. 60-61)

1. **apodal.** Having no feet.

2. **demography.** The statistical study of human populations, including births, deaths, marriages, population movements, and so on.

3. **archetype.** The original pattern or model of a work from which something is made or developed.

4. **monotone.** A single unchanging tone; speech not having any change in pitch; to speak in an unvaried tone.

5. **monotonous.** Changeless; having no variety; uniform; dull

6. **monorail.** A single rail serving as a track for trucks or cars suspended from it or balanced on it.

7. **monophobia.** An abnormal fear of being alone.

8. **monoglot.** A person who knows, speaks, or writes only one language; speaking or writing only one language.

9. **monopoly.** Exclusive control of a commodity or service in a given market; control that makes possible the fixing of prices and the elimination of free competition.

10. **oligarchy.** A form of government in which there is rule by a few (usually a privileged few).

Practice for Additional Words Derived from Combining Forms (p. 61)

(1) e, (2) h, (3) g, (4) i, (5) j, (6) a, (7) d, (8) c, (9) f, (10) b.

Exercise 6 (pp. 62–67)

Practice A

(1) anthropology, (2) generic, (3) bicentennial, (4) legal, bigamy, (5) monogamy, (6) homograph, (7) misanthrope, (8) century, (9) legislature, (10) anthropologist, (11) incredible.

Practice B

(1) misanthrope, (2) polygamist, (3) centennial, (4) homogeneous, (5) legal, (6) century, (7) homograph, (8) bicentennial, (9) homosexual, (10) anthropology, (11) monogamy, (12) generic, (13) bigamy, (14) anthropologist, (15) legislature, (16) decade.

Additional Words Derived from Combining Forms (pp. 66–67)

1. **polyglot.** A person who knows, speaks, or writes many languages; speaking or writing many languages.

2. **polygon.** A closed plane figure with several angles and sides.

3. **podiatrist.** Foot doctor.

4. **bisexual**. Of both sexes; having both male and female organs, as is true of some plants and animals; a person who is sexually attracted by both sexes.

5. **misogamist**. Hater of marriage.

6. **anthropomorphic**. Giving human shape or characteristics to gods, objects, animals, and so on.

7. **anthropoid**. A person resembling an ape either in stature, walk, or intellect; resembling man—used especially of apes such as the gorilla, chimpanzee, and orangutan; resembling or suggesting an ape.

8. **genealogy**. The science or study of one's descent; a tracing of one's ancestors.

9. **genus**. A class, kind, or group marked by shared characteristics or by one shared characteristic.

10. **generate**. To produce; to cause to be; to bring into existence.

Practice for Additional Words Derived from Combining Forms (p. 67)

(1) c, (2) i, (3) f, (4) j, (5) a, (6) g, (7) b, (8) h, (9) d, (10) e.

Crossword Puzzle 2 (pp. 68–69)

¹A	²T				³A	⁴S		
⁵D	E	⁶C	⁷A	⁸A	P	E		
	⁹L	A	¹⁰A	N	T	E		
	¹¹G	E	N	¹²O		¹³L	¹⁴A	
¹⁵M	E			¹⁶H	¹⁷E	E	L	
¹⁸A	N	¹⁹T	²⁰H	²¹R	²²O	²³P	O	²⁴A P ²⁵E
²⁶U	²⁷U	N	I	²⁸W	O	M	²⁹E	N	³⁰A
³¹P	³²O	S	T	³³L	O	S	S	³⁴T ³⁵I ³⁶N
³⁷S	H	³⁸G	³⁹A	⁴⁰M	Y	⁴¹T		⁴²N O
	⁴³O	N	E					

Word Scramble 2 (pp. 69–70)

(1) million, (2) credible, (3) century, (4) decade, (5) import, (6) credential, (7) portable, (8) monarchy, (9) anarchy, (10) atheist, (11) autocrat, (12) alien, (13) theology, (14) alias, (15) anthropology, (16) legal, (17) general, (18) homogeneous, (19) monogamy, (20) bigamy.

Analogies 2 (pp. 70–71)

(1) podiatrist, (2) polyglot, (3) decameter, (4) reporter, (5) polygon, (6) deca, (7) alien, (8) decimal, (9) export, (10) incredible, (11) millennium, (12) decimate, (13) century, (14) anarchy, (15) anthropology, (16) archetype, (17) bigamy, (18) creditor, (19) alienate, (20) credential.

Multiple-Choice Vocabulary Test 2 (pp. 71–74)

Exercise 4

(1) b, (2) a, (3) c, (4) d, (5) a, (6) b, (7) d, (8) d, (9) c, (10) c, (11) d, (12) b, (13) d, (14) b, (15) a, (16) c.

Exercise 5

(17) c, (18) a, (19) b, (20) b, (21) d, (22) b, (23) d, (24) c, (25) c, (26) c, (27) b, (28) a.

Exercise 6

(29) c, (30) b, (31) a, (32) c, (33) b,[2] (34) c, (35) c, (36) c, (37) a, (38) d, (39) b, (40) a.

True/False Test 2 (p. 74–75)

(1) T, (2) F,[3] (3) T,[4] (4) F, (5) F, (6) F, (7) F,[5] (8) F, (9) F, (10) T, (11) T, (12) F, (13) T, (14) F,[6] (15) T, (16) F,[7] (17) F, (18) T, (19) F, (20) T, (21) T, (22) T.

STOP. Turn to page 75 for the scoring of the tests.

[2] Although anthropology is a science, the better answer is *study of mankind,* which describes what kind of science anthropology is and gives more information.

[3] Even if someone hates marriage, it does not mean that he or she must also hate people.

[4] Ten times 100 equals 1,000. One thousand thousands equals 1 million.

[5] Not necessarily.

[6] Not so. Persons who believe in no government rule *may* believe in God.

[7] An *alien* is a foreigner. He or she can legally come to this or any other country. Although there are aliens who enter a country illegally, this is not part of the definition of *alien.*

Additional Practice 1

A. (1) b, (2) e, (3) d, (4) a, (5) c.

B. (1) incredible, (2) century, (3) port, (4) centennial, (5) millennium, (6) credible, (7) credits, (8) million, (9) credentials, (10) porter, (11) portable, (12) reporter, (13) export, (14) bicentennial, (15) imports, (16) decade.

Additional Practice 2

A. (1) d, (2) a, (3) b, (4) e, (5) f, (6) c.

B. (1) alienate, (2) alias, (3) alien, (4) monarchy, (5) autocrat, (6) autocracy, (7) democracy, (8) anarchy, (9) atheist, (10) theocracy, (11) theology, (12) demagogue.

Additional Practice 3

A. (1) e, (2) b, (3) d, (4) g, (5) c, (6) f, (7) a.

B. (1) g, (2) k, (3) l, (4) c, (5) b, (6) i, (7) f, (8) e, (9) d, (10) h, (11) j, (12) a.

CHAPTER FOUR

EXERCISE 7

Step I. Combining Forms

A. Directions: A list of combining forms with their meanings follows. Look at
the combining forms and their meanings. Concentrate on learning each combining form and its meaning. Cover the meanings,
read the combining forms, and state the meanings to yourself.
Check to see if you are correct. Now cover the combining
forms, read the meanings, and state the combining forms to
yourself. Check to see if you are correct.

Combining Forms	Meanings
1. vid, vis	see
2. sci, scio	know
3. poten	powerful
4. omni	all
5. aqua, aqui	water
6. astro	star
7. naut	sailor
8. ven, veni, vent	come

B. Directions: Cover the preceding meanings. Write the meanings of the following combining forms.

Combining Forms   *Meanings*

1. vid, vis   _____

2. sci, scio   _____

3. poten   _____

4. omni   _____

5. aqua, aqui   _____

6. astro   _____

7. naut   _____

8. ven, veni, vent   _____

Step II. Words Derived from Combining Forms

1. **vision** (vi · sion) (vizh′ un) *n.* The sense of sight. *Because the man's **vision** was blocked by the screen, he could not see what the spectators were looking at.*

2. **visible** (vis · i · ble) (viz′ i · bul) *adj.* Able to be seen; evident; apparent; on hand. *On a clear day the skyline of the city is **visible**.*

3. **invisible** (in · vis · i · ble) (in · viz′ i · bul) *adj.* Not able to be seen. *In the film, the **invisible** man was able to appear in many prohibited places because no one was able to see him.*

4. **television** (tel · e · vi · sion) (tel′ e · vizh · un) *n.* An electronic system for the transmission of visual images from a distance; a television receiving set. ***Television** is viewed by so many people all over the country that sponsors pay millions of dollars to advertise their products on it.*

5. **provision** (pro · vi · sion) (pro · vizh′ un) *n.* The act of being prepared beforehand; preparation; something made ready in advance; *pl.* **provisions**: needed materials, especially a supply of food for future needs; a part of an agreement referring to a specific thing. *The army was running out of necessary **provisions**, and the men were beginning to complain that they did not have enough supplies to carry on their operations.*

6. **evident** (ev′ i · dent) *adj.* Obvious; clearly seen; plain. *From everything that you have said, it is **evident** that he is lying about where he was on the night of the murder.*

7. **evidence** (ev · i · dence) (ev′ i · dens̸) *n.* That which serves to prove or disprove something. *The **evidence** was so strong against the defendant that it didn't seem possible that he could prove his innocence.*

8. **science** (sci • ence) (s$¢$ī′ ens$¢$) *n.* Any area of knowledge in which the facts have been investigated and presented in an orderly manner. *New sciences develop as we learn more and more about the universe.*

9. **astrology** (a • strol • o • gy) (a • strol′ o • jē) *n.* The art or practice that claims to tell the future and interpret the influence of the heavenly bodies on the fate of people; a reading of the stars. *There are a large number of people who believe in astrology's ability to predict their futures.*

10. **astronomy** (a • stron • o • my) (a • stron′ o • mē) *n.* The science that deals with stars, planets, and space. *When I studied astronomy, I used a very high-powered telescope to view the stars and planets.*

11. **astronaut** (as′ tro • naut) *n.* One who travels in space, that is, beyond the earth's atmosphere; a person trained to travel in outer space. *The Apollo astronauts shook hands with the Russian astronauts in space during a special space flight in 1975.*

12. **aquanaut** (aq • ua • naut) (ak′ wa • naut) *n.* One who travels undersea; a person trained to work in an underwater chamber. *Jacques Cousteau has many aquanauts on his team who explore the wonders under the seas.*

13. **aquatic** (a • quat • ic) (a • kwat′ ik) *adj.* Living or growing in or near water; performed on or in water. *The best swimmers performed in our aquatic ballet.*

14. **aquarium** (a • quar • i • um) (a • kwar′ ē • um) *n.* A pond, a glass bowl, a tank, or the like, in which aquatic animals and/or plants are kept; a place in which aquatic collections are shown. *The aquatic plants and animals in my aquarium are specially chosen to make sure that they can live together.*

15. **convene** (con • vene) (kon • vēn$¢$′) *v.* To come together; to assemble. *The assemblymen were waiting for everyone to arrive so that they could convene for their first meeting of the year.*

16. **convention** (con • ven • tion) (kon • ven′ shun) *n.* A formal meeting of members for political or professional purposes; accepted custom, rule, or opinion. *The teachers hold their convention annually to exchange professional views and learn about new things.*

17. **convenient** (con • ven • ient) (kon • vēn′ yent) *adj.* Well suited to one's purpose, personal comfort, or ease; handy. *The professional and political conventions are held in cities that have convenient hotels and halls to take care of a great number of people.*

18. **potent** (po • tent) (pōt′ $¢$nt) *adj.* Physically powerful; having great authority; able to influence; strong in chemical effects. *The drug was so potent that it actually knocked out John, who is over 6 feet tall and weighs almost 200 pounds.*

19. **impotent** (im' po · tent) *adj.* Without power to act; physically weak; incapable of sexual intercourse (said of males). *The monarch in England is politically impotent because he or she has hardly any power in the governing of the country.*

20. **potential** (po · ten · tial) (po · ten' shul) *n.* The possible ability or power one has. *adj.* Having force or power to develop. *The acorn has the potential to become a tree.*

21. **omnipresent** (om · ni · pres · ent) (om · ni · prez' ent) *adj.* Being present everywhere at all times. *The omnipresent toothpaste commercial was annoying because it seemed to be on all the channels at the same time.*

Special Notes

1. When the term *potential* is used, it refers to "possible ability." This means that potential is something that a person may have within him or her, but it may or may not necessarily come out. The following cartoon illustrates this idea very nicely.

Understanding the Term *Potential*

© 1959 United Feature Syndicate, Inc.

2. *Astrology* is concerned with the reading of the stars. Astrologists use the stars to try to predict the future of persons. Do not confuse astrology, which is a false science, with astronomy, which is a science that deals with the study of stars, planets, and space.

Step III. Practice

A. Directions: A number of sentences with missing words follows. Choose the word that *best* fits the sentence. Put the word in the blank. There are more words in the list than you need.

Word List

potent, impotent, evidence, evident, vision, invisible, convention, convenient, astronaut, aquanaut, scientist, aquatic, aquarium, astrology, astronomy, provision, science, omnipresent, television, convene, potential.

1. All _____s must be in top physical shape in order to travel in space.

2. If you love swimming and diving and you're very interested in sea life, you may want to be a(n) _____.

3. You find _____ plants in the ocean.

4. Some poisons are so _____ that a one-quarter teaspoon dose will kill you.

5. One of the fish in my _____ grew at an incredible rate.

6. The fortune-teller used her knowledge of _____ to predict my future.

7. I want to study _____ in college because I enjoy learning about stars and planets.

8. Because the stop sign was not clearly _____, the driver went right past it.

9. Have you made any special _____ s for yourself for when you retire?

10. Although he is the head of government, he is politically _____ because he has no say in anything.

11. The district attorney must have some _____ to support his case before he can try to prove the guilt of someone.

12. Astronomy, biology, and geology are all _____ s.

13. _____ s are formal meetings, which are usually held annually.

14. With your good _____, you should be able to see the board from where you're sitting.

15. The _____ warriors seemed to be everywhere.

16. If that time is not _____ for you, we'll change it for a better one.

17. It is difficult to talk about John's ability level, for we do not know what his _____ is.

18. The judge said that the court would _____ in one hour to continue the trial.

STOP. Check answers at the end of Chapter Four (p. 133).

B. Directions: A few paragraphs with missing words follow. Fill the blanks with the words that *best* fit. Words may be used more than once.

Word List

anniversary, visible, convention, evident, omnipresent, decade, television, scientists, reporter, convenient, astrologist, aquanauts, astronauts, evidence, provision, incredible, invisible, aquatic, impotent.

As a(n) 1_____ I get to investigate and write stories. I especially remember one story I wrote about a(n) 2_____ago. I remember it was ten years ago because my wife and I were celebrating our first wedding 3_____ with a special dinner, when the phone rang. It was my boss. His excitement was clearly 4_____. "Joe, did you see what just happened on 5_____?" he asked. "No, we didn't have the 6_____ . . ." Before I could finish answering, he said, "Well, get down here immediately. I want you to cover a special story that just broke." Although it was not a(n) 7_____ time for me, I went to meet him.

It seemed that a group of well-known 8_____ , such as biologists, geologists, astronomists, and so on, were meeting at a national 9_____ held in our city. At the 10_____ there were exhibits of materials that 11_____ had brought back from space. There were also special 12_____ plants that 13_____ had found underseas.

At about ten in the morning, a woman phoned the editor in the newspaper office. She said she was a(n) 14_____ who could foretell the future. She told the editor to watch the 15_____ exhibits that were being shown on 16_____ to people all over the country. She knew that something 17_____ was going to take place shortly and that it would be 18_____ to all who were watching. The editor felt that from the way the woman was talking it was 19_____ she was a "crackpot." He receives so many calls from people telling about things that would happen that never did. There are so many crackpots around that they seem to be 20_____ .

Well, at eight that night, in plain view of all who had their 21_____s tuned to the channel covering the exhibits, a(n) 22_____ robbery took place. The people watching the robbery must have felt 23_____ because they had no power to do anything about it.

Persons dressed as 24_____ who were going on a space flight and 25_____who were going to explore the ocean, stole the priceless materials on display.

Nobody could figure out how they got into the special room. It was as if they were 26_____ , and at the proper moment they materialized and became 27_____ for all to see. They seemed to have had all the 28_____s they needed to carry out the robbery.

92

It was so well planned that no 29 _____ as to who they were or why they did it has ever been found.

STOP. Check answers at the end of Chapter Four (p. 134).

C. Directions: The Combining Form Square contains the combining forms from this exercise as well as many from other exercises. Definitions of combining forms follow. See how many of the combining forms you can find in the square. Fill them in the blanks. If a definition appears more than once, it means that the combining form may have different spellings for the same meaning.

COMBINING FORM SQUARE

```
V   E   N   A   U   T   O   A
I   S   T   Q   V   A   P   N
S   G   E   O   E   L   O   T
E   R   L   A   N   I   R   H
H   O   E   I   B   D   T   R
O   C   S   C   I   I   R   O
M   O   N   O   O   C   O   P
O   N   U   N   I   T   R   O
```

1. _____ self

2. _____ see

3. _____ know

4. _____ man

5. _____ one

6. _____ one who

7. _____ one who

8. _____ one who

9. _____ two

10. _____ carry

11. _____ one

12. _____ sailor

13. _____ earth

14. _____ life

15. _____ come

16. _____ without

17. _____ with; together

18. _____ from a distance

19. _____ other

20. _____ say

21. _____ mankind

STOP. Check answers at the end of Chapter Four (p. 134).

> **less.** Without. When *less* is placed at the end of a word, it means "without." *Less* changes a noun into an adjective. For example: the word *mother* becomes *motherless*—without a mother; *father* becomes *fatherless*—without a father; *blame* becomes *blameless*—without blame; without fault; *harm* becomes *harmless*—without harm; without hurting. For example: *How lucky you are that you have both a mother and a father. Mary is a **motherless** child.* How many more words with *less* can you supply?
>
> **con, co, cor, com, col.** Together; with. When *con* is placed at the beginning of some words, the *n* may change to an *l*, *m*, or *r*. The *n* in some words may be left out altogether. However, *con, com, cor, col,* and *co* all mean "together" or "with." Examples: *co-worker*—someone working with you; *convene*—come together; assemble; *convention*—a meeting where persons come together; *combine*—to join together; unite; *collect*—to gather together; *correspond*—to be equivalent; to write letters to one another.

Additional Words Derived from Combining Forms

From your knowledge of combining forms, can you define the following words?

1. **omnipotent** (om · nip′ o · tent) *adj. No matter how much wealth, power, and prestige someone has, he or she is not **omnipotent**.*

   _____

2. **omniscient** (om · nis · cient) (om · nish′ ent) *adj. With the rapid increase of knowledge, it is not possible for someone to be **omniscient**.*

   _____

3. **omnibus** (om′ ni · bus) *n. Because we had a large group, we chartered an **omnibus** to take us to our destination.*

   _____

4. **visage** (vis · age) (viz′ ij¢) *n. His wolfish **visage** warned me about what he might be thinking.*

   _____

5. **visor** (vi · sor) (vī′ zor) *n. Baseball players wear hats with **visors** because the game is often played in bright sunlight.*

_____

6. **visa** (vi · sa) (vē′ za) *n. We need a **visa** to visit Russia.*

_____

7. **envision** (en · vi · sion) (en · vizh′ un) *v. The shipwrecked crew, who had been drifting on the raft for two days, deliriously **envisioned** a banquet.*

_____

8. **visionary** (vi · sion · ar · y) (vizh′ un · er · ē) *n. (pl. **ies**)· The leader of the newly formed religious group claims that he is a **visionary** who has seen visions of things to come.*

_____

9. **nautical** (nau · tic · cal) (nau′ tik · al) *adj. Because John has a **nautical** bent, he wants to become a sailor.*

_____

10. **venture** (ven · ture) (ven′ chur) *n. Because the business **venture** involved a great amount of speculation, I did not want to become a part of it.*

_____

11. **potentate** (pō′ ten · tāte) *n. The **potentate** of that country is an autocrat whom I would not want as my enemy.*

_____

STOP. Check answers at the end of Chapter Four (pp. 134–135).

Practice for Additional Words Derived from Combining Forms

Directions: Match each word with the *best* definition.

_____ 1. omnipotent   a. a risky, dangerous undertaking

_____ 2. omniscient   b. the face

_____ 3. omnibus   c. person possessing great power

_____ 4. visage   d. pertaining to seamen, ships

_____ 5. visa   e. all-powerful

_____ 6. envision   f. large bus

_____ 7. visionary   g. the projecting front brim of a cap

_____ 8. nautical   h. all-knowing

_____ 9. visor   i. a person who sees visions

_____10. venture   j. to imagine something

_____11. potentate   k. something granting entrance to a country

STOP. Check answers at the end of Chapter Four (p. 135).

EXERCISE 8

Step I. Combining Forms

A. Directions: A list of combining forms with their meanings follows. Look at the combining forms and their meanings. Concentrate on learning each combining form and its meaning. Cover the meanings, read the combining forms, and state the meanings to yourself. Check to see if you are correct. Now cover the combining forms, read the meanings, and state the combining forms to yourself. Check to see if you are correct.

Combining Forms	_Meanings_
1. cide	murder; kill
2. pathy	feeling; suffering
3. syl, sym, syn	same; with; together; along with
4. frater, fratr	brother
5. mors, mort	death
6. capit	head
7. corp, corpor	body
8. em, en	into; in

B. Directions: Cover the preceding meanings. Write the meanings of the following combining forms.

Combining Forms	_Meanings_
1. cide	_____
2. pathy	_____
3. syl, sym, syn	_____
4. frater, fratr	_____
5. mors, mort	_____
6. capit	_____

96

7. corp, corpor   _____

8. em, en   _____

Step II. Words Derived from Combining Forms

1. **homicide** (hom · i · cide) (hom′ i · sīdȼ) *n.* Any killing of one human being by another. *The spectator witnessed a horrible* **homicide,** *in which the victim was beaten to death.*

2. **suicide** (su · i · cide) (sū′ i · sīdȼ) *n.* The killing of oneself. *I wonder if persons who try to kill themselves know that it is against the law to commit* **suicide.**

3. **genocide** (gen · o · cide) (jen′ o · sīdȼ) *n.* The systematic and deliberate killing of a whole racial group or a group of people bound together by customs, language, politics, and so on. *During World War II, Hitler attempted to commit* **genocide** *against the Jewish people because he wanted to wipe them out completely.*

4. **sympathy** (sym · pa · thy) (sim′ pa · thē) *n.* (*pl.* **ies**) Sameness of feeling with another; ability to feel pity for another. *When Mary lost both her parents in an automobile accident, we all felt deep* **sympathy** *for her.*

5. **empathy** (em · pa · thy) (em′ pa · thē) *n.* (*pl.* **ies**) The imaginative putting of oneself into another person's personality; ability to understand how another feels because one has experienced it firsthand or otherwise. *I felt* **empathy** *for the boy with the broken arm because the same thing had happened to me.*

6. **apathy** (ap · a · thy) (ap′ a · thē) *n.* Lack of feeling; indifference. *He had such* **apathy** *regarding the sufferings of persons around him that he didn't care one way or the other what happened to the hurt people.*

7. **fraternity** (fra · ter · ni · ty) (fra · ter′ ni · tē) *n.* (*pl.* **ies**) A group of men joined together by common interests for fellowship; a brotherhood; a Greek letter college organization. *In college I decided to join a* **fraternity** *so that I could make a lot of new friends.*

8. **capital punishment** (cap · i · tal pun · ish · ment) (kap′ i · tal pun′ ish · ment) *n.* The death penalty. *Capital punishment* *has been outlawed in many countries because it is felt that the death penalty is a punishment that is too extreme.*

9. **capitalism** (cap · i · tal · ism) (kap′ i · tal · iz · um) *n.* The economic system in which all or most of the means of production, such as land, factories, and railroads, are privately owned and operated for profit. *Because* **capitalism** *is practiced in the United States, individuals privately own and operate their businesses for profit.*

10. **capital** (cap · i · tal) (kap′ i · tal) *n.* City or town that is the official seat of government; money or wealth; first letter of a word at the beginning of a sentence. *adj.* Excellent. *The capital of the United States is Washington, D.C.*

11. **corpse** (korpse) *n.* Dead body. *After the detective examined the corpse, he was told that there was another dead body in the next room.*

12. **corporation** (cor · po · ra · tion) (kor · po · rā′ shun) *n.* A group of people who get a charter granting them as a body certain of the powers, rights, privileges, and liabilities (legal responsibilities) of an individual, separate from those of the individuals making up the group. *The men formed a corporation so that they would not individually be liable (legally responsible) for the others.*

13. **incorporate** (in · cor · po · rate) (in · kor′ po · rāte) *v.* To unite; combine. *The men decided to incorporate because by joining together, they could be a more potent company.*

14. **corporal punishment** (cor · po · ral pun · ish · ment) (kor′ po · ral pun′ ish · ment) *n.* Bodily punishment; a beating. *Because New Jersey is a state that outlaws corporal punishment in the schools, it is illegal for teachers to hit students.*

15. **mortal** (mor · tal) (mor′ tul) *adj.* Referring to a being who must eventually die; causing death; ending in death; very grave; said of certain sins; to the death, as mortal combat; terrible, as mortal terror. *n.* A human being. *Because he still advanced, after being shot six times, everyone began to wonder whether he was a mortal.*

16. **immortal** (im · mor · tal) (im · mor′ tul) *adj.* Referring to a being who never dies; undying. *n.* One who never dies. *Because a human being must eventually die, he or she is not immortal.*

17. **mortality** (mor · tal · i · ty) (mor · tal′ i · tē) *n.* The state of having to die eventually; proportion of deaths to the population of the region, nation, and so on; death rate; death on a large scale, as from disease or war. *The mortality of children among minority groups is decreasing because the living conditions of such groups are improving.*

18. **mortician** (mor · ti · cian) (mor · ti′ shin) *n.* A funeral director; undertaker. *Morticians are accustomed to handling corpses because their job is to prepare the dead for burial.*

19. **mortgage** (mort · gage) (mor′ gij) *n.* The pledging of property to a creditor (one to whom a sum of money is owed) as security for payment. *v.* To put up property as security for payment; to pledge. *Most persons who buy homes obtain a mortgage from a bank.*

20. **morgue** (morgue) *n.* Place where dead bodies (corpses) of accident victims

and unknown persons found dead are kept; for reporters it refers to the reference library of old newspaper articles, pictures, and so on. *The police took the accident victim's body to the **morgue** because they could find no identification on it.*

Special Notes

1. **empathy** and **sympathy**. **empathy**: The imaginative putting of oneself into another in order to better understand him or her; putting oneself into the personality of another. *When people feel **empathy** for another, they know how the other person feels because they have had the same experience or can put themselves imaginatively into the personality of the other.* **sympathy**: Sameness of feeling with another; ability to feel pity for another. *When you have **sympathy** for someone, you feel pity for him or her. You do not have to go through the same experience as the person.* Empathy is a stronger feeling than sympathy. When you say that you *sympathize* with someone's views, it means that you have the same feeling about the views as the person.

2. **apathy**. Lack of feeling; indifference. *He felt complete **apathy** for the whole situation.* The term *apathy* means that someone has no feeling one way or another. Such a person is indifferent.

3. The term *homicide* is used in the generic sense. You met the term *generic* in an earlier exercise. *Generic* means "referring to all within a group." Therefore, when someone says that *homicide* is used in the generic sense, he or she means that the combining form *homo* (meaning "man" in the word *homocide*) refers to both men and women, not just to males.

4. Remember the term *misanthrope*? *Misanthrope* means "hater of mankind." The word is also used in the generic sense in that *mankind* refers to both men and women, not just to men.

5. There are a number of words that are derived from the combining form *cide* with which you may be familiar. For example: *insecticide* means "an agent that destroys insects"; *germicide* means "an agent that destroys germs"; *herbicide* means "an agent that destroys or holds in check plant growth." In Exercises 16 and 17, you will also meet the terms *patricide* and *matricide*.

Step III. Practice

A. Directions: A number of sentences with missing words follows. Choose the word that *best* fits the sentence. Put the word in the blank. Words may be used in more than one sentence.

99

Word List

capital punishment, corporal punishment, capital, corporation, capitalism, fraternity, suicide, mortality, immortal, morgue, mortgage, genocide, sympathy, mortal, empathy, homicide, incorporate, apathy, mortician.

1. The _____ of New York State is Albany, the _____ of Tennessee is Nashville, and the _____ of California is Sacramento.

2. The five businessmen decided to form a_____ so that each would not be legally responsible for the debts of the others.

3. Under _____ persons can own their businesses and work for a profit.

4. In order to start a business, you need _____ because without _____ you cannot purchase the things you need.

5. As most people do not have enough money to pay for a house, they try to secure a(n)_____ from a bank.

6. We had to go to the_____to identify a relative who had been killed in an accident.

7. We went to a(n)_____ to arrange for the funeral of our relative.

8. The men were happy they had decided to _____, joining in a business venture, because together they were doing better than they had alone.

9. The way George drives his car, he must think that he is_____ and that nothing can kill him.

10. Now that women are more involved in careers, they may be more subject to heart attacks and ulcers, and, as a result, their _____ will increase.

11. On earth only _____ s exist because no one has yet been able to cheat death.

12. More people are trying to get their legislatures to pass a law to bring back _____ _____ because people feel that fear of death will prevent some crimes.

13. When a(n)_____ is committed, the police try to find a suspect who had a motive, the opportunity, and the means to kill the person.

14. Some persons would choose _____ _____ over lesser_____ _____because they cannot stand beatings.

100

15. I felt great _____ for the person whose mother died in an automobile accident because I had experienced the same thing a decade ago.

16. I have no _____ for Alice because I told her beforehand that she would fail if she didn't do any work.

17. It seems incredible that one man was almost able to commit _____ and wipe out a whole race of people.

18. What seems even more incredible is that some people had such _____ about what was going on that they did not care one way or the other.

19. No one could understand why he committed _____ because he seemed to have everything to live for.

20. Many students join a(n) _____ in college in order to be with lots of friendly people and to have a place to go.

STOP. Check answers at the end of Chapter Four (p. 135).

B. Directions: A list of definitions follows. In the space provided, insert the letter for the meaning that *best* fits the word.

_____ 1. The killing of a whole racial, political, or cultural group

   a. homicide   c. genocide
   b. suicide   d. fratricide

_____ 2. Lack of feeling

   a. sympathy   c. fraternity
   b. empathy   d. apathy

_____ 3. Dead body

   a. mortal   c. mortality
   b. corpse   d. immortal

_____ 4. Death rate

   a. mortal   c. mortality
   b. immortal   d. corpse

_____ 5. Ability to put self into another's personality

   a. empathy   c. fraternity
   b. apathy   d. sympathy

_____ 6. A brotherhood

   a. fraternity   c. capitalism
   b. corporation   d. capital

_____ 7. The feeling of pity for another

   a. empathy   c. apathy
   b. sympathy   d. fraternity

_____ 8. Killing of one person by another

   a. homicide   c. mortality
   b. suicide   d. genocide

_____ 9. Killing of oneself

   a. genocide   c. mortality
   b. homicide   d. suicide

_____ 10. To unite

   a. incorporate   c. convene
   b. corporation   d. fraternity

_____11. Money or wealth   a. capitalism   c. capital
  b. corporation   d. incorporate

_____12. Bodily punishment   a. corporal punishment   c. corpse
  b. capital punishment   d. corp-oration

_____13. Death penalty   a. capital punishment   c. mortality
  b. corporal punishment   d. capitalism

_____14. Place where unidentified dead are held   a. mortality   c. corpse
  b. mortal   d. morgue

_____15. Economic system based on profit   a. capital   c. incorporate
  b. corporation   d. capitalism

_____16. An undertaker   a. mortician   c. mortality
  b. mortal   d. immortal

_____17. Referring to one who never dies   a. mortal   c. mortality
  b. immortal   d. corpse

_____18. One who must die   a. immortal   c. mortal
  b. corpse   d. immortal

_____19. The pledging of property to a creditor   a. morgue   c. mortician
  b. mortgage   d. mortality

STOP. Check answers at the end of Chapter Four (p. 135).

C. Directions: Fifteen sentences follow. Define the underlined word or phrase.

1. Very often a homicide is the result of an argument among people who know each other. _____

2. Persons who commit suicide have usually given others around them warnings that they were going to kill themselves._____

3. Meg's apathy toward the upcoming dance was obvious, and she couldn't have cared less whether she went or not._____

4. I felt great sympathy for Jack when he had to drop out of college to help support his family after his father died._____

5. Not everyone likes to join a fraternity because if a person does join one, he tends to spend most of his time with only those fellows in the fraternity.
_____

6. The idea of anyone's attempting genocide to get rid of a whole racial, political, or cultural group seems incredible. _____

7. In geography, when we had to list all the <u>capitals</u> of the states, I always listed Washington, D.C., which is, however, the <u>capital</u> of the United States and not a state <u>capital</u>._____

8. Because I can't stand to look at dead bodies, I did not go to the <u>morgue</u> to help to identify the accident victim._____

9. The <u>mortician</u> made the corpse look lifelike. _____._____

10. The men <u>incorporated</u> and formed a <u>corporation</u> so that each would not be liable for the others in their business._____,_____

11. Because <u>corporal punishment</u> is allowed in most states, school systems have set up regulations regarding when and how a child can be hit._____

12. Do you feel that <u>capital punishment</u> will stop persons from committing horrible crimes because they will be afraid of being put to death?_____

13. Some works of art are called <u>immortal</u> because it is thought that they will live forever. _____

14. I know of no <u>mortal</u> who has lived over 120 years._____

15. If you stop paying the money you owe on your <u>mortgage</u>, the bank will be able to take away your house, because your house was put up as security for the loan._____

STOP. Check answers at the end of Chapter Four (p. 135).

EXTRA WORD
POWER

un. Not. When *un* is placed at the beginning of a word, it means "not." *Un* is used with a very great number of words. Examples: *unwed*—not married; *unaided*—not helped; *unloved*—not loved; *unable*—not able; *uncooked*—not cooked; *unclaimed*—not claimed; *uncaught*—not caught; *uncarpeted*—not carpeted. How many other words can you supply with *un*?

pre. Before. When *pre* is placed in front of a word it means "before in time" or "before in order." *Pre,* like *un,* is used with a very great number of words. Examples: *prehistoric*—referring to time before history was recorded; *pre-Christian*—referring to time before there were Christians; *prerevolutionary*—referring to time before a revolution; *preheat*—to heat before; *prejudge*—to judge or decide before; *prejudice*—an opinion or judgment made beforehand; *preunite*—to join together before; *preset*—to set before;

> *premature*—ripened before; developed before the natural or proper period; *predict*—to say before; to foretell; to forecast, to tell what will happen. See how many more words with *pre* you can supply. Use the dictionary to see the great number of words there are that begin with *un* and *pre*.

Additional Words Derived from Combining Forms

From your knowledge of combining forms, can you define the following words?

1. **fratricide** (frat · ri · cide) (frat′ ri · sīdȼ) *n.* ***Fratricide*** *is an especially horrible crime because it involves the murder of a close relative.*

   _____

2. **corpulent** (cor · pu · lent) (kor′ pū · lent) *adj.* ***Corpulent*** *people usually eat a lot.*

   _____

3. **mortify** (mor · ti · fy) (mor′ ti · fī) *v. The minister was* ***mortified*** *that the people in his church had been involved in the riots.*

   _____

4. **amortize** (am′ or · tīzȼ) *v. The accountant* ***amortized*** *the plant's machinery on a twenty-year schedule.*

   _____

5. **caption** (cap · tion) (kap′ shun) *n. By reading chapter* ***captions***, *I am able in a very short time to gain some idea about the chapter.*

   _____

6. **capitulate** (ca · pit · u · late) (ka · pich′ u · lātȼ) *v. With the criminal gang surrounded by the police and having no possible means of escape, they had no choice but to* ***capitulate.***

   _____

7. **symbol** (sym · bol) (sim′ bul) *n. The dove is a* ***symbol*** *of peace, the cross is a* ***symbol*** *of Christianity, and the Star of David is a* ***symbol*** *of Judaism.*

   _____

8. **syllable** (syl · la · ble) (sil′ ʌa · bul) *n. In the word* pilot *which has two* ***syllables***, pi *is the first* ***syllable***, *and* lot *is the second syllable.*

   _____

9. **monosyllable** (mon · o · syl · la · ble) (mon′ o · sil · ʌa · bul) *n. The word* made *is a* ***monosyllable.***

   _____

10. **symphony** (sym · pho · ny) (sim' fo · nē) *n.* *In the **symphony** the instruments blended together in perfect harmony.*

_____

11. **symptom** (symp · tom) (simp' tum) *n.* *The doctor said that the rash was a definite **symptom** of the disease and that there was a cure for it.*

_____

12. **synthesis** (syn · the · sis) (sin' the · sis) *n.* *(pl.* **theses***) The architect was told that his design must be a **synthesis** of everyone's ideas.*

_____

13. **symmetry** (sym · me · try) (sim' me · trē) *n.* *(pl.* **ies***) He disliked the disorganized pattern because it lacked **symmetry**.*

_____

STOP. Check answers at the end of Chapter Four (pp. 135–136).

Practice for Additional Words Derived form Combining Forms

Directions: Match each word with the *best* definition.

_____ 1. fratricide

_____ 2. corpulent

_____ 3. mortify

_____ 4. caption

_____ 5. amortize

_____ 6. capitulate

_____ 7. symbol

_____ 8. monosyllable

_____ 9. syllable

_____ 10. symphony

_____ 11. symmetry

_____ 12. synthesis

_____ 13. symptom

a. heading of a chapter, section, and the like

b. to cause to feel shame

c. something that stands for another thing

d. to cancel a debt by periodic payments

e. a putting together to form a whole

f. a vowel or a group of letters with one vowel sound

g. balanced form or arrangement

h. harmony of sound

i. the killing of a brother

j. to surrender

k. a condition that results from a disease

l. word consisting of one syllable

m. fat

STOP. Check answers at the end of Chapter Four (p. 136).

EXERCISE 9

Step I. Combining Forms

A. Directions: A list of combining forms with their meanings follows. Look at the combining forms and their meanings. Concentrate on learning each combining form and its meaning. Cover the meanings, read the combining forms, and state the meanings to yourself. Check to see if you are correct. Now cover the combining forms, read the meanings, and state the combining forms to yourself. Check to see if you are correct.

Combining Forms	Meanings
1. man, manu	hand
2. fac, fect, fic	make; do
3. loc, loco	place
4. pseudo	false
5. bene	good
6. cura	care
7. aud, audi	hear
8. nomin, onym	name

B. Directions: Cover the preceding meanings. Write the meanings of the following combining forms.

Combining Forms	Meanings
1. man, manu	_____
2. fac, fect, fic	_____
3. loc, loco	_____
4. pseudo	_____
5. bene	_____
6. cura	_____
7. aud, audi	_____
8. nomin, onym	_____

Step II. Words Derived from Combining Forms

1. **manual** (man' ū · al) *adj.* Referring to the hand; made, done, or used by the hands. *n.* A handy book used as a guide or source of information. *Some persons prefer **manual** labor because they like to work with their hands.*

2. **manicure** (man · i · cure) (man′ i · kur¢) *n.* Care of the hands and fingernails. *v.* To provide care for hands and nails with a manicure; to cut
   closely and evenly. *Because I like my fingernails to look good, I give myself a **manicure** every week.*

3. **manuscript** (man · u · script) (man′ yu · skript) *adj.* Written by hand or
   typed; not printed. *n.* A book or document written by hand; a book
   written by hand and usually sent in for publication; style of penmanship
   in which letters are not joined together, whereas in cursive writing they are.
   *When an author sends a **manuscript** to a publisher, he or she hopes that the
   editor will like it.*

4. **manufacture** (man · u · fac · ture) (man · yu · fak′ chur) *v.* To make goods
   or articles by hand or by machinery; to make something from raw materials
   by hand or machinery. *n.* The act of manufacturing. *Some very special and
   expensive items are still made by hand, but most goods are **manufactured** by
   machine on a large scale.*

5. **factory** (fac · to · ry) (fak′ to · rē) *n.* (*pl.* **ies**) A building or buildings in
   which things are manufactured. *My mother and father work in a **factory**
   where automobiles are made.*

6. **benefactor** (ben · e · fac · tor) (ben′ e · fak · tor) *n.* One who gives help
   or confers a benefit; a patron. *Many times artists have **benefactors** who
   help to support them while they are painting.*

7. **beneficiary** (ben · e · fi · ci · ar · y) (ben · e · fish′ ē · er · ē) *n.* (*pl.* **aries**)
   One who receives benefits or advantages; the one to whom an insurance
   policy is payable. *Joyce, as the only **beneficiary** of her husband's insurance
   policy, did not know that she would receive all the money.*

8. **benefit** (ben′ e · fit) *n.* That which is helpful; advantage; a payment; a performance given to raise funds for a worthy cause. *v.* To be helpful or pro-
   fitable to; to receive benefit; to aid. *The actors gave a **benefit** to
   collect money for the needy children.*

9. **affect** (af · fect) (af · fekt′) *v.* To act upon or to cause something; to
   influence; to produce an effect or change in. *Your poor study habits will
   definitely begin to **affect** your grades and cause them to go down.*

10. **effect** (ef · fect) (ef · fekt′) *n.* Something brought about by some cause;
    the result; consequence. *I told you what the **effects** of your not studying
    would be before the results were in.*

11. **effective** (ef · fec · tive) (ef · fek′ tiv¢) *adj.* Producing or having the
    power to bring about an intended result; producing results with the least
    amount of wasted effort. *His way of doing the job is much more **effective**
    than yours because it takes him so much less time to do the same amount
    of work.*

12. **audible** (au · di · ble) (au′ di · bul) *adj.* Capable of being heard. *He spoke so softly that what he had to say was hardly **audible** to anyone.*

13. **auditorium** (au · di · to · ri · um) (au · di · tor′ ē · um) *n.* A building or hall for speeches, concerts, public meetings, and so on; the room in a building occupied by an audience. *The school **auditorium** was so large that it was able to seat the entire graduating class and their parents.*

14. **audience** (au · di · ence) (au′ dē · ensȼ) *n.* An assembly of listeners or spectators at a concert, play, speech, and so on. *The **audience** listened to the politicians' speeches to learn what their views were on the income tax.*

15. **audit** (au′ dit) *v.* To examine or check such things as accounts; to attend class as a listener. *n.* An examination of accounts in order to report the financial state of a business. *Every year banks have their accounts **audited** to check if everything is in order.*

16. **audition** (au · di · tion) (au · dish′ un) *n.* A trial hearing, as of an actor or singer; the act of hearing. *v.* To try out for a part in an audition. *Carol's first **audition** for the part in the play was so successful that she was told there was no reason to listen to any other person.*

17. **audiovisual** (au′ di · o · vis · u · al) (au•dē · ō · vizh′ ū · al) *adj.* Of, pertaining to, involving, or directed at both hearing and sight. *Many teachers use **audiovisual** aids in the classroom because the added senses of seeing and hearing help in learning.*

18. **local** (lo · cal) (lō′ kal) *adj.* Referring to a relatively small area, region, or neighborhood; limited. *As a child, I always went to the **local** movie theater because it was close to where I lived.*

19. **location** (lo · ca · tion ((lō · kā′ shun) *n.* A place or site; exact position or place occupied; an area or tract of land; a place used for filming a motion picture or a television program (as in the expression *to be on location*). *The **location** for our picnic was perfect because it was such a scenic place.*

20. **allocate** (al · lo · cate) (al′ ĺo · kātȼ) *v.* To set something apart for a special purpose; to divide up something; to divide and distribute something. *Each person was **allocated** a certain share of the profits according to the amount of time and work he or she had put into the project.*

21. **antonym** (an · to · nym) (an′ to · nim) *n.* A word opposite in meaning to some other word. *The words* good *and* bad *are **antonyms** because they are opposite in meaning.*

22. **synonym** (syn · o · nym) (sin′ o · nim) *n.* A word having the same or nearly the same meaning as some other word. *The words* vision *and* sight *are **synonyms** because they have the same meaning.*

23. **homonym** (hom · o · nym) (hom′ o · nim) *n.* A word that agrees in pronunciation with some other word but differs in spelling and meaning.

The color red *and the verb* read *are* **homonyms** *because they sound alike but are spelled differently and have different meanings.*

24. **pseudonym** (pseu · do · nym) (p̸s¢ū′ do · nim) *n.* False name, used by an author to conceal his or her identity; pen name; false name. *Samuel Clemens wrote under the name Mark Twain, his* **pseudonym.**

25. **misnomer** (mis · nō′ mer) *n.* A name wrongly applied to someone or something; an error in the naming of a person or place in a legal document. *It is a* **misnomer** *to call a spider an insect.*

26. **anonymous** (a · non · y · mous) (a · non′ i · m¢us) *adj.* Lacking a name; of unknown authorship. *As it is the policy of the newspaper to publish signed letters only, the* **anonymous** *letter was not published.*

Special Notes

1. Note that *alias* (a word from Exercise 5) and *pseudonym* are basically synonyms. However, the term *alias* is usually used when a criminal uses a name other than his or her own, whereas the term *pseudonym* is usually used when an author uses a name other than his or her own.

   Do not confuse *pseudonym* and *alias* with *misnomer.* The term *misnomer* refers to someone's using a wrong name or word accidentally, that is, *not on purpose.* When someone uses an *alias* or *pseudonym,* he or she is doing it *on purpose* and has not made a mistake.

   The term *anonymous* refers to someone who has not signed his or her name, so that the name of the person is unknown. When you see *anonymous* at the end of a poem or story, it means that the author is unknown.

2. *Affect* and *effect* are terms that are used a great deal. However, they are often used incorrectly. Note the way the words are used in the sentences that follow.

   affect. *v.* To act upon or to cause something; to influence. *You will probably* **affect** *your team's chances to win because you seem to have such a great influence on them.*

   effect. *n.* Something brought about by some cause; the result. *The* **effect** *on the team was that they won the game.*

Step III. Practice

A. Directions: A list of definitions follows. Choose the word that *best* fits the definition. Try to relate your definition to the meanings of the combining forms. All the words are used.

Word List

manual, manicure, manufacture, manuscript, factory, benefactor, beneficiary, benefit, affect, effect, effective, audible, auditorium, audience, audit, audition, audiovisual, local, location, allocate, antonym, synonym, homonym, pseudonym, misnomer, anonymous.

1. A false name _____

2. A name wrongly applied _____

3. A word opposite in meaning to some other word _____

4. A word similar in meaning to some other word _____

5. Lacking a name _____

6. Made by hand _____

7. Written by hand _____

8. Care of the hands and fingernails _____

9. A building in which things are made _____

10. One who gives help _____

11. One who receives aid _____

12. An advantage; payment _____

13. To make goods by hand or machinery _____

14. To influence _____

15. A result _____

16. Producing results with the least amount of wasted effort _____

17. A building or hall for speeches, meetings, and the like _____

18. An assembly of listeners at a concert, play, and so on _____

19. Capable of being heard _____

20. Involving both hearing and sight _____

21. A trial hearing _____

22. To examine or check accounts _____

23. To set apart for a special purpose _____

24. A place or site _____

25. Referring to a relatively small area, region, or neighborhood _____

26. A word that is pronounced the same as some other word but is spelled differently and has a different meaning _____

STOP. Check answers at the end of Chapter Four (p. 136).

B. Directions: A number of sentences with missing words follows. Fill in the word that *best* fits the sentence. Two choices are given for each sentence.

1. As the _____ of the policy, you will receive everything. (benefactor, beneficiary)

2. In the _____ the workers are making a large supply of toy trains. (factory, location)

3. The author did not want to use his own name, so he used a _____ . (misnomer, pseudonym)

4. The police received a(n) _____ letter that gave them information about the murder. (manual, anonymous)

5. In _____ letters are not joined together. (manual, manuscript)

6. The _____ where the people met to listen to the concert was very large. (factory, auditorium)

7. The _____ you are having on your brother is not the one we wanted. (affect, effect)

8. Try not to _____ your brother as much as you do. (affect, effect)

9. *Alias* and *pseudonym* are _____ s. (antonym, synonym)

10. *Happy* and *sad* are _____ s. (antonym, synonym)

11. *Sew* and *so* are _____ s. (synonym, homonym)

12. When something is _____, it brings about results with the least amount of effort. (effective, anonymous)

13. Each employee of the corporation was _____ a certain share of the profits. (affected, allocated)

14. No one was able to hear it, because it was not _____ . (effective, audible)

15. Because I like to stay close to my home, I shop in _____ places. (audiovisual, local)

16. The company decided to _____ its accounts to check for errors. (allocate, audit)

17. If Jennifer doesn't get a(n) _____ soon for a play, she will give up trying to be an actress. (location, audition)

STOP. Check answers at the end of Chapter Four (p. 136).

C. Directions: A few paragraphs with missing words follow. Fill in the blanks
with the word that *best* fits. Words may be used more than
once.

Word List

pseudonym, audible, audition, effect, manicure, location, local, effective, audience, benefit, benefactor, factory, manual, manufacture, beneficiary.

Because Mary Brown enjoys making things and working with her hands, she
doesn't mind 1_____ labor even though she's a woman. However, her parents want her to have lots of 2_____ s. They feel
that the only way she can get the advantages they want her to have is by
finishing college. In order to go to college, she works in a 3_____
in which clothing is 4_____ d on a large scale. She has no
5_____ to help her, and she is not the 6_____ of
any rich old uncle's insurance policy.

This summer they used the 7_____ where she is working as the
8_____ for a movie. It was very exciting! Every day they had a
large 9_____ watch the making of the film. The spectators came
from all over. The movie people were so 10_____ in getting the
11_____ s they wanted for the film that very little time was
wasted. When they worked, no outside sounds were 12_____
because they told the spectators to be silent.

They were going to use a number of 13_____ people in some
of the mob scenes. As Mary Brown lived in the neighborhood, she was chosen
for a(n) 14_____. Mary was told that if they liked what they
saw and heard, they would use her in the movie. Well, Mary tried to make herself look as glamorous as possible. She even decided to give her hands a(n)
15_____.

When the day for her 16_____ came, she was so excited that
she could hardly talk. By the time she got to the 17_____ for
her test, her voice was not 18_____.

The director told all the people in the mob scene that they were to be in a
scene where they all fall into mud. Ugh! And for this Mary Brown had made
herself glamorous and given herself a(n) 19_____. For this
role she would probably use a 20_____ rather than her real
name.

STOP. Check answers at the end of Chapter Four (p. 136).

EXTRA WORD
POWER

> **anti.** Against; opposed to. *Anti,* meaning "against,"
> is found at the beginning of a great number of words.
> For example: *antiwar*—against war; *antigambling*—
> against gambling; *antimachine*—against machines;

antimen—against men; *antiwomen*—against women; *antilabor*—against labor. Note that *anti* changes to *ant* before words that begin with a vowel, as in *antacid*—something that acts against acid; *antonym*— a word opposite in meaning to some other word. As you can see, you can place *anti* at the beginning of a lot of words. Can you think of some words to which you might add *anti*? Use the dictionary to see the great number of words there are with *anti.*

non. Not. When *non* is placed in front of a word, it means a simple negative or the absence of something. The number of words beginning with *non* is so large that the dictionary has them listed in a special section. Check your dictionary to see how many it has. Following are some words with *non*: *nonbeliever*—not a believer; *non-Arab*—not an Arab; *non-Catholic*—not Catholic; *noncapitalist*—not a capitalist; *non-Communist*—not a Communist; *non-efficient*—not efficient; *noncriminal*—not criminal; *non-English*—not English. How many more can you supply?

Additional Words Derived from Combining Forms

From your knowledge of combining forms, can you define the following words?

1. **audiometer** (au · di · om · e · ter) (au · dē · om′ e · ter) *n. The doctor used the **audiometer** to determine if John had a hearing problem.*

   _____

2. **audiology** (au · di · ol · o · gy) (au · dē · ol′ o · jē) *n. Sally decided to major in **audiology** in college because she wanted to help children who had hearing problems.*

   _____

3. **benediction** (ben · e · dic · tion) (ben · e · dik′ shun) *n. At the end of the church service the minister gave the **benediction**.*

   _____

4. **antipathy** (an · tip · a · thy) (an · tip′ a · thē) *n. Mary had great **antipathy** toward the persons who injured her brother.*

   _____

5. **pseudopodium** (pseu · do · po · di · um) (p̸se̸u · do · pō′ dē · um) *n.*
(*pl.* **dia**) *Some one-celled animals have **pseudopodia**, which are used for taking in food and for movement.*

6. **curator** (cu · ra · tor) (kū · rā′ tor) *n. A good **curator** of a museum should know everything that is going on in the museum.*

7. **pedicure** (ped · i · cure) (ped′ i · kur̸e) *n. I always have a **pedicure** before I wear open sandals.*

8. **pseudoscience** (pseu · do · sci · ence) (p̸se̸u · dō · s̸ci′ ens̸e) *n. Astrology is a **pseudoscience** because it involves only the reading of the stars to foretell the future and is not based on rational principles.*

9. **manipulation** (ma · nip · u · la · tion) (ma · nip′ yu · lā · shun) *n. By his clever **manipulation** of all those around him, he was able to gain the position he desired.*

10. **emancipate** (e · man · ci · pate) (ē · man′ si · pāt̸e) *v. After enslaved people have been **emancipated**, they must learn how to live like free people.*

11. **personification** (per · son · i · fi · ca · tion) (per · son · i · fi · kā′ shun) *n. "The clouds wept a torrent of tears that almost flooded the city," is an example of **personification**.*

12. **facsimile** (fac · sim · i · le) (fak · sim′ i · lē) *n. v. The little girl was the **facsimile** of her mother at the same age.*

13. **faction** (fac · tion) (fak′ shun) *n. There was a special **faction** in the union that was trying to gain power so that its members could further their own desires.*

STOP. Check answers at the end of Chapter Four (p. 137).

Practice for Additional Words Derived from Combining Forms

Directions: Match each word with the *best* definition.

———— 1. audiometer

———— 2. audiology

———— 3. benediction

———— 4. antipathy

———— 5. pseudopodia

———— 6. curator

———— 7. pedicure

———— 8. pseudoscience

———— 9. manipulation

————10. emancipate

————11. personification

————12. facsimile

————13. faction

a. a blessing

b. an exact copy

c. to free from servitude or slavery

d. a figure of speech in which human qualities are given to nonliving things

e. a dislike for someone

f. a group in an organization or government, often self-seeking, with common ends

g. one in charge, as of a department in a museum

h. an instrument used to measure hearing

i. the study of hearing

j. a false science

k. the skillful handling of something

l. false feet

m. care or treatment of the feet

STOP. Check answers at the end of Chapter Four (p. 137).

Question: When doesn't it pay to increase your vocabulary?

© 1975 by NEA, Inc.

"MY MOTHER JUST DECREASED MY VOCABULARY BY ONE WORD!"

Answer: When the words you use hurt.

CROSSWORD PUZZLE 3

Directions: The meanings of many of the combining forms from Exercises 7–9 follow. Your knowledge of these combining forms will help you to solve this crossword puzzle. Note that *combining form* is abbreviated as *comb. f.*

Across

3. Comb. f. for *without*
4. A misanthrope is a____of mankind
8. Same as #1 Down
9. Squirrels eat these
12. Two-wheeler
15. Comb. f. for *place*
16. To be
17. Comb. f. for *in*
18. An artificial waterway
19. Meaning of *vis*; *vid*
20. Comb. f. for *care*
24. Rhymes with *ham*
26. Opposite of *off*
27. Comb. f. for *hand*
30. Same as #3 Across
31. Word for *strong feeling against*
34. Same as #26 Across
35. Word for *written by hand*
41. Rhymes with *hit*
42. Comb. f. for *wrong*; *hate*

Down

1. Comb. f. for *make*; *do*
2. Comb. f. for *come*
3. Comb. f. for *water*
4. A sound you make when you laugh
5. A monarch is a____of a monarchy
6. Comb. f. for *see*
7. Comb. f. for *good*
8. You put this around a picture
10. A homonym of *two*
11. Comb. f. for *know*
12. Marriage to two spouses at the same time
13. Opposite of *no*
14. Comb. f. for *without*
18. Something to sleep on
20. Comb. f. for *body*
21. Comb. f. for *not*; *lack of*
22. Word meaning *yearly*
23. Comb. f. for *head*
25. A way of saying *mother*

116

43. Comb. f. for *star*
45. To hand out something a little at a time
46. A period of time
48. Comb. f. for *from a distance*
50. You do this in a chair
51. Abbreviation for *advertisement*
52. A long slippery fish
53. Opposite of *friend*
54. Comb. f. for *sail*
55. Comb. f. for *powerful*
56. Comb. f. for *kill*
59. Comb. f. for *all*

28. Comb. f. for *name*
29. Word meaning *to join*
30. Comb. f. for *hear*
31. Same as #3 Across
32. Past tense of *eat*
33. A farmer uses this tool
35. Comb. f. for *death*
36. A homonym of *sew*
37. You can do this when you put two hands together
38. When you do something again, you____it
39. A pronoun
40. He is a____-ager
43. Same as #3 Across
44. Comb. f. for *same*
47. Comb. f. for *again, back*
49. Same as #15 Across
50. To be in appearance
57. Same as #39 Down
58. When you carry out an act, you ____it

STOP. Check answers at the end of Chapter Four (p. 137).

WORD SCRAMBLE 3

Directions: Word Scramble 3 is based on words from Exercises 7–9. The meanings are your clues to arranging the letters in correct order. Write the correct word in the blank.

		Meanings
1. siivno	_____	sense of sight
2. eeiilotvns	_____	electronic system for transmitting images from a distance
3. niiibelvs	_____	not able to be seen
4. vrooiisnps	_____	food or supplies
5. cendeive	_____	that which serves to prove or disprove something
6. cciseen	_____	an area of knowledge in which facts have been investigated and presented in an orderly manner

7. taslrygoo   _____   the false science of foretelling the future from the stars

8. tysaromno   _____   the study of stars, planets, and space

9. tnaoaustr   _____   one who travels in space

10. catuaiq   _____   referring to water

11. noecnev   _____   to come together

12. ivnenocnte   _____   well suited to one's purposes

13. tentop   _____   powerful

14. apenotlit   _____   ability or power you might have

15. restennopim   _____   being present everywhere at all times

16. deoiimhc   _____   the killing of one person by another

17. thapya   _____   lack of feeling

18. nodeigce   _____   the killing of a whole racial, political, or cultural group

19. ymethap   _____   the imaginative putting of oneself into the personality of another

20. patcalmisi   _____   economic system based on profit

21. notareorpic   _____   to unite; combine

22. persoc   _____   dead body

23. troaimlm   _____   referring to a being who never dies

24. gtromega   _____   the pledging of property to a creditor

25. luaanm   _____   referring to hands

26. eeaotfbnrc   _____   one who gives help

27. carytfo   _____   a building in which things are manufactured

28. fcteef   _____   a result

29. catffe   _____   to influence

30. eaubild   _____   capable of being heard

31. tiadu   _____   to examine accounts

32. lotaaecl   _____   to divide and distribute something

33. duesypnom   _____   false name

34. yysmonn   _____   a word having the same meaning as another

35. sanyonuom   _____   lacking a name

STOP. Check answers at the end of Chapter Four (p. 138).

ANALOGIES 3

Directions: Find the word from the following list that *best* completes each analogy. There are more words in the list than you need.

Word List

deny, pedestrian, capitulate, capital, convenient, creed, creditor, apathy, stars, underwater, pseudoscience, facsimile, omnipresent, omniscient, omnipotent, effect, affect, impotent, potential, convene, convention, anonymous, pseudo-podal, mortify, audible, caption, audiometer, audiology, audition, suicide, homicide, genocide, corpulent, antipathy, love, feel, sympathy, empathy, visage.

1. Astronaut : space :: aquanaut :_____.

2. Visible : evident : : everywhere :_____.

3. Incredible : credible : : potent : _____.

4. Mortal : immortal : : adjourn : _____.

5. Astronomy : science : : astrology :_____.

6. Snake : apodal : : amoeba :_____.

7. Incorporate : unite : : humiliate : _____.

8. Benediction : blessing : : heading : _____.

9. Pseudonym : alias : : face :_____.

10. Autograph : signature : : copy : _____.

11. Life : biology : : hearing :_____.

12. Vest : clothing :: fratricide : _____.

13. Deny : contradict : : fleshy :_____.

14. Symmetry : balance : : dislike :_____.

15. Assembly : meeting : : handy : _____.

16. Benefit : advantage : : indifference :_____.

17. Noise : clamor : : faith : _____.

18. Handbook : manual : : result :_____.

19. Location : site : : nameless :_____.

20. Anarchy : order : : resist : _____.

STOP. Check answers at the end of Chapter Four (p. 138).

MULTIPLE-CHOICE VOCABULARY TEST 3

Directions: This is a test on words in Exercises 7–9. Words are presented according to exercises. *Do all exercises before checking answers.* Underline the meaning that *best* fits the word.

Exercise 7

1. vision
   a. able to be seen
   b. system for the transmission of visual images from a distance
   c. sense of sight
   d. easily recognized

2. visible
   a. sense of sight
   b. system for the transmission of visual images from a distance
   c. able to be seen
   d. not seen

3. television
   a. sense of sight
   b. system for the transmission of visual images from a distance
   c. able to be seen
   d. plain

4. invisible
   a. not able to be seen
   b. in disguise
   c. out of sight
   d. to view from inside

5. provision
   a. something made ready in advance
   b. something to see from a distance
   c. something to see
   d. to see for someone

6. evident
   a. clearly seen
   b. sense of sight
   c. able to see from a distance
   d. to view

7. evidence
   a. that which seems to prove or disapprove something
   b. able to see clearly
   c. that which is seen from a distance
   d. that which shows something

8. science
   a. a knowing person
   b. able to know
   c. the sense of knowing
   d. area of ordered and investigated knowledge

9. astrology
   a. the study of heavenly bodies
   b. the reading of the stars to foretell the future
   c. a true science
   d. refers to stars

10. astronomy
   a. the study of stars, planets, and space
   b. the reading of the stars
   c. a true science
   d. refers to stars

11. astronaut
   a. refers to space
   b. refers to stars
   c. one who travels underwater
   d. one who travels in space

12. aquanaut
   a. refers to undersea
   b. one who travels undersea
   c refers to water
   d. refers to one who travels in space

13. aquatic
   a. referring to a water plant
   b. referring to a water flower
   c. referring to water
   d. referring to undersea plants

14. aquarium
   a. a water bowl
   b. refers to water
   c. a globelike bowl or rectangular container for water plants and animals
   d. an area of study

15. convene
   a. something suitable
   b. a meeting
   c. to come together
   d. to call a special meeting

16. convention
   a. a friendly get-together
   b. a formal meeting of members for professional purposes
   c. something suitable
   d. to come together

17. convenient
   a. suited to one's purpose
   b. a get-together
   c. joining together
   d. a special meeting

18. potent
   a. a drug
   b. a perfume
   c. powerful
   d. refers to money

19. impotent
   a. refers to sex
   b. without power
   c. refers to power
   d. refers to males only

20. potential
   a. the ability or power one may have
   b. refers to sex
   c. refers to males only
   d. refers to feeling

121

21. omnipresent   a. referring to a gift   c. referring to everyone
                               b. referring to all   d. being present every-
                                                                       where at all times

Exercise 8

22. homicide   a. killing of a brother   c. killing of one person
                               b. killing of oneself   by another
                                                      d. killing of a whole group
                                                      of people

23. suicide   a. killing of oneself   c. killing of a brother
                               b. killing of a whole   d. killing of one person
                                    group of people   by another

24. genocide   a. killing of man   c. killing of a brother
                               b. killing of a whole racial,   d. killing of oneself
                                   political, or cultural
                                   group

25. sympathy   a. feeling sad   c. self-pity
                               b. ability to put oneself   d. ability to feel pity
                                   into the personality   for another
                                   of another

26. empathy   a. ability to feel pity for   c. self-pity
                               b. ability to imaginatively   d. feeling sad
                                   put oneself into the per-
                                   sonality of another

27. apathy   a. refers to pity   c. lack of feeling
                               b. self-pity   d. feeling sad

28. fraternity   a. a Greek letter college   c. killing of a brother
                               organization   d. refers to friends and
                               b. a brother   relatives

29. capital punishment   a. bodily harm   c. death penalty
                               b. head punishment   d. beatings

30. capitalism   a. refers to profit   c. an economic system in
                               b. an economic system   which all or most of the
                                   in which all or most of   means of production are
                                   the means of production   not privately owned
                                   are privately owned   d. an economic system in
                                                          which all or most of the
                                                         means of production are
                                                         privately owned and op-
                                                         erated for profit

31. capital
   a. official seat of govern-
      ment
   b. relevant
   c. refers to an economic
      system
   d. refers to death

32. corpse
   a. a body
   b. a dead body
   c. a group of people
   d. refers to beatings

33. corporation
   a. men getting together
   b. a business
   c. a group of people with
      a charter granting them
      certain powers and
      making them not le-
      gally responsible for
      each other
   d. a group of people with
      a charter granting them
      certain powers to rule

34. incorporate
   a. to unite
   b. to join a club
   c. refers to a body
   d. men getting together

35. corporal
    punishment
   a. death penalty
   b. a beating
   c. refers to the body
   d. refers to punishment of
      an officer in the service

36. mortal
   a. referring to death
   b. referring to a dead
      person
   c. referring to any dead
      animal
   d. referring to someone who
      must die

37. immortal
   a. referring to all
      living persons
   b. referring to all
      dead persons
   c. referring to death
   d. referring to a being who
      never dies

38. mortality
   a. dead persons
   b. death rate
   c. one who never dies
   d. one who must die

39. mortician
   a. a dead man
   b. one who must die
   c. a person who counts
      the dead
   d. an undertaker

40. mortgage
   a. refers to death
   b. pledging property
   c. giving up your property
   d. pledging property to a
      creditor as security for
      payment

41. morgue
   a. refers to the dead
   b. place to keep all dead
      bodies
   c. an undertaker's office
   d. place where unidentified
      dead bodies are kept

Exercise 9

42. manual
    a. referring to the hands
    b. referring to manly work
    c. referring to men
    d. referring to help

43. manicure
    a. refers to cure
    b. refers to hands
    c. the curing of hand problems
    d. the care of the hands and fingernails

44. manuscript
    a. a newspaper
    b. a role in a play
    c. to write by hand
    d. a letter

45. manufacture
    a. to make machinery
    b. to store in a factory
    c. to make by hand or machine from raw material
    d. made to sell

46. factory
    a. a building
    b. a house
    c. a place for storing things only
    d. a place for manufacturing things

47. benefactor
    a. one who gets help
    b. one who gives help
    c. someone good
    d. a blessing

48. beneficiary
    a. one who gives help
    b. one who needs help
    c. one who gets help
    d. a blessing

49. benefit
    a. a performance for some charity or cause
    b. a blessing
    c. a performance
    d. charity

50. affect
    a. the result
    b. to bring
    c. an action
    d. to influence

51. effect
    a. to influence
    b. the result
    c. the action
    d. to bring something

52. effective
    a. producing no results after a while
    b. producing
    c. making something do
    d. producing results in a minimum of time

53. audible
    a. referring to hearing
    b. referring to a listener
    c. capable of being heard
    d. not heard

54. auditorium
    a. a building in which things are made
    b. a special building
    c. a place for workers
    d. a place for speeches, concerts, and so on.

55. audience
    a. a group of listeners or spectators at a play, concert, and so on
    b. spectacles
    c. people
    d. a building

56. audit
    a. to hear
    b. to examine accounts
    c. to examine
    d. to be a spectator

57. audition
    a. an examination of books
    b. an examination
    c. a hearing for a jury trial
    d. a trial hearing for an actor or singer

58. audiovisual
    a. instruction using books
    b. instruction using printed matter
    c. instruction using only television
    d. pertaining to hearing and seeing

59. local
    a. referring to a neighborhood area
    b. referring to a distant place
    c. referring to a place
    d. referring to a situation

60. location
    a. in the neighborhood
    b. a place or site
    c. a situation
    d. any place close

61. allocate
    a. to place
    b. to set
    c. to divide and distribute
    d. to put together

62. antonym
    a. a word similar to another in meaning
    b. a word opposite in meaning to another
    c. a word that is pronounced the same as another
    d. a word that is spelled like another

63. synonym
    a. a word similar in pronounciation to another
    b. a word opposite in meaning to another
    c. a word similar to another in spelling
    d. a word similar to another in meaning

64. homonym
    a. a word similar to another in spelling
    b. a word similar to another in pronunciation
    c. a word different from another in meaning and spelling but similar in pronunciation
    d. a word different in meaning from another

65. pseudonym
    a. wrong name
    b. same name
    c. lacking a name
    d. false name

66. misnomer
    a. false name
    b. lacking a name
    c. same name
    d. wrong name

67. anonymous
    a. wrong name
    b. false name
    c. lacking a name
    d. same name

True/False Test 3

Directions: This is a true/false test on Exercises 7–9. Read each sentence carefully. Decide whether it is true or false. Put a *T* for *true* or an *F* for *false* in the blank. The number after the sentence tells you if the word is from Exercise 7, 8, or 9.

_____ 1. A fratricide would also be a homicide. 8

_____ 2. A suicide is also a homicide. 8

_____ 3. Corporal punishment refers to a beating. 8

_____ 4. Some mortals are able to survive forever. 8

_____ 5. If the proportion of minority group children who die is higher, then the mortality of such children is lower than that for children as a whole. 8

_____ 6. A person who receives capital punishment is not executed. 8

_____ 7. Astrology is a science. 7

_____ 8. Astronauts travel undersea. 7

_____ 9. If something is convenient for you, it occurs at a bad time. 7

_____10. You can hear your potential. 7

_____11. An omnipresent thing is present everywhere all the time. 7

_____12. You can have sympathy for someone even if you can't experience how he or she feels. 8

_____13. Genocide is a fatal illness. 8

_____14. The words *antipathy* and *apathy* are synonyms. 8, 9

_____15. The words *synonym* and *antonym* are antonyms. 9

_____16. To audit the books means to examine them. 9

_____17. The words *alias* and *pseudonym* are synonyms. 9

_____18. Man is immortal. 8

_____19. A morgue is where all dead bodies are stored. 8

_____20. A manuscript can refer to a book written by hand and sent in for publication. 9

_____21. Something audible can be heard. 9

_____22. The words *pseudonym* and *misnomer* are synonyms. 9

_____23. The words *bury* and *berry* are synonyms. 9

_____24. The words *fat* and *corpulent* are synonyms. 8, 9

_____25. The words *anonymous* and *alias* are synonyms. 9

STOP. Check answers for both tests at the end of Chapter Four (pp. 138–139).

SCORING OF TESTS

Multiple-Choice Vocabulary Test

Number Wrong	Score
0–4	Excellent
5–10	Good
11–14	Weak
Above 14	Poor

Score_____

True/False Test

Number Wrong	Score
0–2	Excellent
3–5	Good
6–7	Weak
Above 7	Poor

Score_____

1. If you scored in the excellent or good range on *both tests,* you are doing well. Go on to Chapter Five.

2. If you scored in the weak or poor range on either test, look below and follow directions for Additional Practice. Note that the words on the tests are arranged so that you can tell in which exercise to find them. This will help you if you need additional practice.

ADDITIONAL PRACTICE SETS

A. Directions: Write the words you missed on the tests from the three exercises in the space provided. Note that the tests are presented so that you can tell to which exercises the words belong.

Exercise 7 Words Missed

1. _____   6. _____
2. _____   7. _____
3. _____   8. _____
4. _____   9. _____
5. _____   10. _____

Exercise 8 Words Missed

1. _____   6. _____
2. _____   7. _____

3. _____   8. _____

4. _____   9. _____

5. _____   10. _____

Exercise 9 Words Missed

1. _____   6. _____

2. _____   7. _____

3. _____   8. _____

4. _____   9. _____

5. _____   10. _____

B. Directions: Restudy the words that you have written down on p. 127 and this page. Study the combining forms from which those words are derived. Do Step I and Step II for those you missed. Note that Step I and Step II of the combining forms and vocabulary derived from these combining forms are on the following pages:

Exercise 7—pp. 87–90

Exercise 8—pp. 96–99

Exercise 9—pp. 106–109

C. Directions: Do Additional Practice 1 on this page and pp. 129–130 if you missed words from Exercise 7. Do Additional Practice 2 on pp. 130–131 if you missed words from Exercise 8. Do Additional Practice 3 on pp. 132–133 if you missed words from Exercise 9. Now go on to Chapter Five.

Additional Practice 1 for Exercise 7

A. Directions: Following are the combining forms presented in Exercise 7. Match the combining form with its meaning.

_____ 1. vid, vis   a. star

_____ 2. sci, scio   b. all

_____ 3. poten   c. see

_____ 4. omni   d. come

_____ 5. aqua, aqui   e. sailor

_____ 6. astro   f. water

_____ 7. naut   g. powerful

_____ 8. ven, veni, vent   h. know

STOP. Check answers at the end of Chapter Four (p. 139).

B. Directions: Sentences containing the meanings of vocabulary presented in Exercise 7 follow. Chose the word that *best* fits the meaning of the word or phrase underlined in the sentence. A word may be used only once.

Word List

potent, convenient, astrology, conventions, astronomy, aquatic, convene, astronauts, aquarium, television, visible, evident, provisions, science, evidence, invisible, impotent, potential, omnipresent, aquanauts, vision.

1. If you are blind, you do not have your sense of sight. _____

2. In the film, a man played a ghost who was not able to be seen. _____

3. I enjoy visual image shows that come from New York and California in my own home. _____

4. The sign was able to be seen, but I went past it. _____

5. We will take enough supplies for our trip. _____

6. I am studying astronomy, which is a field of organized knowledge concerning heavenly bodies. _____

7. The lawyer needed something that would prove that his client was innocent of the charges. _____

8. It is plain from the way you are acting that you want me to leave.

   _____

9. Some people believe that a reading of the stars will predict their futures.

   _____

10. What do you call men who travel in space?_____

11. What do you call men who travel undersea? _____

12. My favorite course is the study of stars, planets, and space.

    _____

13. I enjoy studying about water plants and animals. _____

14. I keep my water plants and animals in a large tank where I can watch them.

    _____

15. The judge said that the people in court should come together again at two in the afternoon. _____

129

16. I enjoy attending formal professional meetings. _____

17. Attending classes in the afternoon is not suitable for me because I work in the afternoon. _____

18. That is powerful medicine you are taking. _____

19. The person in charge was merely a figurehead who was without power. _____

20. If I knew what my possible ability was, I would try to do something with it. _____

21. The bandits seemed to be present everywhere at all times. _____

STOP. Check answers at the end of Chapter Four (p. 139).

Additional Practice 2 for Exercise 8

A. Directions: The combining forms presented in Exercise 8 follow.
   Match the combining form with its meaning.

_____ 1. cide   a. into; in

_____ 2. pathy   b. kill; murder

_____ 3. syl, sym, syn   c. death

_____ 4. frater, fratr   d. same; with; together; along with

_____ 5. mors, mort   e. brother

_____ 6. capit   f. feeling; suffering

_____ 7. corp, corpor   g. head

_____ 8. em, en   h. body

STOP. Check answers at the end of Chapter Four (p. 139).

B. Directions: Sentences containing the meanings of vocabulary presented in Exercise 8 follow. Choose the word that *best* fits the meaning of the word or phrase underlined in the sentence.

Word List

genocide, apathy, empathy, sympathy, suicide, homicide, capitalism, immortals, fraternity, capital, mortals, capital punishment, corporation, incorporate, corporal punishment, corpse, mortality, mortgage, mortician, morgue.

1. More and more persons are involved in <u>the act of killing others</u>.
   _____

2. Only a madman would attempt the <u>destruction of a whole race of people</u>.
   _____

3. I have <u>the ability to understand how you feel</u> because I had the same experience. _____

4. I have <u>no feeling</u> about that. _____

5. I have <u>pity</u> for the child who lost both parents in an accident. _____

6. The man resorted to <u>the act of killing himself</u> when he lost all his money.
   _____

7. I am joining <u>a Greek letter college organization</u> next semester. _____

8. My father's friends formed <u>an association of a number of businessmen, which took out a special charter granting it certain rights</u>. _____

9. In the United States we have <u>an economic system based on private ownership and profit</u>. _____

10. Are you and the other men going to <u>join together to form a business</u>?
    _____

11. All <u>human beings</u> must eventually die. _____

12. <u>Undying beings</u> do not exist on earth. _____

13. We found a <u>dead body</u> in the woods. _____

14. I wonder if <u>the death penalty</u> will return. _____

15. Many persons believe that children should not be subjected to <u>a beating</u> in school. _____

16. Do you know <u>the death rate</u> of teen-agers involved in automobile accidents?
    _____

17. Because it was unidentified, the body was taken to <u>a special place where unidentified bodies are held</u> until it could be claimed. _____

18. They had difficulty paying off <u>the loan on their property</u> because of other very large unexpected expenses. _____

19. She went to <u>an undertaker</u> to arrange for her father's funeral. _____

20. Do you have enough <u>money</u> to start such a business venture? _____

STOP. Check answers at the end of Chapter Four (p. 139).

A. Directions: The combining forms presented in Exercise 9 follow. Match the combining form with its meaning.

_____	1. man, manu	a. make; do
_____	2. fac, fect, fic	b. place
_____	3. loc, loco	c. hear
_____	4. pseudo	d. care
_____	5. bene	e. name
_____	6. aud, audi	f. false
_____	7. cura	g. good
_____	8. nomin, onym	h. hand

STOP. Check answers at the end of Chapter Four (p. 139).

B. Directions: Sentences containing the meanings of vocabulary presented in Exercise 9 follow. Choose the word that *best* fits the meaning of the word or phrase underlined in the sentence.

Word List

manual, beneficiary, benefit, affect, effect, effective, audible, misnomer, anonymous, pseudonyms, allocate, antonyms, synonyms, auditorium, audience, audit, audition, manufacture, audiovisual, location, local, homonyms, benefactor, factory, manicure, manuscript.

1. She goes to the beauty shop for the care of her fingernails. _____
2. We learned the style of writing our letters without joining them together. _____
3. My husband works in a building that makes furniture. _____
4. Many artists have a person who supports them so that they do not have to worry about money. _____
5. Hand labor does not bother me. _____
6. The speaker was just capable of being heard. _____
7. When they examine the accounts, they had better balance, or you will be in trouble. _____
8. There will be a tryout for the new play next week. _____
9. In my school we use a lot of television, radio, records, and picture aids. _____

10. The method you have for studying is really <u>productive in getting results</u> for you. _____

11. The concert is being held in <u>a large special room</u> used for such performances in the school._____

12. In this day and age we <u>make goods by machinery</u> on a large scale in order to have enough available for so many people. _____

13. What <u>result</u>, if any, did you find?_____

14. I just found out that I am <u>the receiver of a large amount of money</u> that was left to me by an old uncle who recently died. _____

15. What is the major <u>advantage</u> of going to college?_____

16. <u>The group of listeners at the concert</u> was so quiet that you could hear a pin drop. _____

17. I am not going to <u>influence</u> your brother in any way. _____

18. *Bear* and *bare* are <u>words that sound alike but are spelled differently and have different meanings.</u> _____

19. *Corpulent* and *fat* are <u>words similar in meaning.</u> _____

20. *Antonym* and *synonym* are <u>words opposite in meaning.</u> _____

21. Some authors use <u>pen names or names other than their own names.</u>

    _____

22. When I used the term *misanthrope* to mean a hater of marriage, I was using <u>a wrong word.</u>_____

23. The poem was <u>without an author's name.</u> _____

24. I shop only in <u>neighborhood</u> stores. _____

25. The men will <u>set aside</u> a certain number of tickets for us. _____

26. Our house is in a lovely <u>place.</u> _____

STOP. Check answers at the end of Chapter Four (p. 139).

ANSWERS: Chapter Four

Exercise 7 (pp. 87–96)

Practice A

(1) astronaut, (2) aquanaut, (3) aquatic, (4) potent, (5) aquarium, (6) astrology, (7) astronomy, (8) evident, (9) provision, (10) impotent, (11) evidence, (12) science, (13) Convention, (14) vision, (15) omnipresent, (16) convenient, (17) potential, (18) convene.

Practice B

(1) reporter, (2) decade, (3) anniversary, (4) evident, (5) television, (6) television, (7) convenient, (8) scientists, (9) convention, (10) convention, (11) astronauts, (12) aquatic, (13) aquanauts, (14) astrologist, (15) convention, (16) television, (17) incredible, (18) visible,[1] (19) evident, (20) omnipresent, (21) television, (22) incredible, (23) impotent, (24) astronauts, (25) aquanauts, (26) invisible, (27) visible, (28) provision, (29) evidence.

Practice C

(1) auto, (2) vis, (3) sci, (4) homo, (5) mono, (6) er, (7) ist, (8) or, (9) bi, (10) port, (11) uni, (12) naut, (13) geo, (14) bio, (15) ven, (16) a, (17) con, (18) tele, (19) ali, (20) dict, (21) anthropo.

COMBINING FORM SQUARE

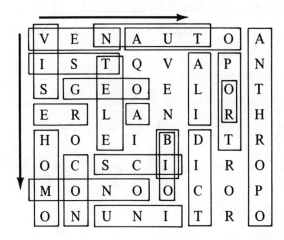

Additional Words Derived from Combining Forms (pp. 94–95)

1. **omnipotent.** All-powerful.

2. **omniscient.** All-knowing.

3. **omnibus.** A large bus designed to carry a number of people as passengers, An *omnibus* bill is a legislative bill that carries a mixture of provisions.

4. **visage.** The face; the appearance of the face or its expression.

5. **visor.** The projecting front brim of a cap for shading the eyes.

6. **visa.** Something stamped or written on a passport that grants an individual entry to a country.

---

[1] Answer can be either *evident* or *visible*.

7. **envision.** To imagine something; to picture in the mind.

8. **visionary.** A person who sees visions.

9. **nautical.** Pertaining to seamen, ships, or navigation.

10. **venture.** A risky or dangerous undertaking, especially a business enterprise in which there is a danger of loss as well as a chance for profit.

11. **potentate.** A person possessing great power; a ruler; a monarch.

Practice for Additional Words Derived from Combining Forms (pp. 95–96)

(1) e, (2) h, (3) f, (4) b, (5) k, (6) j, (7) i, (8) d, (9) g, (10) a, (11) c.

Exercise 8 (pp. 96–105)

Practice A

(1) capital, (2) corporation, (3) capitalism, (4) capital, (5) mortgage, (6) morgue, (7) mortician, (8) incorporate, (9) immortal, (10) mortality, (11) mortal, (12) capital punishment, (13) homicide, (14) capital punishment, corporal punishment, (15) empathy, (16) sympathy, (17) genocide, (18) apathy, (19) suicide, (20) fraternity.

Practice B

(1) c, (2) d, (3) b, (4) c, (5) a, (6) a, (7) b, (8) a, (9) d, (10) a, (11) c, (12) a, (13) a, (14) d, (15) d, (16) a, (17) b, (18) c, (19) b.

Practice C

(1) killing of one person by another, (2) killing of oneself, (3) lack of feeling, (4) ability to feel sorry for, (5) a men's organization at college, (6) the killing of a whole group of people, (7) city or town that is the official seat of government, (8) place where unidentified dead are kept, (9) undertaker, (10) joined together, group of people who get a charter granting them certain rights as a body, (11) a beating, (12) death penalty, (13) that which never dies, (14) person who must die or human being, (15) pledge of property as security with a creditor.

Additional Words Derived from Combining Forms (pp. 104–105)

1. **fratricide.** The killing of a brother; may also refer to the killing of a sister.

2. **corpulent.** Fat; fleshy; obese.

3. **mortify.** To cause to feel shame; to punish (one's body) or control (one's physical desires or passions) by self-denial, fasting, and the like, as a means of religious or ascetic (severe) discipline.

135

4. **amortize.** The gradual extinction of a debt such as a mortgage or a bond issue by payment of a part of the principal at the time of each periodic interest payment.

5. **caption.** The heading of a chapter, section, or page in a book; a title or subtitle of a picture.

6. **capitulate.** To give up; surrender.

7. **symbol.** Something that stands for or represents another thing; an object used to represent something abstract.

8. **syllable.** A vowel or a group of letters with one vowel sound.

9. **monosyllable.** A word consisting of a single syllable.

10. **symphony.** Harmony of sound; harmony of any kind.

11. **symptom.** In medicine, a condition that results from a disease and serves as an aid in diagnosis; a sign or token that indicates the existence of something else.

12. **synthesis.** A putting together of two or more things to form a whole.

13. **symmetry.** Balanced form or arrangement; balance on both sides.

Practice for Additional Words Derived from Combining Forms (p. 105)

(1) i, (2) m, (3) b, (4) a, (5) d, (6) j, (7) c, (8) l, (9) f, (10) h, (11) g, (12) e, (13) k.

Exercise 9 (pp. 106–115)

Practice A

(1) pseudonym, (2) misnomer, (3) antonym, (4) synonym, (5) anonymous, (6) manual, (7) manuscript, (8) manicure, (9) factory, (10) benefactor, (11) beneficiary, (12) benefit, (13) manufacture, (14) affect, (15) effect, (16) effective, (17) auditorium, (18) audience, (19) audible, (20) audiovisual, (21) audition, (22) audit, (23) allocate, (24) location, (25) local, (26) homonym.

Practice B

(1) beneficiary, (2) factory, (3) pseudonym, (4) anonymous, (5) manuscript, (6) auditorium, (7) effect, (8) affect, (9) synonym, (10) antonym, (11) homonym, (12) effective, (13) allocated, (14) audible, (15) local, (16) audit, (17) audition.

Practice C

(1) manual, (2) benefit, (3) factory, (4) manufacture, (5) benefactor, (6) beneficiary, (7) factory, (8) location, (9) audience, (10) effective, (11) effect, (12) audible, (13) local, (14) audition, (15) manicure, (16) audition, (17) location, (18) audible, (19) manicure, (20) pseudonym.

Additional Words Derived from Combining Forms (pp. 113–114)

1. **audiometer.** An instrument used to measure hearing.

2. **audiology.** The study of hearing.

3. **benediction.** A blessing; the expression of good wishes.

4. **antipathy.** A dislike for someone.

5. **pseudopodium.** False foot.

6. **curator.** Head of a department of a museum; one in charge.

7. **pedicure.** Care of the feet, toes, and nails.

8. **pseudoscience.** A false science.

9. **manipulation.** The act of handling or operating; the act of managing or controlling skillfully or by shrewd use of influence; the act of changing or falsification for one's own purposes or profit.

10. **emancipate.** To set free from servitude or slavery; to set free.

11. **personification.** A figure of speech in which a nonliving thing or idea is made to appear as having the qualities of a person.

12. **facsimile.** An exact copy; to make an exact copy of.

13. **faction.** A number of persons in an organization, group, government, party, and so on, having a common goal, often self-seeking and reckless of the common good.

Practice for Additional Words Derived from Combining Forms (p. 115)

(1) h, (2) i, (3) a, (4) e, (5) l, (6) g, (7) m, (8) j, (9) k, (10) c, (11) d, (12) b, (13) f.

Crossword Puzzle (pp. 116–117)

137

(1) vision, (2) television, (3) invisible, (4) provisions, (5) evidence, (6) science, (7) astrology, (8) astronomy, (9) astronaut, (10) aquatic, (11) convene, (12) convenient, (13) potent, (14) potential, (15) omnipresent, (16) homicide, (17) apathy, (18) genocide, (19) empathy, (20) capitalism, (21) incorporate, (22) corpse, (23) immortal, (24) mortgage, (25) manual, (26) benefactor, (27) factory, (28) effect, (29) affect, (30) audible, (31) audit, (32) allocate, (33) pseudonym, (34) synonym, (35) anonymous.

Analogies 3 (p. 119)

(1) underwater, (2) omnipresent, (3) impotent, (4) convene, (5) pseudoscience, (6) pseudopodal, (7) mortify, (8) caption, (9) visage, (10) facsimile, (11) audiology, (12) homicide, (13) corpulent, (14) antipathy, (15) convenient, (16) apathy, (17) creed, (18) effect, (19) anonymous, (20) capitulate.

Multiple-Choice Vocabulary Test 3 (pp. 120–125)

Exercise 7

(1) c, (2) c, (3) b, (4) a, (5) a, (6) a, (7) a, (8) d, (9) b, (10) a, (11) d, (12) b, (13) c, (14) c, (15) c, (16) b, (17) a, (18) c, (19) b, (20) a, (21) d.

Exercise 8

(22) c, (23) a, (24) b, (25) d, (26) b, (27) c, (28) a, (29) c, (30) d, (31) a, (32) b, (33) c, (34) a, (35) b, (36) d, (37) d, (38) b, (39) d, (40) d, (41) d.

Exercise 9

(42) a, (43) d, (44) c, (45) c, (46) d, (47) b, (48) c, (49) a,[2] (50) d, (51) b, (52) d, (53) c, (54) d, (55) a, (56) b, (57) d, (58) d, (59) a, (60) b, (61) c, (62) b, (63) d, (64) c, (65) d, (66) d, (67) c.

True/False Test 3 (pp. 126–127)

(1) T,[3] (2) F,[4] (3) T, (4) F, (5) F,[5] (6) F, (7) F, (8) F, (9) F, (10) F, (11) T,

---

[2] *Performance* or *charity* is not specific enough by itself. A benefit performance is a performance for some charity or cause. Not *all* performances are for benefits.

[3] Although a fratricide is the killing of a brother or a sister, it is also a homicide.

[4] A suicide is *not* a homicide because it does not involve another person.

[5] As proportionally more minority group children die than children as a whole, the mortality or death rate for minority group children would be *higher*.

(12) T[6], (13) F, (14) F, (15) T, (16) T, (17) T, (18) F, (19) F,[7] (20) T, (21) T, (22) F, (23) F, (24) T, (25) F.

STOP. Turn to p. 127 for the scoring of the tests.

Additional Practice Sets (pp. 127–133)

Additional Practice 1

A. (1) c, (2) h, (3) g, (4) b, (5) f, (6) a, (7) e, (8) d.
B. (1) vision, (2) invisible, (3) television, (4) visible,[8] (5) provisions, (6) science, (7) evidence, (8) evident,[8] (9) astrology, (10) astronauts, (11) aquanauts, (12) astronomy, (13) aquatic, (14) aquarium, (15) convene, (16) conventions, (17) convenient, (18) potent, (19) impotent, (20) potential, (21) omnipresent.

Additional Practice 2

A. (1) b, (2) f, (3) d, (4) e, (5) c, (6) g, (7) h, (8) a.
B. (1) homicide, (2) genocide, (3) empathy, (4) apathy, (5) sympathy, (6) suicide, (7) fraternity, (8) corporation, (9) capitalism, (10) incorporate, (11) mortals, (12) immortal, (13) corpse, (14) capital punishment, (15) corporal punishment, (16) mortality, (17) morgue, (18) mortgage, (19) mortician, (20) capital.

Additional Practice 3

A. (1) h, (2) a, (3) b, (4) f, (5) g, (6) c, (7) d, (8) e.
B. (1) manicure, (2) manuscript, (3) factory, (4) benefactor, (5) manual, (6) audible, (7) audit, (8) audition, (9) audiovisual, (10) effective, (11) auditorium, (12) manufacture, (13) effect, (14) beneficiary, (15) benefit, (16) audience, (17) affect, (18) homonyms, (19) synonyms, (20) antonyms, (21) pseudonyms, (22) misnomer, (23) anonymous, (24) local, (25) allocate, (26) location.

---

[6] Only for empathy must you experience how the other person feels.

[7] A morgue is a place where only accident victims and other unidentified bodies are kept.

[8] Although *visible* and *evident* are synonyms, *visible* is the more specific and therefore *better* answer for 4; *evident* is the *better* answer for 8.

CHAPTER FIVE

EXERCISE 10

Step I. Combining Forms

A. Directions: A list of combining forms with their meanings follows. Look at
the combining forms and their meanings. Concentrate on learning each combining form and its meaning. Cover the meanings,
read the combining forms, and state the meanings to yourself.
Check to see if you are correct. Now cover the combining forms,
read the meanings, and state the combining forms to yourself.
Check to see if you are correct.

Combining Forms	Meanings
1. dia	through
2. cata	down
3. log, logo	speech; word
4. fin	end
5. biblio	book
6. fer	bring; bear; yield (give up)
7. epi	upon; beside; among
8. pro	before; forward

B. Directions: Cover the preceding meanings. Write the meanings of the following combining forms.

Combining Forms	Meanings
1. dia	_____
2. cata	_____
3. log, logo	_____
4. fin	_____
5. biblio	_____
6. fer	_____
7. epi	_____
8. pro	_____

Step II. Words Derived from Combining Forms

1. **logical** (log · i · cal) (loj′ i · kal) *adj.* Relating to the science concerned with correct reasoning. *The arguments that you are giving are not very **logical** because the reasoning is faulty.*

2. **prologue** (prō′ logᴜͤ) *n.* An introduction, often in verse (poetry), spoken or sung before a play or opera; any introductory or preceding event; a preface. *The **prologue** of the play comes at the beginning and sometimes introduces the characters or sets the mood for the play.*

3. **epilogue** (ep′ i · logᴜͤ) *n.* A short section added at the end to a book, poem, and so on; a short speech added to a play and given at the end. *We were very moved by the actor's **epilogue** at the end of the play.*

4. **catalog** (cat · a · log) (kat′ a · log) *n.* A listing of names, titles, and so on, in some order; a book containing such a list. *v.* To make a catalog. *The card **catalog** in the library lists books in alphabetical order according to topics, authors, and titles.*

5. **dialogue** (dī′ a · logᴜͤ) *n.* A conversation in which two or more take part; the conversation in a play. *John and Mary had such a good **dialogue** going that, when the bell rang, they still continued their conversation.*

6. **diagram** (dī′ a · gram) *n.* An outline figure that shows the relationship among parts or places; a graph or chart. *The **diagram** showing the circulatory system of the body helped me to see the relationship between the veins and arteries.*

142

7. **diameter** (dī · am′ e · ter) *n.* A straight line passing through the center of a circle. *The **diameter** of a circle divides the circle in half because it passes through the center of it from one end to the other.*

8. **bibliography** (bib · li · og · ra · phy) (bib · lē · og′ ra · fē) *n.* (*pl.* **phies**) A listing of books on a subject or by an author (the description includes author's name, title, publisher, date of publication, and so on). *The **bibliography** for my paper was large because our teacher wanted us to list at least twenty books on the topic we were writing about.*

9. **final** (fī′ nal) *adj.* Conclusive; last; coming at or relating to the end. *Most instructors give a **final** examination at the end of the semester.*

10. **finite** (fī′ nīt) *adj.* Having a limit or end; able to be measured. *Because there are a **finite** number of places where the missing item can be, we'll find it.*

11. **infinite** (in′ fi · nīt) *adj.* Having no limit or end; not able to be measured. *If the universe is **infinite**, it has no beginning or end.*

12. **fertile** (fer′ tīl) *adj.* Able to produce a large crop; able to produce; capable of bearing offspring, seeds, fruit, and so on; productive in mental achievements; inventive; having abundant resources. *The land was so **fertile** that each year it produced a very large crop*

13. **fertilization** (fer · til · i · za · tion) (fer · til · i · zā′ shun) *n.* The act of making something able to produce; in biology, the union of a male and female germ cell; impregnation. *Human **fertilization** takes place when a sperm cell and egg cell unite.*

14. **reference** (ref · er · ence) (ref′ er · ens) *n.* A referring or being referred; the giving of a problem to a person, a committee, or an authority for settlement; a note in a book that sends the reader for information to another book; the name of another person who can offer information or recommendation; the mark or sign, as a number or letter, directing the reader to a footnote, and so on; a written statement of character, qualification, or ability; testimonial. *My biology and geology instructors said that they would give me good **references** for a job after college.*

15. **preference** (pref · er · ence) (pref′ er · ens) *n.* The choosing of one person or thing over another; the valuing of one over another; a liking better. *Her **preference** for science courses is obvious, for she chooses those over all others.*

16. **transfer** (trans′ fer) *v.* To carry or send from one person or place to another; to cause to pass from one person or place to another. *n.* An act of transferring or being transferred. *When my boss said he would **transfer** me to another department, I was very pleased because I wanted to go to the other place.*

17. **conference** (con · fer · ence) (kon' fer · ens) *n.* A discussion or meeting on some important matter. *Because the dean wanted a **conference** with the students involved in the fight, he asked his secretary to call in the students for a meeting with him.*

18. **suffer** (suf' · fer) *v.* To feel pain or distress. *The woman who lost five sons in World War II must have **suffered** a great deal.*

19. **circumference** (cir · cum · fer · ence) (sir · kum' fer · ens) *n.* The distance around a circle; a boundary line of any rounded area. *When we speak of the **circumference** of the globe, we refer to the distance around the globe.*

Special Notes

1. *Prologue* and *preface* are both introductory statements. However, a *prologue* is usually found at the beginning of a play or poem but usually not in a book such as a novel or textbook. In a book, article, or speech, the introduction found at the beginning is usually called a *preface*. The preface sets forth the plan, purpose, and so on, of the book, article, or speech.

2. **logical.** Relating to correct reasoning. A person who is *logical* is able to present arguments in a carefully thought out manner so that each statement correctly follows the other.

Step III. Practice

A. Directions: A number of sentences with missing words follows. Fill in the word that *best* fits the sentence. Two choices are given for each sentence.

1. _____ in plants also involves the union of egglike and spermlike cells. (Circumference, Fertilization)

2. A _____ is an outline figure that shows the relationship between parts or places. (diameter, diagram)

3. A(n) _____ is found at the end of a book. (prologue, epilogue)

4. In order to engage in a _____ , you need two or more people interested in the topic of discussion. (dialogue, prologue)

5. When a limited number of something exists, it means that the number is _____. (final, finite)

6. The biologists held a number of _____s to discuss important topics. (conference, circumference)

7. The _____ is a listing of books that usually comes at the end of a research paper, a report, or an essay. (bibliography, catalog)

144

8. When someone has a _____ for something, he or she usually chooses that thing over another. (reference, preference)

9. An introduction to a play or poem is called a _____. (dialogue, prologue)

10. The _____ exam will come on the last day of class. (finite, final)

11. Time is considered _____ because it goes on without end. (infinite, final)

12. A(n) _____ lists items in some kind of order. (epilogue, catalog)

13. Both lawyers presented arguments that sounded reasonable and appeared _____. (logical, fertile)

14. The author of the book I am reading made a _____ to another author who has written on the same topic. (reference, preference)

15. When a tomato plant is _____, it can produce a lot. (fertile, finite)

STOP. Check answers at the end of Chapter Five (p. 190).

B. Directions: A number of sentences with missing words follows. Choose the word that *best* fits the sentence. Put the word in the blank. All words are used.

Word List

diagram, infinite, circumference, fertile, transfer, fertilization, suffer, catalog, diameter, finite, epilogue, dialogue, final, logical, preference, prologue, bibliography, reference, conference.

1. At the beginning of some plays there may be a(n)_____.

2. The _____ between the main characters in the play was interesting to listen to.

3. Some authors add a(n) _____ at the end of their books.

4. _____s have always helped me in learning something because I can understand better when I see an outline picture.

5. Our instructor asked us to list at least twenty-five books for our topic and to make sure that we gave the author, name of book, publisher, and date in the proper form for our_____.

6. As a senior, do you have to take _____ s at the end of the semester?

7. Only a(n)_____number of people can attend the jazz concert because there is limited seating.

8. The number system is_____because you can go on counting numbers without end.

9. At the science convention, a group of scientists had_____s to discuss some important matters.

10. The _____ cuts a circle in half.

11. The boundary of a circle is called its_____.

12. I am going to _____ my funds from the State National Bank to the Security Bank because the Security Bank pays more interest.

13. Because your argument is full of holes, it is not very_____.

14. A file clerk has to _____ things in some order.

15. The soil in our garden is so _____ that we can grow practically anything.

16. I asked Professor Jones, from whom I received an *A*, if I could use his name as a(n)_____for a job.

17. Because she has a(n) _____ for certain kinds of clothing, I know exactly what she will choose.

18. He was willing to_____and bear the pain of another operation if it meant that he would walk again.

19. In the process of sexual reproduction, the union of sperm and egg is called _____ .

STOP. Check answers at the end of Chapter Five (p. 190).

C. Directions: The Combining Form and Word Square that follows contains the combining forms from this exercise as well as the words derived from these combining forms. Definitions of the combining forms and words follow. There are *more definitions* than words in the square. Some of the definitions are for words from previous exercises.

1. Fill in the combining form that matches the meaning. Find the combining form in the square.

2. Fill in the blanks of those vocabulary definitions that have words in the square.

3. List the letters of the vocabulary definitions that do not have words in the square.

4. List the words that *best* fit the definitions that do not have words in the square.

COMBINING FORM AND WORD SQUARE

I	P	C	C	O	T	E	F	I	N	A	L	C
A	R	I	A	B	R	P	B	I	B	L	I	O
F	E	R	T	I	L	I	Z	A	T	I	O	N
D	F	C	A	B	A	L	B	I	O	E	C	F
I	E	U	L	L	L	O	G	I	C	A	L	E
A	R	M	O	I	S	G	D	N	F	P	O	R
M	E	F	G	O	U	U	I	F	E	R	R	E
E	N	E	E	G	F	E	A	I	R	O	A	N
T	C	R	E	R	F	O	G	N	T	S	R	C
E	E	E	R	A	E	A	R	I	I	C	C	E
R	M	N	E	P	R	I	A	T	L	I	H	O
O	A	C	I	H	L	A	M	E	E	I	S	T
R	B	E	C	Y	D	I	A	L	O	G	U	E

1. Combining Forms
    a. through_____
    b. down _____
    c. speech; word _____
    d. end _____
    e. book _____
    f. bring; bear, yield _____
    g. upon; beside; among _____
    h. before; forward _____

147

2. Vocabulary Definitions

    a. Endless _____

    b. A listing of books _____

    c. Last _____

    d. Killing of oneself _____

    e. An introduction _____

    f. Not believable _____

    g. Not legal _____

    h. Able to produce _____

    i. Able to be measured; having an end _____

    j. Relating to correct reasoning _____

    k. A listing of names, titles, and so on, in some order _____

    l. A conversation _____

    m. The act of making something able to produce _____

    n. The distance around a circle _____

    o. A straight line passing through the center of a circle _____

    p. A short section added to the end of a book _____

    q. An outline figure that shows the relationship among parts _____

    r. To feel pain or distress _____

    s. A note in a book that sends the reader to another book _____

    t. The choosing of one person or thing over another _____

    u. A discussion or meeting of some important matter _____

    v. To carry from one place to another _____

3. List the letters of the vocabulary definitions that do not have words in the square. _____

4. List the words that *best* fit the definitions that do not have words in the square. _____

_____

STOP. Check answers at the end of Chapter Five (pp. 190–191).

im, in. Into. **in, im, il, ir.** Not. Note than when *in* is placed at the beginning of a word, it can mean either "into" or "not." Note also that the *n* changes to an *m* when *in* is added to a word beginning with an *m*, *b*, or *p*. Example of *in* meaning "into": *inspection*—the act of looking into something. *The inspector gave the restaurant a careful* **inspection** *to see if everything was in order.* Examples of *in* meaning "not": *infinite*—not ending; *ineffectual*—not being able to bring about results. *The lifeguard was* **ineffectual** *in his efforts to save the drowning child.* Examples of *in* meaning "into" changing to *im*: *import*—to carry in; *important*—deserving of notice; of great value. *The materials being* **imported** *were so* **important** *that fifteen extra guards were hired to watch them as they came off the ship.* Examples of *in* meaning "not" changing to *im*: *imperfect*—not perfect; having a fault. Note that *in* meaning "not" also changes to *il* and *ir* when *in* is added to words beginning with *l* or *r*. For example: *illegal*—not legal; *irregular*—not uniform; not the same.

trans. Across; beyond; through; on the other side of; over. When *trans* is placed at the beginning of a word such as the following, it means "across," "beyond," "through," "on the other side of." For example: *transatlantic*—across the Atlantic; on the other side of the Atlantic; *transhuman*—beyond human limits; *transport*—to carry from one place to another; *transparent*—able to be seen through; *transfer*—to move from one place to another.

Additional Words Derived from Combining Forms

From your knowledge of combining forms, can you define the following words?

1. **inference** (in • fer • ence) (in′ fer • ens¢) *n. Although he did not say it exactly, the* **inference** *I got was that he was quitting his job.*

2. **proficient** (pro · fi · cient) (pro · fish′ ent) *adj.* *It was obvious that he was a **proficient** skier because he was able to ski from the highest and steepest mountain paths with ease.*

---

3. **dialect** (di · a · lect) (dī′ a · lekt) *n.* *It's evident that Jane comes from the South because she speaks a Southern **dialect**.*

---

4. **monologue** (mon′ o · logue) *n.* *Jim's **monologue** was so long that after a while nobody was listening to what he was saying.*

---

5. **definitive** (de · fin′ i · tive) *adj.* *The results from the studies are not **definitive** because there are too many different conclusions.*

---

6. **finale** (fi · na′ lē) *n.* *The play's **finale** was completely unexpected on the basis of everything that went before.*

---

7. **affinity** (af · fin · i · ty) (af · fin′ i · tē) *n.* *We knew that our relationship would grow into more than just being acquaintances, because of the **affinity** we had for one another when we first met.*

---

8. **infinitesimal** (in · fin · i · tes′ i · mal) *adj.* *The size of the microorganism was almost **infinitesimal** because it could be seen only with the most high-powered microscope.*

---

9. **deference** (def · er · ence) (def′ er · ense) *n.* *In **deference** to his age and position, the group decided to give him a chance to speak.*

---

10. **defer** (de · fer′) *v.* *I will **defer** to my partner because he has studied the matter very closely.*

STOP. Check answers at the end of Chapter Five (p. 191).

Practice for Additional Words Derived from Combining Forms

Directions: Match each word with the *best* definition.

_____ 1. inference   a. respect

_____ 2. proficient   b. too small to be measured

_____ 3. dialect   c. able to do something very well

_____ 4. monologue   d. a conclusion drawn from statements

_____ 5. infinitesimal   e. to leave to another's opinion

_____ 6. affinity   f. conclusive

_____ 7. definitive   g. long speech by one person

_____ 8. finale   h. close relationship

_____ 9. deference   i. the last part

_____10. defer   j. a variety of speech

STOP. Check answers at the end of Chapter Five (p. 192).

©1960 United Feature Syndicate, Inc.

EXERCISE 11

Step I. Combining Forms

A. Directions: A list of combining forms with their meanings follows. Look at the combining forms and their meanings. Concentrate on learning each combining form and its meaning. Cover the meanings, read the combining forms, and state the meanings to yourself. Check to see if you are correct. Now cover the combining forms, read the meanings, and state the combining forms to yourself. Check to see if you are correct.

Combining Forms	*Meanings*
1. cap, cep	take, receive
2. gnosi, gnosis	knowledge
3. ped, pedo	child

4. tox, toxo	poison
5. gyn, gyno	woman
6. temp, tempo, tempor	time
7. hypo	under
8. derm, dermo	skin
9. ri, ridi, risi	laughter

B. Directions: Cover the preceding meanings. Write the meanings of the following combining forms.

Combining Forms	Meanings
1. cap, cep	_____
2. gnosi, gnosis	_____
3. ped, pedo	_____
4. tox, toxo	_____
5. gyn, gyno	_____
6. temp, tempo, tempor	_____
7. hypo	_____
8. derm, dermo	_____
9. ri, ridi, risi	_____

Step II. Words Derived from Combining Forms

1. **capable** (ca · pa · ble) (kā′ pa · bul) *adj.* Able to be affected; able to understand; having ability; having qualities that are able to be developed. *Although he is capable of many things, time will tell whether he will use all his abilities.*

2. **captive** (cap · tive) (kap′ tive̸) *n.* One who is taken prisoner; one who is dominated. *When the daughter of a wealthy man was held a captive by dangerous criminals, one million dollars was paid to the criminals to release the girl.*

3. **conceive** (con · ceive) (kon · sēi̸ve̸′) *v.* To become pregnant with; to form in the mind; to understand; to think; to believe; to imagine; to develop mentally. *I cannot conceive of him as a scientist because the image I have of him is as a playboy.*

4. **deceive** (de · ceive) (de · sēi̸ve̸′) *v.* To mislead by lying; to lead into error. *I couldn't believe that my best friend told all those lies to deceive me.*

5. **reception** (re · cep · tion) (re · sep′ shun) *n.* The act of receiving or being received; a formal social entertainment; the manner of receiving someone;

the receiving of a radio or television broadcast. *I received a warm reception when I attended Laura's wedding reception, which was the social event of the year.*

6. **exception** (ex · cep · tion) (ek · sep′ shun) *n.* The act of taking out; something or one that is taken out or left out; an objection. *In English spelling rules there always seems to be an exception to which the rule does not apply.*

7. **perception** (per · cep · tion) (per · sep′ shun) *n.* The act of becoming aware of something through the senses of seeing, hearing, feeling, tasting and/or smelling. *If you have something wrong with your senses, your perception will be faulty.*

8. **capsule** (cap · sule) (kap′ sul¢) *n.* A small container made of gelatin (or other material that melts) that holds a dose of medicine; a special removable part of an airplane or rocket. *Each capsule contained the exact amount of medicine the doctor wanted me to take.*

9. **ridiculous** (ri · dic · u · lous) (ri · dik′ yu · l¢us) *adj.* Unworthy of consideration; absurd (senseless); preposterous. *His suggestion was so ridiculous that no one would even consider it.*

10. **ridicule** (rid · i · cule) (rid′ i · kūl¢) *n.* The language or actions that make a person the object of mockery or cause one to be laughed at or scorned. *v.* To mock or view someone in a scornful way; to hold someone up as a laughingstock; to make fun of. *I think it is cruel when someone ridicules another person and holds him or her up as a laughingstock.*

11. **diagnose** (dī · ag · nōs¢′) *v.* To determine what is wrong with someone after an examination. *It is very important for a doctor to be able to diagnose a person's illness correctly so that the doctor will know how to treat it.*

12. **prognosis** (prog · nō′ sis) *n.* (*pl.* **ses**) (sēz) A prediction or conclusion regarding the course of a disease and the chances of recovery; a prediction. *Because the doctor's prognosis regarding John's illness was favorable, we knew that he would recover.*

13. **pediatrician** (pe · di · a · tri · cian) (pē · dē · a · trish′ un) *n.* A doctor who specializes in children's diseases. *I like to take my children to a pediatrician for a checkup rather than to a general doctor because a pediatrician deals only with children's diseases.*

14. **gynecologist** (gyn · e · col · o · gist) (gī · ne · kol′ o · jist) *n.* A doctor dealing with women's diseases, especially in reference to the reproductive organs. *Many women go to a gynecologist for an annual checkup even if they have no symptoms of anything wrong.*

15. **toxic** (tox · ic) (tok′ sik) *adj.* Relating to poison. *Children should not be allowed to lick the walls because some of the paints have toxic materials in them.*

16. **dermatologist** (der · ma · tol · o · gist) (der · ma · tol′ o · jist) *n.* A doctor who deals with skin disorders. *When I broke out in a rash, I went to a dermatologist to find out what was wrong with me.*

17. **hypodermic** (hy · po · der · mic) (hī · po · der′ mik) *adj.* Referring to the area under the skin; used for injecting under the skin. *n.* A hypodermic injection; a hypodermic syringe or needle. *The doctor injected the hypodermic needle so far under my skin that my arm hurt all day.*

18. **hypothesis** (hy · poth · e · sis) (hī · poth′ e · sis) *n.* (*pl.* ses) (sēz). An unproved scientific conclusion drawn from known facts; something assumed as a basis for argument; a possible answer to a problem that requires further investigation. *The hypothesis that was put forth as the solution to the problem seemed logical, but it required further investigation to prove whether it was correct.*

19. **temporary** (tem · po · rar · y) (tem′ po · rar · ē) *adj.* Lasting for a short period of time. *I was not upset when I was dismissed from my job because I had been told, when hired, that it was only a temporary position.*

20. **contemporary** (con · tem · po · rar · y) (kon · tem′ po · rar · ē) *adj.* Belonging to the same age; living or occurring at the same time; current. *n.* (*pl.* ies) One living in the same period as another or others; a person or thing of about the same age or date of origin. *Even though they act like contemporaries, they are a generation apart.*

Special Notes

1. The term *exception,* meaning "something or one that is left out," has a special meaning when it is used in the phrase *to take exception. To take exception* means "to disagree," "to object." For example: *I take exception to what you are saying.*

2. *Hypothesis* is a term that is much used in the area of logic and science. An hypothesis may be defined as an unproved scientific conclusion drawn from known facts and used as a basis for further investigation. In science, an *hypothesis* is thus a possible explanation of observed facts and must be found true or false by more experiments.

3. You met the combining forms *ped, pod* in Exercise 1 of Chapter One. *Ped, pod* means "foot" in such words as *biped, pedestrian, apodal, pseudopodia,* and *podiatrist. Ped, pedo* means "child" in such words as *pediatrician* and *pedagogue.*

4. *Capsule* can also mean "something extremely brief" such as an outline or survey. When *capsule* is used as an adjective, it means "extremely brief or small and very compact." When someone asks for a capsule report of something, he or she wants a very brief report.

Step III. Practice

A. Directions: The words presented in Exercise 11 follow. Match the
word with its meaning.

_____ 1. diagnose

_____ 2. prognosis

_____ 3. pediatrician

_____ 4. gynecologist

_____ 5. toxic

_____ 6. dermatologist

_____ 7. capable

_____ 8. captive

_____ 9. deceive

_____ 10. reception

_____ 11. conceive

_____ 12. perception

_____ 13. exception

_____ 14. ridicule

_____ 15. capsule

_____ 16. ridiculous

_____ 17. hypodermic

_____ 18. hypothesis

_____ 19. temporary

_____ 20. contemporary

a. having ability

b. a small container that holds
a dose of medicine

c. the act of taking out

d. to become pregnant with; to
think

e. a prisoner

f. a formal social entertainment;
act of receiving

g. the act of becoming aware of
something through the senses

h. to mislead by lying

i. referring to the area under
skin

j. an unproved scientific conclusion

k. to mock or view someone in a
scornful way

l. absurd; beyond belief

m. a doctor who specializes in skin
diseases

n. referring to poison

o. a doctor who specializes in
children's diseases

p. a prediction

q. to determine what is wrong with
someone after an examination

r. a doctor who specializes in
women's diseases

s. of the same age; current

t. for a short period of time

STOP. Check answers at the end of Chapter Five (p. 192).

B. Directions: Each sentence has a missing word. Choose the word that *best* completes the sentence. Write the word in the blank.

Word List

diagnose, hypothesis, perception, hypodermic, prognosis, contemporary, conceive, ridiculous, ridicule, dermatologist, capsule, captive, temporary, toxic, capable, exception, reception, pediatrician, deceive, gynecologist.

1. The scientists came up with a(n) _____, which they felt needed further testing to determine if it was the solution to their problem.

2. It is _____ to believe that an eighty-five-year-old man can ride a bicycle across the whole United States, so I will not even consider the idea.

3. As I don't know what these spots on my face and hands are, I'm going to visit a(n) _____ .

4. The space _____ left the rocket at the proper time.

5. Because the patient could not take any medicine by mouth, the doctor told the nurse to give the patient the medicine using a(n) _____ needle.

6. When I am ill, I want a doctor who is able to _____ what is wrong with me.

7. After being _____ s for three years or more, some prisoners of war had a difficult time adjusting to normal life.

8. The help I need is _____ because we are leaving in a short period of time.

9. The doctor's _____ for the patient's recovery was favorable.

10. _____ materials are dangerous and should be clearly marked as poisonous.

11. It's a shame that someone who is as _____ as you are is not doing anything with his ability.

12. I dislike people who _____ others by making fun of them.

13. It is incredible that in _____ times there are still people in the United States who do not have indoor bathrooms and other modern conveniences.

14. A(n) _____ to a rule is something that does not fit in.

15. The wedding _____ of the two wealthiest persons in the world was held in the largest ballroom the reporters ever saw, and it was a spectacular affair.

156

16. Many parents like to take their young children to_____s because they prefer doctors who specialize in children's diseases.

17. Nobody was able to_____of a plan that was agreeable to all because everyone thought of a different one.

18. Some husbands or wives _____ their spouses by telling them lies.

19. Because I prefer a doctor who specializes in women's diseases, I go to a(n)_____.

20. A person who is deaf has no _____ of what it is to hear.

STOP. Check answers at the end of Chapter Five (p. 192).

C. Directions: Twenty sentences containing the meanings of vocabulary presented in Exercise 11 follow. Choose the word that *best* fits the meaning of the word or phrase underlined in the sentence.

Word List

ridiculous, reception, ridicule, hypothesis, capable, contemporaries, toxic, captive, hypodermic, temporary, gynecologist, dermatologist, diagnose, prognosis, capsules, deceive, conceive, exception, pediatrician, perception.

1. As a person having ability, you should do well in college. _____

2. I knew they were happy to see us because of the manner in which they received us when we visited them. _____

3. I become very upset when I learn how some leaders of our country mislead us by lying to us. _____

4. I can't think of you as someone interested in astrology. _____

5. What you have said is so unworthy of consideration that I will not even repeat it to anyone. _____

6. How cruel of those children to make fun of the poor man. _____

7. Would you believe that I have to take ten tiny containers of medicine like this every day? _____

8. Blind persons seem to have a more developed sense of hearing because they seem to be able to hear things that others can't. _____

9. Almost every general rule has an example that does not belong. _____

10. When I received an injection by needle under my skin, I broke out in a cold sweat. _____

11. The geologist has come up with a possible solution to a problem he has been working on, and now he would like to test it to determine if it is correct.
_____

157

12. At the political rally, I met a lot of people of my same age group.

    _____

13. We waited anxiously to hear what the doctor's prediction would be concerning our mother's heart condition. _____

14. After an examination, the doctor was able to tell what was wrong with our mother. _____

15. I feel that it's best to take a child to a doctor who specializes in children's diseases. _____

16. I feel that a doctor who specializes in women's diseases would know more about some female problems than other doctors. _____

17. When I have a skin problem, I go to a doctor who specializes in skin disorders. _____

18. Parents should keep poisonous materials out of the reach of children.

    _____

19. Although this job will be lasting for a short period of time only, I will still try to do my best at it. _____

20. The warden of the jail was held a prisoner by three men who were trying to escape. _____

STOP. Check answers at the end of Chapter Five (p. 192).

EXTRA WORD
POWER

> **e, ex.** Out of; from; lacking. When *ex* or *e* is placed at the beginning of a word, it means "out of" or "from." When *ex* is placed at the beginning of a word and a hyphen (-) is attached to the word, *ex* means "former" or "sometime." For example: *ex-president*—former president; *ex-wife*—former wife. Examples of *ex* meaning "out of" or "from": *exclude*—to keep from; *exit*—to go out of; *expect*—to look out for; *excuse*—to forgive; to apologize for; *exhale*—to breathe out.
>
> **de.** Away; from; off; completely. *De* is found at the beginning of many words. For example: *deport*—to send someone away. *An alien who was involved in many holdups was* **deported** *to his own country.* Other words with *de*: *deflea*—to take off fleas; *delouse*—to free from lice; *decolor*—to take color away; *decode*—to change from code to plain language; *dextoxify*—to take away poison; to destroy

the poison; *decapitate*—to take off the head; to kill; *deprive*—to take something away from; *denude*— to strip the covering from completely. Can you supply more words with *ex, e,* or *de*?

Additional Words Derived from Combining Forms

From your knowledge of combining forms, can you define the following words?

1. **misogynist** (mi · sog · y · nist) (mi · soj′ i · nist) *n. Although Tom is a misogamist, he isn't a **misogynist** because he likes women.*

   _____

2. **agnostic** (ag · nos · tic) (ag · nos′ tik) *adj. n. Pat must be an **agnostic** because she believes that there is no way for anyone to know for sure about the existence of God.*

   _____

3. **epidermis** (ep · i · der′ mis) *n. The **epidermis** is the layer of skin that is the most exposed.*

   _____

4. **pedagogue** (ped′ a · gogue) *n. A **pedagogue** is a person who teaches students.*

   _____

5. **antitoxin** (an · ti · tox · in) (an · ti · tok′ sin) *n. The doctor injected my brother with an **antitoxin** in order to prevent his getting a certain disease.*

   _____

6. **toxicologist** (tox · i · col · o · gist) (tok · si · kol′ o · jist) *n. A **toxicologist** was called in to help in the homicide investigation because all symptoms pointed to a possible death by poisoning.*

   _____

7. **derisive** (de · rī′ sive) *adj. The **derisive** laughter of the class toward all student comments kept me from saying anything because I did not want to be ridiculed.*

   _____

8. **intercept** (in · ter · cept) (in · ter · sept′) *v. When the ball was **intercepted** before a goal could be made, the home team audience screamed with delight.*

   _____

9. **susceptible** (sus · cep · ti · ble) (sus · sep′ ti · bul) *adj. When he heard that he was **susceptible** to tuberculosis, he asked the doctor to help him to prevent the onset of the disease.*

10. **perceptive** (per · cep · tive) (per · sep′ tiv) *adj. Being a **perceptive** individual, she knew that this was not the right time to ask her father for use of the car.*

11. **tempo** (tem′pō) *n. (pl. **tempi**) The **tempo** of modern living is very fast.*

12. **extemporaneous** (ex · tem · po · ra · ne · ous) (ek · stem · po · rā′ nē · ous) *adj. When she was called upon to express her views, her **extemporaneous** talk was so logical and well expressed that she couldn't have done better if she had spent hours preparing it.*

STOP. Check answers at the end of Chapter Five (pp. 192–193).

Practice for Additional Words Derived from Combining Forms

Directions: Match each word with the *best* definition.

_____ 1. misogynist	a. outermost layer of skin
_____ 2. agnostic	b. rate of speed
_____ 3. pedagogue	c. being aware
_____ 4. antitoxin	d. hater of women
_____ 5. epidermis	e. mocking; jeering
_____ 6. toxicologist	f. something used against poison
_____ 7. derisive	g. done or spoken without preparation
_____ 8. intercept	
_____ 9. susceptible	h. professing uncertainty about ultimates
_____ 10. perceptive	i. specialist in poisons
_____ 11. extemporaneous	j. a teacher
_____ 12. tempo	k. especially liable to
	l. to stop or interrupt the course of

STOP. Check answers at the end of Chapter Five (p. 193).

EXERCISE 12

Step I. Combining Forms

A. Directions: A list of combining forms with their meanings follows. Look at the combining forms and their meanings. Concentrate on learning each combining form and its meaning. Cover the meanings, read the combining forms, and state the meanings to yourself. Check to see if you are correct. Now cover the combining forms, read the meanings, and state the combining forms to yourself. Check to see if you are correct.

Combining Forms	Meanings
1. tain, ten, tent	hold
2. cede, ceed	go; give in; yield (give in)
3. sequi	follow
4. cycl, cyclo	circle; wheel
5. chron, chrono	time
6. archae, archaeo	ancient
7. crypt, crypto	secret; hidden
8. duc	lead
9. brevi	short; brief

B. Directions: Cover the preceding meanings. Write the meanings of the following combining forms.

Combining Forms	Meanings
1. tain, ten, tent	_____
2. cede, ceed	_____
3. sequi	_____
4. cycl, cyclo	_____
5. chron, chrono	_____
6. archae, archaeo	_____
7. crypt, crypto	_____
8. duc	_____
9. brevi	_____

1. **tenant** (ten′ ant) *n.* A person who holds property; one who lives in property belonging to another; one who rents or leases from a landlord; one who lives in a place. *The **tenants** told the landlord, who owned the building, that they would not pay the rent unless the landlord made the needed repairs to their apartments.*

2. **content** (con · tent) (kon′ tent) *n.* What something holds (usually plural in this sense); subject matter; the material that something is made up of; the main substance or meaning. *The course **content** was supposed to deal with the earth's crust or makeup, but the instructor had not yet covered any subject matter related to geology.*

3. **content** (con · tent) (kon · tent′) *adj.* Satisfied; not complaining; not desiring something else. *It is obvious that Sally is **content** with her life because she never complains and always seems free from worry.*

4. **maintain** (main · tain′) *v.* To carry on or continue; to keep up; to keep in good condition. *When Mr. Jones lost his job, he found that he could not **maintain** his house because the needed repairs were too costly.*

5. **sequence** (se · quence) (sē′ kwens) *n.* The following of one thing after another; order; a continuous or related series, with one thing following another. *The detectives investigating the suicide were trying to get the **sequence** of events, step-by-step and in order, to try to figure out why the man took his life.*

6. **consequence** (con · se · quence) (kon′ se · kwens) *n.* That which follows from any act; a result; an effect. *I had no idea what the **consequence** of my leaving home would be until I found out that my mother became ill as a result of it.*

7. **subsequent** (sub · se · quent) (sub′ se · kwent) *adj.* Following soon after; following in time, place, or order; resulting. *The **subsequent** chapter, which follows this one, is the last chapter in Part I of this book.*

8. **cycle** (cy · cle) (sī′ kul) *n.* A period that keeps coming back, in which certain events take place and complete themselves in some definite order; a round of years or ages; a pattern of regularly occurring events; a series that repeats itself. *We seem to be going through an economic **cycle** that is similar to one we had a decade ago.*

9. **cyclone** (cy · clone) (sī′ klōn) *n.* A system of violent and destructive whirlwinds. *When the **cyclone** hit the small town, its winds were so strong that it destroyed everything in its path.*

10. **archaeology** (ar · chae · ol · o · gy) (ar · kē · ol′ o · jē) *n.* The study of the life and culture of ancient people, as by the digging up of old settlements, ruins from the past, and old man-made or other objects. *I knew*

*that I'd enjoy studying **archaeology** because I have always loved to dig in old places and hunt for things from the past so that I could learn more about ancient times.*

11. **archaic** (ar · cha · ic) (ar · kā′ ik) *adj.* Belonging to an earlier period; ancient; old-fashioned; no longer used. *It is surprising to find someone in our times who believes in such an **archaic** practice as bloodletting for curing disease.*

12. **chronological** (chron · o · log · i · cal) (kron · o · loj′ i · kal) *adj.* Arranged in time order (earlier things or events precede later ones). *In order to arrange our outline on wars in the United States in **chronological** order, we needed to know the dates of the wars.*

13. **chronic** (chron′ ic) (kron′ ik) *adj.* Continuing for a long time; prolonged; recurring. *Because he had a **chronic** cough, it lasted for a long period of time and always came back.*

14. **concede** (con · cede) (kon · sēdȼ′) *v.* To give in; surrender; yield; grant; admit. *After a long discussion and debate on an issue, the union said it would **concede** on this particular issue because the employers had given in on other issues.*

15. **precede** (pre · cede) (prē · sēdȼ′) *v.* To go or come before. *In the circus parade the clowns were to **precede** the others because, by entering first, they would put the spectators in a good mood for the rest of the show.*

16. **proceed** (pro · ceed) (prō · sēȼd′) *v.* To go on; to go forward; to carry on an action. *We will **proceed** the way we have been going unless someone knows some reason why we should not continue.*

17. **succeed** (suc · ceed) (suk · sēȼd′) *v.* To accomplish what is attempted; to come next in order; to come next after or replace another in an office or position. *The people who **succeed** seem to be those who do not stop until they have accomplished what they set out to do.*

18. **abbreviation** (ab · bre · vi · a · tion) (aḃ · brē · vē · ā′ shun) *n.* A short-ened form of a word or phrase. *It is usual to give an **abbreviation** of the spelling of the states rather than write them out completely because it's much faster and easier.*

19. **conductor** (con · duc · tor) (kon · duk′ tor) *n.* One who guides or leads; a guide or director; one who has charge of a railroad train; the director of an orchestra or chorus; any substance that conducts electricity, heat, and so on. *You could tell from the applause that the **conductor** of the orchestra was greatly admired by the large audience that had come to see him lead the orchestra.*

20. **deduction** (de · duc · tion) (de · duk′ shun) *n.* The act of drawing a con-clusion by reasoning or reasoning that goes from the general to the particular; the subtraction of something; an inference or conclusion. *How much money are you able to get back by having so many **deductions** on your income tax?*

21. **cryptic** (cryp · tic) krip′ tik) *adj.* Having a hidden or secret meaning; mysterious. *The **cryptic** message was very difficult to decode because no one was familiar with the meanings of the letters used in the code.*

22. **crypt** (kript) *n.* An underground vault. *The **crypt** was buried fifty feet underground in a special cave.*

Special Notes

1. Note that the terms *content* (con′ tent) *n.* and *content* (con · tent′) *adj.* are spelled identically but are *pronounced differently* and have *different meanings.* Many of the words you have met have had more than one meaning. However, they were *pronounced identically.* Because *content* (con′ tent) *n.* and *content* (con tent′) *adj.* are pronounced differently and each word has meanings different from those of the other, they are presented separately.
    a. **content** (con′ tent) *n.* What something holds (usually plural in this sense). *The **contents** of the box contained all her childhood toys.*
    b. **content** (con′ tent) *n.* Subject matter. *The course **content** was so boring that I decided not to take any other courses in that subject.*
    c. **content** (con′ tent) *n.* The material that something is made up of. *When I checked the **content** of the ice cream I was eating, I found that it was made up almost completely of artificial products.*
    d. **content** (con · tent′) *adj.* Satisfied; not complaining; not desiring something else. *I am **content** with my job, so there is no need for me to look for another.*

2. You met the term *bicycle,* meaning "two-wheeler," in Exercise 1. You can now see that *cycle* in *bicycle* comes from the combining form *cyclo* meaning *wheel.*

3. The term **deduction** has a few meanings.
    a. **deduction.** A subtraction; something taken away. A *deduction* refers to your being able to subtract or take away a certain amount from something else. This meaning of *deduction* is much used in relation to the income tax. You can subtract or take away a certain amount of money from your income taxes on the basis of the number of *deductions* you have.
    b. **deduction.** Reasoning from the general to the particular or reasoning from given statements to conclusions. This meaning of *deduction* is used in *logic,* which is the *science of correct reasoning.* You met the term *logical,* which deals with correct reasoning, in Exercise 10. An example of deduction—going from the general to the specific—follows:

    All men are good.
    Arthur is a man.
    Therefore, Arthur is good.

    In the preceding example, we can decide, on the basis of a general statement that all men are good, that a particular man, Arthur, must be good.

c. **deduction**. An inference; a conclusion. It is important for readers to be able to make *deductions* in reading because many times writers do not directly state what they mean but present ideas in a more "roundabout" way, or *indirectly.*

In Exercise 10 you met the word *inference* in the section entitled Additional Words Derived from Combining Forms. *Deduction* and *inference* have the same meaning. Remember that an *inference* is drawn from information that is not directly stated. The same is true of *deduction.* When all the information is given in statements but the information is given indirectly, you must make *deductions* or *inferences.* In order to get the information, you must "read between the lines." Mystery writers often use *inference* to make their stories more interesting and enjoyable. Following is an example of inference. Can you draw the proper inferences or make the correct deductions from the information given?

Read the following short selection, and answer the two questions.

The six remaining boys were worn out from walking all day with such heavy knapsacks. They headed toward the mountain range, hoping to reach it before the sun finally set behind it. One third of their original number had turned back earlier.

(1) In what direction were the six boys headed?

(2) How many boys had there been at the beginning of the trip?

In order to answer the first question, you must collect the following clues:

(1) Boys walking toward mountain range.

(2) Sun sets behind the mountain range.

From this information you should conclude that the answer to the first question is "west" because the sun sets in the west and the boys were heading toward the setting sun.

To answer the second question, you must collect the following clues:

(1) Six boys remaining.

(2) One third had turned back.

From this information you should conclude that the answer to the second question is "nine" because two thirds of the boys equals six, one third must be three, and six plus three equals nine.

PEANUTS ®   **By Schulz**

A. Directions: Each sentence has a missing word. Choose the word that *best*
    completes the sentence. Write the word in the blank. Note
    that one word is used in two sentences, once as a noun and
    once as an adjective.

Word List

*concede, maintain, cycle, abbreviation, subsequent, precede, proceed, chronic,
cyclone, conductor, archaic, cryptic, content, sequence, crypt, succeed, chronological, deduction, archaeology, tenant, consequence.*

1. As that is a(n)_____word, it is not used anymore.

2. Whenever I have an argument with anyone, it always seems that I'm the
    one to _____ , because the other person just won't give
    in.

3. The _____ writing that they found on the box has still
    not been decoded because no one can figure out the code.

4. I've heard that some banks store their gold in a(n) _____
    that is buried so far in the ground that it is almost impossible for robbers
    to get to it.

5. A(n) _____ is a person who usually pays rent to occupy
    property.

6. I am perfectly _____ with the place where I live, so there
    is no reason for me to complain about it.

7. Because our landlord will not_____the property and keep
    it in good condition, we are withholding our rent.

8. The_____of events was easy to follow because there was a
    definite order to the events.

9. After the fire it was difficult to tell what the_____s of the
    house had been because everything in the house was so badly burned.

10. The doctor told my friend that unless he followed the doctor's orders, the
    _____s would be bad, and he might have to go to the
    hospital.

11. How many_____s will you be able to subtract from your
    income tax this year?

12. Because _____ deals with ancient cultures, we are going to
    visit an ancient cave and dig for things from the past for our _____
    class.

13. The dates were listed in _____ order, starting with ancient times and continuing to contemporary times.

14. I can tell that I'm starting my losing _____ all over again because the events that happened before seem to be repeating themselves.

15. The problem with a(n) _____ illness is that even though it may go away, it always comes back.

16. When the _____ hit our area, we were lucky that our house was not in the path of the violent winds because it would have been completely destroyed.

17. I attempt to do only things that I feel I can accomplish because I like to _____ in what I do.

18. You usually use a(n) _____ for name titles rather than write out the whole word.

19. _____ with your work because you seem to be doing it correctly.

20. I was surprised that you did not _____ him in the lineup of players because you always go up to bat before he does.

21. The audience was quiet when the _____ came on stage to begin directing the orchestra.

22. The _____ chapters should be easier for you because they come after the more difficult material.

STOP. Check answers at the end of Chapter Five (p. 193).

B. Directions: A short story with missing words follows. Fill in the blanks with the words that *best* fit. Words are used only once. Note that *content* is given twice because it us used in two different ways.

Word List

cyclone, homicide, corpse, morgue, television, consequence, description, sequence, local, cryptic, conductor, deduction, hypothesis, illegal, tenant, maintain, chronic, succeed, concede, content, content, abbreviation, subsequent, cycle, proceed.

I am a(n) 1 _____ in a large apartment building. I have been 2 _____ living there and really had nothing much to complain about until last month. A(n) 3 _____ of events took place that has made it very difficult for me to 4 _____ my former way of living. What I am saying is that as a(n) 5 _____ of one particular night my whole life has changed.

I remember the night very well for three reasons. First, we had such a violent 6_____ during the day that some of my windows had been broken. Second, the night was very dark because the moon was completing its monthly 7_____ just before the new moon. Third, a(n) 8_____ took place right outside my broken window.

I should tell you that I live on the ground floor in a rather quiet neighborhood. My building is across the street from a large park, and during the summers we have many famous 9_____ s leading orchestras in outdoor concerts. I live on the ground floor because I have a(n) 10_____ back problem, and I never know when it will give me trouble.

Let me 11_____ with my story of the murder. At about 10 P.M. I thought I heard some sounds from outside, but I had the 12_____ on, so I wasn't sure. The third time I thought I heard something, I went to my broken window to look outside. It was so dark that I saw nothing. However, on my floor I found a paper attached to a broken piece of glass. Although I tried to read it, I did not 13_____ in figuring out the 14_____s of the paper. The paper contained a(n) 15_____ message, which I could not decode. The only thing I could make out was *Dr.*, a(n) 16_____ of the word *doctor.*

I immediately phoned the police. While waiting for the police, I again tried to decode the message. I finally had to 17_____ to myself that I could not figure it out. The police arrived. I told them my story. They went out to investigate. It was then that they found the 18_____ . I was asked to look at the body. Frightened and trembling, I did. However, I had never seen the person before. The dead body was then taken to the 19_____ because there was no identification on it. 20_____ to that, the police came to question me. They wanted to know if I had any 21_____ that might be a possible explanation for the murder. I stated that I had none and that I knew nothing.

I told them that the only 22_____ I could make or conclude was that the person couldn't have died right away because he had time to pick up a piece of broken glass, attach some paper to it, and throw it through my already broken window.

The police were able to decode the message. The message gave such a good 23_____ of the murderer that the police were able to have a picture drawn of him. It turned out to be a(n) 24_____doctor from the neighborhood who was involved with the 25_____ sale of drugs.

STOP. Check answers at the end of Chapter Five (p. 193).

C. Directions: In the Word Square there are fifteen words from Exercise 12. Find the words in the square, and match them with their correct meanings. Note that there are *more* meanings than words.

If there is no word in the square for a meaning, write *none* and give the word.

Word Square

D	E	D	U	C	T	I	O	N	E	S	A
C	O	N	S	E	Q	U	E	N	C	E	B
R	A	C	U	M	A	I	N	T	H	E	B
Y	R	Y	B	C	Y	C	L	E	R	M	R
P	C	C	S	O	P	C	E	N	O	A	E
T	H	L	E	N	U	O	C	A	N	I	V
I	O	O	Q	T	C	N	O	N	I	N	I
C	O	N	U	E	O	T	N	T	C	T	A
H	L	E	E	N	N	E	T	E	A	A	T
R	O	I	N	T	A	N	E	O	N	I	I
O	G	N	T	C	O	T	C	E	D	N	O
N	Y	A	R	C	H	A	I	C	A	O	N

Meanings	*Words*
1. Satisfied; not complaining	_____
2. To continue; to keep up; to keep in good condition	_____
3. A continuous series	_____
4. A result; an effect	_____
5. A person who rents or leases from a landlord	_____
6. Following soon after	_____
7. The study of the life and culture of ancient people	_____
8. Referring to what is ancient	_____
9. A round of years or ages	_____
10. A violent, destructive whirlwind	_____
11. Arranged in time order	_____
12. To go forward	_____

169

13. To give in _____

14. To go or come before _____

15. Continuing for a long time and
    coming back _____

16. To accomplish what is attempted;
    to come after _____

17. A shortened form of a word or
    phrase _____

18. One who guides or leads _____

19. The act of drawing a conclusion
    by reasoning; an inference _____

20. Having a hidden meaning _____

21. An underground vault _____

22. Subject matter _____

STOP. Check answers at the end of Chapter Five (p. 193).

EXTRA WORD
POWER

> **dis.** Away from; apart; not. When *dis* is placed in front of a word, it may give it the opposite meaning. It may result in undoing something that was done. It may take away some quality, power, rank, and so on. For example: *disrobe*—take off clothes; *disband*—break up the group; *disable*—make an object or someone not able to do something; *disloyal*—not loyal; *disapprove*—to not approve of; to regard as not worthy; *dishonest*—not honest; not to be trusted. How many more words with *dis* can you supply?
>
> **sub.** Under; beneath; below; lower in rank. *Sub* is added to the beginning of many words. For example: *submarine*—undersea ship; *subfloor*—floor beneath; *subtraction*—the act of taking something away; *subset*—something that is under the larger set; *subcommittee*—a committee under the original committee. Check your dictionary to find many more words beginning with *sub*.

Additional Words Derived from Combining Forms

From your knowledge of combining forms, can you define the following words?

1. **chronometer** (chro • nom • e • ter) (kro • nom' e • ter) *n. As the car's* **chronometer** *was always correct, I usually went by that time.*

2. **anachronism** (a • nach • ro • nism) (a • nak' ro • niz • um) *n. An example of an* **anachronism** *in a film would be to have an automobile present in a set representing the Middle Ages.*

3. **synchronize** (syn • chro • nize) (sin' kro • nīz¢) *v. We* **synchronized** *our watches to make sure that we all had the same time.*

4. **concession** (con • ces • sion) (kon • sesh' un) *n. In order to settle the strike, both sides had to make a number of* **concessions.**

5. **procession** (pro • ces • sion) (pro • sesh' un) *n. The* **procession** *continued to move forward in an orderly manner even though it was raining very hard.*

6. **recession** (re • ces • sion) (re • sesh' un) *n. During a* **recession,** *when unemployment is high, economists try to figure out ways to stimulate the economy.*

7. **secede** (se • cede) (se • sēd¢') *v. During the Civil War, the South* **seceded** *from the Union.*

8. **subscription** (sub • scrip • tion) (sub • skrip' shun) *n. Each year when I take out a* **subscription** *for my favorite magazine, I sign a form promising to pay a certain amount of money for the delivery of the magazine.*

9. **untenable** (un • ten • a • ble) (un • ten' a • bul) *adj. Her position on the issue was such an* **untenable** *one that we all agreed not to support her.*

10. **detain** (de • tāín') *v. The man at the airport was* **detained** *by the police because they thought that he was a criminal attempting to flee the country.*

11. **retentive** (re • ten' tiv¢) *adj. Arthur has such a* **retentive** *memory that he can recall details from things he studied or read over twenty years ago.*

12. **tenacious** (te · na · cious) (te · nā′ shus) *adj. He had such **tenacious** feelings on that issue that no one could change his mind.*

STOP. Check answers at the end of Chapter Five (pp. 194–195).

©1966 United Feature Syndicate, Inc.

Practice for Additional Words Derived from Combining Forms

Directions: Match each word with the *best* definition.

_____ 1. chronometer

_____ 2. concession

_____ 3. anachronism

_____ 4. recession

_____ 5. synchronize

_____ 6. untenable

_____ 7. tenacious

_____ 8. retentive

_____ 9. secede

a. having the ability to keep things in

b. to withdraw from

c. an instrument used to measure time

d. the act of going back

e. a parade

f. an act of giving in

g. something out of time order

h. to cause to agree in rate or speed

172

_____ 10. subscription

_____ 11. procession

_____ 12. detain

i. an agreement to pay some money for something

j. to stop; to delay

k. stubborn

l. not able to be held or defended

STOP. Check answers at the end of Chapter Five (p. 195).

CROSSWORD PUZZLE 4

Directions: The meanings of many of the combining forms from Exercises 10–12 follow. Your knowledge of these combining forms will help you to solve this crossword puzzle. Note that *combining form* is abbreviated as *comb. f.*

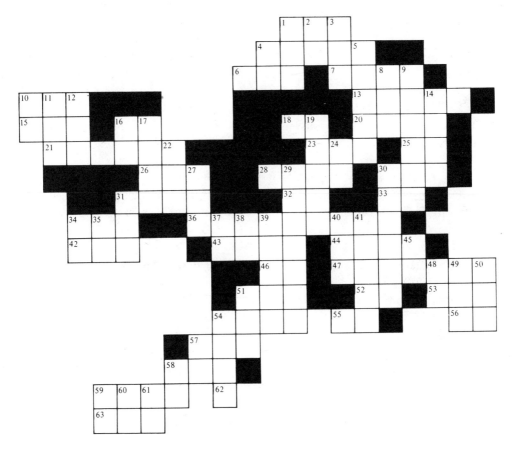

Across

1. Meaning of comb. f. *deca*

Down

1. You pay this on money you earn

4. Salesmen like to make lots of ___
6. Comb. f. for *poison*
7. Comb. f. for *skin*
10. Comb. f. for *other*
13. Sound a duck makes
15. Homonym of *two*
16. Comb. f. for *one who*
18. Rhymes with *ham*
20. Until, to
21. Comb. f. for *knowledge*
23. Comb. f. for *upon*
25. Homonym of *two*
26. Comb. f. for *lead*
28. Comb. f. for *down*
30. Comb. f. for *take*
31. Belonging to me
32. Comb. f. for *back*
33. Abbreviation for *railroad*
34. Comb. f. for *before*
36. Rule by the people
42. Intention
43. Geometry is a ___ course
44. Comb. f. for *under*
46. Exclamation of surprise, suspicion, or triumph
47. Antonym of *actor*
51. Used to express surprise, enthusiasm
52. Means *look*; ___ and behold
53. Comb. f. for *through*
54. A courageous man admired for his brave deeds
55. Sound made when laughing
56. Abbreviation for *New York*
57. Something small is a little ___
58. Comb. f. for *woman*
59. Comb. f. for *time*
62. Fourth letter of the alphabet
63. Meaning of *uni*

2. Abbreviation for *elevated train*
3. Boy's name
4. Homonym of *sew*
5. Comb. f. for *follow*
8. You ___ faster than you walk
9. What a thing is made of
10. A preposition meaning "on" or "near"
11. Comb. f. for *speech; word*
12. Comb. f. for state of, act of, or result of
14. Home for chickens
16. Rhymes with *has*
17. Comb. f. for *laughter*
18. Comb. f. for *without*
19. Comb. f. for *measure*
22. On a nice day it shines
24. Way of saying *father*
27. Comb. f. for *go*
29. Comb. f. for *ancient*
30. Comb. f. for *secret*
31. Way of saying *mother*
34. Same as #24 Down
35. Comb. f. for *laughter*
37. Comb. f. for *in*
38. Way of saying *mother*
39. Meaning of *ali*
40. Sound made when surprised
41. Comb. f. for *circle; wheel*
45. Comb. f. for *one who*
48. Ending for the past tense of regular verbs
49. When you do a wrong, you commit a ___
50. Meaning of *dict*
51. Rhymes with *let*
54. Refers to the rear
57. You say this when you leave
58. Abbreviation for a doctor who has a general practice
59. Same as #25 Across
60. Comb. f. for *in*
61. A pronoun

STOP. Check answers at the end of Chapter Five (p. 195).

WORD SCRAMBLE 4

Directions: Word Scramble 4 is based on words from Exercises 10–12. The meanings are your clues to arranging the letters in correct order. Write the correct word in the blank.

Meanings

1. aenttn   _____ a person who occupies property

2. nctonte   _____ subject matter

3. cuneqsee   _____ the following of one thing after another

4. busqseetnu   _____ following soon after

5. rhicaac   _____ belonging to an earlier period

6. iloglohcnroac   _____ arranged in time order

7. eenocdc   _____ to give in

8. cereped   _____ to go before

9. yccrtip   _____ mysterious

10. onedidtuc   _____ the act of drawing a conclusion

11. noceylc   _____ system of violent and destructive whirlwinds

12. notcroucd   _____ one who leads or guides

13. geuorplo   _____ an introduction to a play

14. gloclia   _____ relating to correct reasoning

15. eeiuoglp   _____ something added to the end of a book

16. metadire   _____ a straight line passing through the center of a circle

17. ffuesr   _____ to feel pain

18. enofrencec   _____ a discussion or meeting on some important matter

19. libbyoipragh   _____ a listing of books

20. eiifnt   _____ having a limit or end

21. literef   _____ able to produce a large crop

22. laeapcb   _____ having ability

23. pitacve   _____ a prisoner

24. onticpere   _____ the manner of receiving someone

25. cceeiovn   _____ to think; to believe

26. ceideve   _____ to mislead by lying

27. urdiclei   _____ to make fun of

28. cionxpete   _____ something or one that is left out

29. rontippece   _____ the act of being aware of something through the senses

30. nosegdai   _____ to determine what is wrong with

31. orgpsonsi   _____ a prediction or conclusion regarding the course of a disease

32. armedlottsigo   _____ a skin doctor

33. dipetraiinac   _____ a children's doctor

34. oxict   _____ referring to poison

35. ropetmrya   _____ lasting for a short period of time

36. redopyhcim   _____ under the skin

STOP. Check answers at the end of Chapter Five (pp. 195–196).

ANALOGIES 4

Directions: Find the word from the following list that *best* completes each analogy. There are more words in the list than you need.

Word List

infinitesimal, infinite, dialogue, dialect, finite, diagram, diameter, chronometer, reference, captor, bibliography, biography, pediatrician, epilogue, inference, deride, prognosis, diagnosis, catalog, tenacious, deceive, transparent, toxicologist, preface, procession, agnostic, adult, decimate, pedagogue, content, fertile, mouth, visage, cyclone, contemporary, ancient, archaic, consequence.

1. Clock : chronometer :: stubborn :_____.

2. Beginning : end :: prologue :_____.

3. Enthusiasm : apathy :: immeasurable : _____ .

4. Deference : respect :: ridicule : _____.

5. Skin : dermatologist :: poison :_____.

6. Limp : wilted :: parade :_____.

7. Extemporaneous : prepared :: dissatisfied :_____ .

8. Woman : gynecologist :: child :_____.

9. Lawyer : counselor :: teacher :_____.

10. Potentate : monarch :: current :_____.

11. Deportment : behavior :: effect :_____ .

12. Snow : blizzard :: wind :_____.

13. Wrist : arm :: nose :_____ .

14. Archaic : ancient :: bluff :_____.

15. Salary : employee :: ransom :_____ .

16. Alarm : warn :: dynamite :_____.

17. Sheer : opaque :: sterile :_____.

18. God : atheist :: knowing :_____.

19. Shawl : scarf :: deduction :_____.

20. Gait : trot :: speech :_____.

STOP. Check answers at the end of Chapter Five (p. 196).

MULTIPLE-CHOICE VOCABULARY TEST 4

Directions: This is a test on words in Exercises 10–12. Words are presented according to exercises. *Do all exercises before checking answers.* Underline the meaning that *best* fits the word.

Exercise 10

1. prologue
   a. added to the end of a book
   b. introduction to a play
   c. correct reasoning
   d. conversation

2. logical
   a. relating to correct reasoning
   b. relating to an introduction
   c. a listing of names
   d. added to the end of a book

177

3. catalog
   a. added to the end of a book
   b. an introduction
   c. conversation
   d. a listing of names, titles, and so on, in some order

4. epilogue
   a. conversation
   b. a listing of books
   c. addition to the end of a book
   d. an introduction

5. dialogue
   a. introduction
   b. conversation
   c. at the end of a book
   d. refers to reasoning

6. diagram
   a. divides circle in half
   b. conversation
   c. outline figure showing relationships
   d. introduction

7. diameter
   a. line dividing a circle in half
   b. an outline showing relationships in a circle
   c. an outline
   d. a map

8. bibliography
   a. a listing of books on a subject
   b. a note in a book
   c. refers to books
   d. the study of spelling

9. final
   a. able to produce
   b. limited number
   c. last
   d. refers only to tests

10. finite
    a. the end of a play
    b. at the end of a book
    c. added to a book
    d. having a limit or an end

11. infinite
    a. ends in time
    b. endless
    c. ends
    d. certain number

12. fertile
    a. a producer
    b. able to produce a large crop
    c. refers to soil
    d. refers to children

13. fertilization
    a. a producer
    b. what one puts on soil
    c. union of sperm and egg
    d. refers to children

14. reference
    a. a person who sends things
    b. a chapter in a book
    c. a recommendation from a person
    d. a letter

15. preference
    a. a note in a book
    b. a note in a book sending you for information
    c. a recommendation
    d. someone or something you choose over another

16. transfer
   a. to carry or send from one place to another
   b. a sender
   c. a carrier
   d. to cross

17. conference
   a. a convention
   b. a friendly get-together
   c. a discussion or meeting on some important matters
   d. refers to science meetings

18. suffer
   a. to be able to take pain
   b. to put up with pain
   c. to feel pain
   d. refers to pain

19. circumference
   a. the distance across a circle
   b refers to measurement
   c. the distance around a circle
   d. refers to a globe

Exercise 11

20. capable
   a. something for the head
   b. able to wear hats
   c. refers to power
   d. having ability

21. captive
   a. a prisoner
   b. a hunter
   c. a kidnapper
   d. a searcher

22. conceive
   a. to learn
   b. to conceal
   c. to teach
   d. to think

23. deceive
   a. to believe
   b. to lead
   c. to mislead by lying
   d. to tell

24. reception
   a. to receive something
   b. the manner of receiving someone
   c. the manner of thinking
   d. the act of taking

25. exception
   a. something or one that is left out
   b. being included
   c. being invited
   d. refers to leaving

26. perception
   a. a sense
   b. senses of seeing and hearing
   c. act of knowing something
   d. act of becoming aware of something through the senses

27. capsule
   a. a spaceship
   b. a rocket
   c. an instrument
   d. a removable part of a rocket or an airplane

28. ridiculous   a. funny   c. something not nice
                  b. unworthy of consid-   d. something not helpful
                      eration

29. ridicule   a. to laugh   c. to make someone the
                  b. to joke   object of mockery
                                         d. to be cruel

30. diagnose   a. to make a predic-   c. to give an examination
                     diction   d. to determine what is
                  b. to make a prediction   wrong with someone
                     concerning someone's   after an examination
                     illness

31. prognosis   a. refers to recovery   c. refers to knowing
                  b. refers to illness   what is wrong
                                         d. a prediction concern-
                                         ing an illness

32. pediatrician   a. a woman who is   c. a doctor who special-
                     a doctor   izes in foot diseases
                  b. a doctor   d. a children's doctor

33. gynecologist   a. a woman who is   c. a doctor who is a
                     a doctor   specialist
                  b. a doctor   d. a doctor who special-
                                         izes in women's diseases

34. toxic   a. deadly   c. unsafe
                  b. poisonous   d. unclear

35. dermatologist   a. a skin disease   c. a skin doctor
                  b. a doctor   d. refers to skin

36. hypodermic   a. a needle   c. area above the skin
                  b. referring to the area   d. skin
                     under the skin

37. hypothesis   a. any guess   c. an unproved conclusion
                  b. any idea   d. an unproved conclusion
                                         drawn from known facts

38. temporary   a. referring to time   c. referring to a short time
                  b. referring to a   period
                     waiting period   d. referring to a time period

39. contemporary   a. referring to what is   c. referring to a short
                     ancient   period of time
                  b. referring to a time   d. referring to what is
                     period   modern

Exercise 12

40. tenant
    a. one who takes care of apartments for a salary
    b. one who lives on property belonging to another
    c. one who takes care of buildings for a salary
    d. one who holds things

41. content
    a. subject matter
    b. refers to courses
    c. refers to teaching
    d. refers to learning

42. maintain
    a. to keep up in good repair
    b. to help someone
    c. to carry
    d. to hold

43. content
    a. worried
    b. unsure
    c. unhappy
    d. satisfied

44. sequence
    a. coming before
    b. coming after
    c. following
    d. following one after the other

45. consequence
    a. an arrangement
    b. in order
    c. an effect
    d. following

46. subsequent
    a. in order
    b. following
    c. a result
    d. an arrangement

47. cycle
    a. refers to time
    b. refers to the wind
    c. refers to the mind
    d. a round of years or ages

48. cyclone
    a. a wind
    b. a rainstorm
    c. system of violent and destructive whirlwinds
    d. a round of years or ages

49. archaeology
    a. study of rocks
    b. study of rulers
    c. ancient life
    d. study of the life and culture of ancient people

50. archaic
    a. refers to rulers
    b. the study of ancient cultures
    c. ancient
    d. a time period

51. chronological   a. referring to disease   c. referring to an outline
                                  b. arranged in time order   d. referring to an ancient time

52. chronic   a. time   c. continuing for a long time
                       b. time period   d. not returning

53. concede   a. going before   c. to accomplish what one started out to do
                        b. coming after   d. to give in

54. precede   a. to go forward   c. to give in
                       b. to come before   d. to accomplish things

55. proceed   a. to come before   c. to go back
                       b. to go forward   d. to give in

56. succeed   a. to accomplish what one started out to do   c. to go forward
                       b. to give in   d. to go back

57. abbreviation   a. a short person   c. refers to short
                               b. a shortened form of a word or phrase   d. a cutoff of something

58. conductor   a. head of a company   c. one who takes
                        b. an orchestra leader   d. one who takes away

59. deduction   a. act of leading away   c. a conclusion
                       b. act of leading   d. act of leading to

60. cryptic   a. a hidden vault   c. an underground vault
                       b. a mysterious vault   d. having a hidden or secret meaning

61. crypt   a. having a hidden meaning   c. a vault
                   b. having a secret meaning   d. an underground vault

TRUE/FALSE TEST 4

Directions: This is a true/false test on Exercises 10–12. Read each sentence carefully. Decide whether it is true or false. Put a *T* for *true* or an *F* for *false* in the blank. The number after the sentence tells you if the word is from Exercise 10, 11, or 12.

_____ 1. A bibliography is a listing of reference words. 10

_____ 2. *Prologue* and *dialogue* are antonyms. 10

_____ 3. A diagram helps to give a description of something by using an outline figure to show relationships among things. 10

_____ 4. *Podiatrist* and *pediatrician* are synonyms. 11

_____ 5. Something contemporary must be archaic. 11, 12

_____ 6. *Content* meaning "subject matter" and *content* meaning "satisfied" are homographs. 12

_____ 7. When I was preceded by Alan in the parade, Alan came after me. 12

_____

8. The number of deductions on my paycheck refers to money I get from savings bonds. 12

_____ 9. Antitoxin is used by scientists to diagnose a patient's condition. 11

_____10. A prognosis is usually based on a doctor's diagnosis and makes a prediction about a patient's recovery. 11

_____11. An agnostic is one who is sure of his or her beliefs. 11

_____12. *Demagogue* and *pedagogue* are synonyms. 11

_____13. A pediatrician is a foot doctor. 11

_____14. A misanthrope is also a misogynist. 11

_____15. A bachelor must be a misogynist. 11

_____16. An archaeologist is one who is ancient. 12

_____17. The word *conceive* can mean "to become pregnant" and "to think of." 11

_____18. Something that is finite must end. 10

_____19. When something is an exception to a rule, it means that it belongs to the rule. 11

_____20. *Crypt* refers to a hidden message. 12

_____21. In order to be logical, you must use correct reasoning. 10

_____22. An epilogue is what is sometimes given at the beginning of a play to the audience. 10

_____23. A capable person is one with ability. 11

_____24. *Consequence* and *affect* are synonyms. 12

_____25. When something is subsequent to something else, it comes before it. 12

183

_____ 26. Chronological order does not have to refer to time order. 12

_____ 27. When someone maintains something, he or she keeps it up. 12

_____ 28. It is logical to assume that if *A* is taller than *B* and *B* is taller than *C*, then *A* is taller than *C*. 10

_____ 29. The consequences of actions would be the results of them. 12

_____ 30. The terms *deduction* and *inference* can be synonyms. 12, 10

_____ 31. When someone is able to make a conclusion from the general to the particular, that is a deduction. 12

_____ 32. When someone is able to gain information from statements that are indirectly stated, that is a deduction. 12

_____ 33. When you are a captive, you are always a prisoner in jail. 11

_____ 34. Something temporary can last for an infinite time period. 11

_____ 35. When fertilization takes place, it means a woman has conceived. 10, 11

STOP. Check answers for both tests at the end of Chapter Five (pp. 196–197).

SCORING OF TESTS

Multiple-Choice Vocabulary Test			True/False Test	
Number Wrong	*Score*		*Number Wrong*	*Score*
0–4	Excellent		0–4	Excellent
5–9	Good		5–7	Good
10–13	Weak		8–10	Weak
Above 13	Poor		Above 10	Poor
Score_____			Score_____	

1. If you scored in the excellent or good range on *both tests,* you are doing well. Go on to Chapter Six.

2. If you scored in the weak or poor range on either test, turn to the next page and follow directions for Additional Practice. Note that the words on the test are arranged so that you can tell in which exercise to find them. This will help you if you need additional practice.

ADDITIONAL PRACTICE SETS

A. Directions: Write the words you missed on the tests from the three exercises in the space provided. Note that the tests are presented so that you can tell to which exercises the words belong.

Exercise 10 Words Missed

1. _____   6. _____
2. _____   7. _____
3. _____   8. _____
4. _____   9. _____
5. _____   10. _____

Exercise 11 Words Missed

1. _____   6. _____
2. _____   7. _____
3. _____   8. _____
4. _____   9. _____
5. _____   10. _____

Exercise 12 Words Missed

1. _____   6. _____
2. _____   7. _____
3. _____   8. _____
4. _____   9. _____
5. _____   10. _____

B. Directions: Restudy the words that you have written down on this page. Study the combining forms from which those words are derived. Do Step I and Step II for those you missed. Note that Step I and Step II of the combining forms and vocabulary derived from these combining forms are on the following pages:

Exercise 10—pp. 141–144.

Exercise 11—pp. 151–154.

Exercise 12—pp. 161–165.

C. Directions: Do Additional Practice 1 on pp. 186–187 if you missed words from Exercise 10. Do Additional Practice 2 on pp. 187–188 if you missed words from Exercise 11. Do Additional Practice 3 on pp. 188–190 if you missed words from Exercise 12. Now go on to Chapter Six.

A. Directions: The combining forms presented in Exercise 10 follow.
Match the combining form with its meaning.

_____ 1. dia   a. end

_____ 2. cata   b. down

_____ 3. log, logo   c. through

_____ 4. fin   d. book

_____ 5. biblio   e. speech; word

_____ 6. fer   f. before; forward

_____ 7. epi   g. bring; bear; yield (give up)

_____ 8. pro   h. upon; beside; among

STOP. Check answers at the end of Chapter Five (p. 197).

B. Directions: The words presented in Exercise 10 follow. Match the
word with its meaning.

_____ 1. prologue   a. to feel pain

_____ 2. logical   b. outline figure showing relationships

_____ 3. catalog

                             c. last

_____ 4. epilogue

                             d. someone or something chosen
over another

_____ 5. dialogue

_____ 6. diagram   e. a listing of books on a subject

_____ 7. diameter   f. endless

_____ 8. bibliography   g. a discussion or meeting on an
important matter

_____ 9. final

_____10. finite   h. section added to the end of a
book

_____11. infinite

                             i. a listing of names, titles, and so
on, in some order

_____12. fertile

_____13. reference   j. distance around a circle

_____14. fertilization
k. having an end

_____15. preference

                             l. the union of sperm and egg

_____16. transfer

_____17. conference

_____18. suffer

_____19. circumference

m. able to produce

n. referring to correct reasoning

o. a recommendation

p. introduction to a play

q. to carry or send from one place
to another

r. a line that divides a circle in half

s. conversation

STOP. Check answers at the end of Chapter Five (p. 197).

Additional Practice 2 for Exercise 11

A. Directions: The combining forms presented in Exercise 11 follow.
Match the combining form with its meaning.

_____ 1. cap, cep   a. skin

_____ 2. gnosi, gnosis   b. laughter

_____ 3. ped, pedo   c. under

_____ 4. tox, toxo   d. take; receive

_____ 5. gyn, gyno   e. child

_____ 6. temp, tempo, tempor   f. woman

_____ 7. hypo   g. knowledge

_____ 8. derm, dermo   h. time

_____ 9. ri, ridi, risi   i. poison

STOP. Check answers at the end of Chapter Five (p. 197).

B. Directions: The words presented in Exercise 11 follow. Match the
word with its meaning.

_____ 1. capable   a. to mock or view in a scornful way

_____ 2. captive   b. modern

_____ 3. conceive   c. a children's doctor

_____ 4. deceive   d. prediction concerning an illness

_____ 5. reception   e. poisonous

187

_____ 6. exception

_____ 7. perception

_____ 8. capsule

_____ 9. ridiculous

_____ 10. ridicule

_____ 11. diagnose

_____ 12. prognosis

_____ 13. pediatrician

_____ 14. gynecologist

_____ 15. toxic

_____ 16. dermatologist

_____ 17. hypodermic

_____ 18. hypothesis

_____ 19. temporary

_____ 20. contemporary

f. having ability

g. doctor who specializes in women's diseases

h. an unproved conclusion drawn from known facts

i. to think

j. something or one that is left out

k. to mislead by lying

l. referring to the area under the skin

m. unworthy of consideration

n. a becoming aware of something through the senses

o. a prisoner

p. manner of receiving someone

q. lasting for a short period of time

r. to determine what is wrong with someone after an examination

s. a removable part of a rocket or airplane

t. a skin doctor

STOP. Check answers at the end of Chapter Five (p. 197).

Additional Practice 3 for Exercise 12

A. Directions: The combining forms presented in Exercise 12 follow. Match the combining form with its meaning.

_____ 1. tain, ten, tent

_____ 2. cede, ceed

_____ 3. sequi

_____ 4. cycl, cyclo

a. short; brief

b. ancient

c. hold

d. lead

_____ 5. chron, chrono   e. circle; wheel

_____ 6. archae, archaeo   f. secret; hidden

_____ 7. crypt, crypto   g. follow

_____ 8. duc   h. go; give in; yield (give in)

_____ 9. brevi   i. time

STOP. Check answers at the end of Chapter Five (p. 197).

B. Directions: The words presented in Exercise 12 follow. Match the word with its meaning.

_____ 1. tenant

_____ 2. content

_____ 3. content

_____ 4. maintain

_____ 5. sequence

_____ 6. consequence

_____ 7. subsequent

_____ 8. cycle

_____ 9. cyclone

_____ 10. archaeology

_____ 11. archaic

_____ 12. chronological

_____ 13. chronic

_____ 14. concede

_____ 15. precede

_____ 16. proceed

_____ 17. succeed

_____ 18. abbreviation

_____ 19. conductor

_____ 20. deduction

_____ 21. cryptic

_____ 22. crypt

a. the study of the life and culture of ancient people

b. to go forward

c. to come before

d. to give in

e. one who lives on property belonging to another

f. a result

g. satisfied

h. a round of years or ages

i. the following of one thing after another

j. a system of violent and destructive whirlwinds

k. subject matter

l. to keep up

m. following

n. a shortened form of a word or phrase

o. ancient

p. having a hidden meaning

q. a conclusion

r. underground vault

s. continuing for a long time
and returning

t. orchestra leader; one in charge
of a train

u. arranged in time order

v. to accomplish what one started
out to do

STOP. Check answers at the end of Chapter Five (p. 197).

ANSWERS: Chapter Five

Exercise 10 (pp. 141–151)

Practice A

(1) Fertilization, (2) diagram, (3) epilogue, (4) dialogue, (5) finite, (6) conference, (7) bibliography, (8) preference, (9) prologue, (10) final, (11) infinite, (12) catalog, (13) logical, (14) reference, (15) fertile.

Practice B

(1) prologue, (2) dialogue, (3) epilogue, (4) Diagram, (5) bibliography, (6) final, (7) finite, (8) infinite, (9) conference, (10) diameter, (11) circumference, (12) transfer, (13) logical, (14) catalog, (15) fertile, (16) reference, (17) preference, (18) suffer, (19) fertilization.

Practice C

(1) (a) dia, (b) cata, (c) log, (d) fin, (e) biblio, (f) fer, (g) epi, (h) pro.
(2) (a) infinite, (b) bibliography, (c) final, (h) fertile, (i) finite, (j) logical, (k) catalog, (l) dialogue, (m) fertilization, (n) circumference, (o) diameter, (p) epilogue (q) diagram, (r) suffer, (s) reference, (t) preference, (u) conference.
(3) (d), (e), (f), (g), (v).
(4) (d) suicide, (e) prologue, (f) incredible, (g) illegal, (v) transfer.

COMBINING FORM AND WORD SQUARE

```
I  P  C  C  O  T  E  F  I  N  A  L  C
A  R  I  A  B  R  P  B  I  B  L  I  O
F  E  R  T  I  L  I  Z  A  T  I  O  N
D  F  C  A  B  A  L  B  I  O  E  C  F
I  E  U  L  L  L  O  G  I  C  A  L  E
A  R  M  O  I  S  G  D  N  F  P  O  R
M  E  F  G  O  U  U  I  F  E  R  R  E
E  N  E  E  G  F  E  A  I  R  O  A  N
T  C  R  E  R  F  O  G  N  T  S  R  C
E  E  E  R  A  E  A  R  I  I  C  C  E
R  M  N  E  P  R  I  A  T  L  I  H  O
O  A  C  I  H  L  A  M  E  E  I  S  T
R  B  E  C  Y  D  I  A  L  O  G  U  E
```

Additional Words Derived from Combining Forms (pp. 149–150)

1. **inference.** Something derived by reasoning; something that is not directly stated but suggested in the statement; a logical conclusion that is drawn from statements; a deduction.

2. **proficient.** Knowing something very well; able to do something very well.

3. **dialect.** A variety of speech; a regional form of a standard language.

4. **monologue.** A long speech by one person; a dramatic sketch performed by one actor.

5. **definitive.** Conclusive; final; most nearly complete or accurate.

6. **finale.** The last part; end; the concluding movement of a musical composition; the last scene of an entertainment.

7. **affinity.** Close relationship; attraction to another.

8. **infinitesimal.** Too small to be measured; very minute.

9. **deference.** Respect; a giving in to another's opinion or judgment.

10. **defer.** To leave to another's opinion or judgment; to delay; to postpone; to put off for a future time.

Practice for Additional Words Derived from Combining Forms (p. 151)

(1) d, (2) c, (3) j, (4) g, (5) b, (6) h, (7) f, (8) i, (9) a, (10) e.

Exercise 11 (pp. 151–160)

Practice A

(1) q, (2) p, (3) o, (4) r, (5) n, (6) m, (7) a, (8) e, (9) h, (10) f, (11) d, (12) g, (13) c, (14) k, (15) b, (16) l, (17) i, (18) j, (19) t, (20) s.

Practice B

(1) hypothesis, (2) ridiculous, (3) dermatologist, (4) capsule, (5) hypodermic, (6) diagnose, (7) captive, (8) temporary, (9) prognosis, (10) Toxic, (11) capable, (12) ridicule, (13) contemporary, (14) exception, (15) reception, (16) pediatrician, (17) conceive, (18) deceive, (19) gynecologist, (20) perception.

Practice C

(1) capable, (2) reception, (3) deceive, (4) conceive, (5) ridiculous, (6) ridicule, (7) capsules, (8) perception, (9) exception, (10) hypodermic, (11) hypothesis, (12) contemporaries, (13) prognosis, (14) diagnose, (15) pediatrician, (16) gynecologist, (17) dermatologist, (18) toxic, (19) temporary, (20) captive.

Additional Words Derived from Combining Forms (pp. 159–160)

1. **misogynist.** Hater of women.

2. **agnostic.** Professing uncertainty; one who is not for or against; one who doubts that the ultimate cause (God) and the essential nature of things are knowable.

3. **epidermis.** Outermost layer of skin.

4. **pedagogue.** A teacher.

5. **antitoxin.** Something used against bacterial poison; a substance formed in the body that counteracts a specific toxin; the antibody formed in immunization with a given toxin, used in treating certain infectious diseases or in immunizing against them.

6. **toxicologist.** One who specializes in the study of poisons.

7. **derisive.** Mocking; jeering.

8. **intercept.** To stop or interrupt the course of.

9. **susceptible.** Easily influenced by or affected with; especially liable to.

10. **perceptive.** Being aware; having insight, understanding, or intuition, as a *perceptive* analysis of the problems involved.

11. **tempo.** The rate of speed at which a musical composition is supposed to be played; rate of activity.

12. **extemporaneous.** Done or spoken without special preparation; makeshift.

Practice for Additional Words Derived from Combining Forms (p. 160)

(1) d, (2) h, (3) j, (4) f, (5) a, (6) i, (7) e, (8) l, (9) k, (10) c, (11) g, (12) b.

Exercise 12 (pp. 161–173)

Practice A

(1) archaic, (2) concede, (3) cryptic, (4) crypt, (5) tenant, (6) content,
(7) maintain, (8) sequence, (9) content, (10) consequence, (11) deduction,
(12) archaeology, (13) chronological, (14) cycle, (15) chronic, (16) cyclone,
(17) succeed, (18) abbreviation, (19) Proceed, (20) precede, (21) conductor,
(22) subsequent.

Practice B

(1) tenant, (2) content, (3) sequence, (4) maintain, (5) consequence, (6) cyclone, (7) cycle, (8) homicide, (9) conductor, (10) chronic, (11) proceed,
(12) television, (13) succeed, (14) content, (15) cryptic, (16) abbreviation,
(17) concede, (18) corpse, (19) morgue, (20) Subsequent, (21) hypothesis,
(22) deduction, (23) description, (24) local, (25) illegal.

Practice C

(1) content, (2) maintain, (3) sequence, (4) consequence, (5) tenant, (6) subsequent, (7) none–archaeology, (8) archaic, (9) cycle, (10) cyclone, (11) none–
chronological, (12) none–proceed, (13) none–concede, (14) none–precede,
(15) chronic, (16) none–succeed, (17) abbreviation, (18) none–conductor,
(19) deduction, (20) cryptic, (21) crypt, (22) content.

WORD SQUARE

D	E	D	U	C	T	I	O	N	E	S	A
C	O	N	S	E	Q	U	E	N	C	E	B
R	A	C	U	M	A	I	N	T	H	E	B
Y	R	Y	B	C	Y	C	L	E	R	M	R
P	C	C	S	O	P	C	E	N	O	A	E
T	H	L	E	N	U	O	C	A	N	I	V
I	C	O	Q	T	C	N	O	N	I	N	I
C	O	N	U	E	O	T	N	T	C	T	A
H	L	E	E	N	N	E	T	E	A	A	T
R	O	I	N	T	A	N	E	O	N	I	I
O	G	N	T	C	O	T	C	E	D	N	O
N	Y	A	R	C	H	A	I	C	A	O	N

Additional Words Derived from Combining Forms (pp. 171–172)

1. **chronometer.** A very accurate clock or watch; an instrument used to measure time.

2. **anachronism.** Something out of time order; an error in chronology (the science of measuring time in fixed periods, and arranging dates in their proper order) in which a person, an object, or an event is assigned an incorrect date or period.

3. **synchronize.** To cause to agree in rate or speed; to happen or take place at the same time.

4. **concession.** An act of giving in; a right granted by the government or other authority for a specific purpose.

5. **procession.** A parade, as a funeral *procession*; any continuous course.

6. **recession.** The act of going back; in economics, the decline of business activity.

7. **secede.** To withdraw from.

8. **subscription.** An agreement; a promise in writing to pay some money; an agreement to receive something and pay for it.

9. **untenable.** Not able to be held or defended.

10. **detain.** To stop; to hold; to keep from proceeding; to delay.

11. **retentive.** Having the ability to retain or keep in things; tenacious, as a *retentive* memory; having a good memory.

12. **tenacious.** Stubborn; tough; holding or tending to hold strongly to one's views, opinions, rights, and so on; retentive, as a *tenacious* memory.

Practice for Additional Words Derived from Combining Forms (pp. 172–173)

(1) c, (2) f, (3) g, (4) d, (5) h, (6) l, (7) k, (8) a, (9) b, (10) i, (11) e, (12) j.

Crossword Puzzle 4 (pp. 173–174)

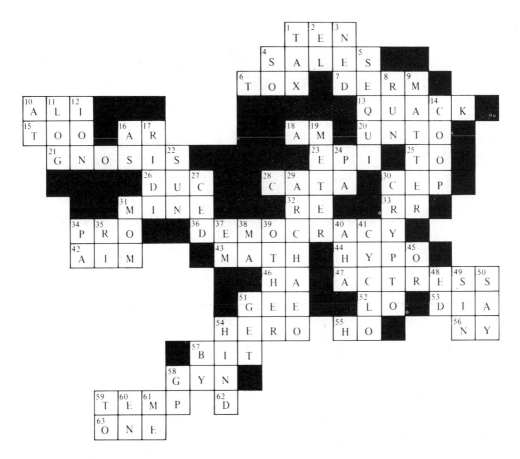

Word Scramble 4 (pp. 175–176)

(1) tenant, (2) content, (3) sequence, (4) subsequent, (5) archaic, (6) chrono-logical, (7) concede, (8) precede, (9) cryptic, (10) deduction, (11) cyclone, (12) conductor, (13) prologue, (14) logical, (15) epilogue, (16) diameter, (17) suffer, (18) conference, (19) bibliography, (20) finite, (21) fertile, (22) capable, (23) captive, (24) reception, (25) conceive, (26) deceive, (27) ridicule, (28) ex-

ception, (29) perception, (30) diagnose, (31) prognosis, (32) dermatologist, (33) pediatrician, (34) toxic, (35) temporary, (36) hypodermic.

Analogies 4 (pp. 176-177)

(1) tenacious, (2) epilogue, (3) finite, (4) deride, (5) toxicologist, (6) procession, (7) content, (8) pediatrician, (9) pedagogue, (10) contemporary, (11) consequence, (12) cyclone, (13) visage, (14) deceive, (15) captor, (16) decimate, (17) fertile, (18) agnostic, (19) inference, (20) dialect.

Multiple-Choice Vocabulary Test 4 (pp. 177-182)

Exercise 10

(1) b, (2) a, (3) d, (4) c, (5) b, (6) c, (7) a, (8) a, (9) c, (10) d, (11) b, (12) b, (13) c, (14) c, (15) d, (16) a, (17) c, (18) c, (19) c.

Exercise 11

(20) d, (21) a, (22) d, (23) c, (24) b, (25) a, (26) d, (27) d, (28) b, (29) c, (30) d, (31) d, (32) d, (33) d, (34) b, (35) c, (36) b,[1] (37) d,[2] (38) c, (39) d.

Exercise 12

(40) b, (41) a, (42) a, (43) d, (44) d, (45) c, (46) b, (47) d, (48) c,[3] (49) d, (50) c, (51) b, (52) c, (53) d, (54) b, (55) b, (56) a, (57) b, (58) b, (59) c, (60) d, (61) d.

---

[1] *Referring to the area under the skin* is a better answer than a *needle* because *hypodermic* refers to an area under the skin. The term *hypodermic* also means "a needle that is injected under the skin" or "a hypodermic needle." However, the best answer is *b* because a needle could refer to any needle, including a sewing needle.

[2] *An unproved conclusion drawn from known facts* is a better answer than *an unproved conclusion* because it is a more complete answer.

[3] *System of violent and destructive whirlwinds* is a better answer than *a wind* because it is more complete and less general. This is also true for numbers 32, 33, and 35 in Exercise 11. It is not enough to state *doctor* as the answer. That is too general. You must state the kind of doctor the person is.

196

(1) F, (2) F, (3) T, (4) F, (5) F, (6) T, (7) F, (8) F, (9) F, (10) T, (11) F, (12) F, (13) F, (14) T^4, (15) F^5, (16) F, (17) T, (18) T, (19) F, (20) F, (21) T, (22) F, (23) T, (24) F^6, (25) F, (26) F, (27) T, (28) T, (29) T, (30) T, (31) T, (32) T, (33) F, (34) F, (35) T.

STOP. Turn to p. 184 for the scoring of the tests.

Additional Practice Sets (pp. 185-190)

Additional Practice 1

A. (1) c, (2) b, (3) e, (4) a, (5) d, (6) g, (7) h, (8) f.
B. (1) p, (2) n, (3) i, (4) h, (5) s, (6) b, (7) r, (8) e, (9) c, (10) k, (11) f, (12) m, (13) o, (14) l, (15) d, (16) q, (17) g, (18) a, (19) j.

Additional Practice 2

A. (1) d, (2) g, (3) e, (4) i, (5) f, (6) h, (7) c, (8) a, (9) b.
B. (1) f, (2) o, (3) i, (4) k, (5) p, (6) j, (7) n, (8) s, (9) m, (10) a, (11) r, (12) d, (13) c, (14) g, (15) e, (16) t, (17) l, (18) h, (19) q, (20) b.

Additional Practice 3

A. (1) c, (2) h, (3) g, (4) e, (5) i, (6) b, (7) f, (8) d, (9) a.
B. (1) e, (2) $g,^7$ (3) $k,^8$ (4) l, (5) i, (6) f, (7) m, (8) h, (9) j, (10) a, (11) o, (12) u, (13) s, (14) d, (15) c, (16) b, (17) v, (18) n, (19) t, (20) q, (21) p, (22) r.

---

[4] Because a misanthrope is a hater of mankind, in the generic sense, he or she would also have to be a hater of women.

[5] It does not necessarily follow that a man who is not married is a hater of women. He may be unmarried for many reasons—one might be that he likes many women a lot.

[6] *Consequence* and *effect* have the same meanings. *Affect* means "to influence."

[7] The answer for 2 can be either *g* or *k*.

[8] The answer for 3 can be either *k* or *g*.

197

CHAPTER SIX

EXERCISE 13

Step I. Combining Forms

A. Directions: A list of combining forms with their meanings follows. Look at the combining forms and their meanings. Concentrate on learning each combining form and its meaning. Cover the meanings, read the combining forms, and state the meanings to yourself. Check to see if you are correct. Now cover the combining forms, read the meanings, and state the combining forms to yourself.

Combining Forms	*Meanings*
1. tend, tens, tent	stretch; strain
2. belli, bello	war
3. civ, civis	citizen
4. polis	city
5. pac, pax	peace
6. voc, vox	voice; call
7. post	after
8. ambi	both

199

B. Directions: Cover the preceding meanings. Write the meanings of the following combining forms.

Combining Forms	Meanings
1. tend, tens, tent	_____
2. belli, bello	_____
3. civ, civis	_____
4. polis	_____
5. pac, pax	_____
6. voc, vox	_____
7. post	_____
8. ambi	_____

Step II. Words Derived from Combining Forms

1. **attention** (at · ten · tion) (aṯ · ten′ shun) *n.* Mental concentration; care; a position of readiness; act of courtesy. *When children are tired, they cannot pay* **attention** *because they have lost their ability to concentrate.*

2. **intention** (in · ten · tion) (in · ten′ shun) *n.* Aim; goal; purpose. *Although, as a child, her* **intention** *was to become a famous archaeologist, she never thought that she would achieve her goal.*

3. **tension** (ten · sion) (ten′ shun) *n.* The act of stretching or the condition of being stretched tight; mental strain. *The parents'* **tension** *was so great when their child was kidnapped that they did not know how long they could stand the mental strain.*

4. **intense** (in · tensé′) *adj.* Having great or extreme force; very strong; existing or occurring to a high or extreme degree. *The heat was so* **intense** *from the fire that the firemen could not enter the building.*

5. **belligerent** (bel · lig · er · ent) (beḻ · lij′ er · ent) *adj.* Warlike. *n.* Any nation, person, or group engaged in fighting or war. *Because he has such a* **belligerent** *manner, he gets into a lot of fights.*

6. **civilian** (ci · vil · ian) (si · vil′ yun) *n.* One who is not in the military; *adj.* Of civilians; nonmilitary. *It is good to be a* **civilian** *again after spending three years in the army.*

7. **civics** (civ · ics) (siv′ iks) *n.* (Used in the singular.) The part of political science dealing with the study of civic affairs and the rights and responsibilities of citizenship. *In school I took a course in* **civics** *because I wanted to learn more about the individual citizen's rights and responsibilities.*

200

8. **civilization** (civ · i · li · za · tion) (siv′ i · li · zā · shun) *n.* A state of human society that has a high level of intellectual, social, and cultural development; the cultural development of a specific people, country, or region. *In a **civilization**, a high level of intellectual, social, and cultural development is supposed to exist.*

9. **civil** (siv′ il) *adj.* Of a citizen or citizens; relating to citizens and their government; relating to ordinary community life as distinghished from military or church affairs; courteous or polite. ***Civil** liberties are the rights that individual citizens have.*

10. **politics** (pol · i · tics) (pol′ i · tiks) *n.* (Although plural, it is usually looked upon as singular.) The science or art of government or of the direction and management of public or state affairs. *Persons who are in **politics** are interested in the management of public or state affairs.*

11. **politician** (pol · i · ti · cian) (pol′ i · tish · un) *n.* A person engaged in politics; a person involved in the science or art of government; a person who seeks advancement or power within an organization by dubious (doubtful) means. *The **politicians** met to determine whom they would support for office.*

12. **metropolitan** (met · ro · pol · i · tan) (met · ro · pol′ i · tun) *adj.* Referring to a major city center and its surrounding area. *n.* A person who inhabits a metropolis or one who has the manners and tastes associated with a metropolis. *I like to live in a **metropolitan** area so that I can be close to the kinds of stores, theaters, and restaurants that are found in large cities.*

13. **vocal** (vo · cal) (vō′ kul) *adj.* Referring to the voice; having voice; oral; freely expressing oneself in speech, usually with force; speaking out. *When we strained our **vocal** cords from yelling at the basketball game, we could hardly use our voices the next day.*

14. **vocabulary** (vo · cab · u · lar · y) (vō · kab′ yu · lar · ē) *n.* (*pl.* ies) A list of words and phrases, usually arranged alphabetically, that are defined or translated from another language; a stock of words possessed by an individual or a group. *You are gaining a larger **vocabulary** from doing the exercises involving lists of words and their definitions.*

15. **vocation** (vo · ca · tion) (vō · kā′ shun) *n.* A calling; a person's work or profession. *Sharon chose a **vocation** similar to her father's because she wanted to follow in his footsteps.*

16. **ambiguous** (am · big′ ū · ⌀us) *adj.* Having two or more meanings. *What he said was so **ambiguous** that I couldn't figure out if he wanted me to stay or go.*

201

© 1973 National News Syndicate. Reprinted by permission of Bob Cordray.

17. **postscript** (post · script) (pōst′ skript) *n.* Something added to a letter after the writer's signature; something added to written or printed legal papers. *The abbreviation of* **postscript,** *something added to a letter after the writer has signed his or her name, is P.S.*

18. **pacify** (pac · i · fy) (pas′ i · fī) *v.* To bring peace to; to calm; to quiet. *The speaker tried to* **pacify** *the mob, but he could not calm them down.*

Special Note

The term *civilian,* which refers to someone who is not in the military, is used also by policemen and by others who wear special uniforms to refer to someone out of uniform.

Step III. Practice

A. Directions: Each sentence has a missing word. Choose the word that *best* completes the sentence. Write the word in the blank.

Word List

postscript, metropolitan, attention, vocabulary, vocal, pacify, intention, belligerent, ambiguous, tension, civics, politics, vocation, civil, intense, civilian, civilization, politician.

1. Some people pay a lot of _____ to their appearance because they want to look their best.

2. His _____ is to be on time, but he is always late.

3. Too much_____ gives me a headache because I can't take mental strain.

4. Try to be less _____about everything you do because your forcefulness is beginning to annoy us.

202

5. The homeowners were so angry at their increase in taxes that it was difficult to _____ them.

6. The crowd had become so _____ that the police had to call for reinforcements to help control the crowd.

7. My course in _____ helped me gain a better understanding of the individual citizen's rights and responsibilities.

8. After being in military service for a decade, I decided to leave and become a(n) _____ again.

9. Being in _____ has opened my eyes to a lot of problems that exist in the management and direction of state affairs.

10. As a(n) _____ who was elected to office, I hope to be able to make some contribution to society.

11. Some people are _____ on purpose because they do not want to say exactly how they stand on an issue.

12. This is not the _____ I planned for in school, but it's the only work I could get.

13. Although we have reached a high level of _____ , wars still exist among nations.

14. Persons involved in the _____ rights movement try to protect citizens' rights as established in the Constitution.

15. The singer had to cancel her performance because she had something wrong with her _____ cords.

16. Because I need a good _____ to read successfully, I am studying words and their meanings.

17. After I signed my name to the letter I was writing, I had to add a(n) _____ because I thought of something else I wanted to say.

18. When we moved to a(n) _____ area, I sold my car and decided to become a pedestrian because it was too difficult to keep a car in the city.

STOP. Check answers at the end of Chapter Six (p. 246).

B. Directions: Underline the word that *best* fits the definition(s).

1. Mental concentration; act of courtesy

   a. tension   c. attention
   b. intense   d. intention

2. Aim; goal

   a. attention   c. tension
   b. intense   d. intention

3. Mental strain

    a. intense   c. attention
    b. tension   d. intention

4. Very strong

    a. tension   c. intention
    b. attention   d. intense

5. Warlike

    a. intense   c. belligerent
    b. tension   d. civil

6. One not in the military

    a. civil   c. civilian
    b. civilization   d. civics

7. Cultural development of a people

    a. civics   c. civilian
    b. civilization   d. civil

8. Polite; of a citizen or citizens

    a. civics   c. civilian
    b. politician   d. civil

9. Science of government dealing with the management of public affairs

    a. civilization   c. politics
    b. civics   d. civilian

10. The part of political science dealing with citizens' rights and responsibilities

    a. civics   c. civilization
    b. politics   d. civilian

11. A person involved in the science or art of government

    a. civilian   c. politics
    b. vocation   d. politician

12. Referring to a major city center and its surrounding area

    a. civilization   c. politics
    b. metropolitan d. civilian

13. Something added to a letter after the signature

    a. vocabulary   c. metropolitan
    b. ambiguous   d. postscript

14. List of words that are defined

    a. vocation   c. vocal
    b. vocabulary   d. postscript

15. Referring to the voice

    a. vocal   c. vocabulary
    b. vocation   d. ambiguous

16. A person's work

    a. vocation   c. politics
    b. civilization   d. vocal

17. To calm

    a. civil   c. pacify
    b. vocal   d. postscript

18. Having two or more meanings

    a. vocabulary   c. vocal
    b. attention   d. ambiguous

STOP. Check answers at the end of Chapter Six (p. 246).

C. Directions: In the following sentences give the meaning that *best* fits the underlined word.

1. During the president's speech we paid very close <u>attention</u> to what he was saying because we did not want to miss one word._____

2. From his conflicting actions, I can't figure out what his <u>intentions</u> are.

    _____

3. There was considerable <u>tension</u> in the room after the instructor told the students that they needed to do more work. _____

4. The light was so <u>intense</u> that it hurt my eyes._____

5. Pat avoids <u>belligerent</u> people because she is peaceful._____

6. How do you feel now that you're out of uniform and a <u>civilian</u> again?

    _____

7. Courses in <u>civics</u> will help me because I want to become a politician.

    _____

8. Western <u>civilization</u> is different from Eastern <u>civilization</u> because the cultural development of the West and that of the East have been different.

    _____

9. There have been so many scandals in <u>politics</u> in the past decade that many people feel that elected officials are more concerned with selfish interests than with the proper management of public affairs. _____

10. It is sometimes difficult to be <u>civil</u> to persons who are rude and impolite.

    _____

11. As a <u>politician</u>, Kim intends to serve wisely the people who elected her to office. _____

12. What a change it was when we moved from a rural area, which is all farmland, to a <u>metropolitan</u> area. _____

13. The students were very <u>vocal</u> in their demands. _____

14. After studying so many words and their meanings, I have a larger <u>vocabulary</u>.

    _____

15. Jack's <u>vocation</u> is one that requires a lot of time, effort, and study._____

16. The directions for the exam were so <u>ambiguous</u> that half the class did one thing, and the other half did something else._____

17. I needed to add a <u>postscript</u> to my letter because I thought of more things to say after I had already signed my letter. _____

18. The mother tried to <u>pacify</u> her screaming child by giving him a toy.

    _____

STOP. Check answers at the end of Chapter Six (p. 246).

ance, ence. Act of; state of; quality of. When *ance* is found at the end of a word, it means "act of," "state of," or "quality of." In an earlier exercise you met *tion,* which also means "state of" or "act of." If *ance* or *ence* is added to a word, the word changes to a noun. For example: **maintain.** To carry on or continue; to keep up. *I will maintain your car while you are away so that it will be in good working condition when you get home.* **maintenance.** The act of keeping up. *The maintenance of your car is important if it is to stay in good running condition.* Examples of words with *ance, ence: dependence*—act of trusting; act of relying on someone for support; *assistance*—act of helping; *sequence*—the state of following; *conferance*—the act of meeting in a group. How many more words can you supply?

al. Relating to. When *al,* meaning "relating to," is added to the end of a word, the word is usually an adjective. For example: *vocal*—relating to the voice; *local*—relating to a place; *manual*—relating to the hand; *annual*—relating to the year; *universal*—relating to all; *legal*—relating to law; *apodal*—relating to being without feet; *nautical*—relating to sailing. How many more words can you supply?

Additional Words Derived from Combining Forms

From your knowledge of combining forms, can you define the following words?

1. **postmortem** (pōst · mor′ tem) *adj. n. The doctor performed a postmortem examination on the victim in order to determine the cause of his death.*

_____

2. **posterior** (pos · te · ri · or) (pos · tir′ ē · or) *adj. n. This blueprint shows the posterior section of the new airplane our company is building.*

_____

3. **posterity** (pos · ter · i · ty) (pos · ter′ i · tē) *n. Artists hope that their works will be admired by posterity.*

_____

4. **posthumously** (post · hu · mous · ly) (pos′ chū · mǿus · lē) *adv. Many artists gain recognition **posthumously** rather than during their lifetime.*

5. **provoke** (pro · vōkǿ′) *v. The speaker's words so **provoked** some of the people in the audience that they stood up and booed.*

6. **pacifist** (pac · i · fist) (pas′ i · fist) *n. As George was a **pacifist**, he would not join the armed forces or any other military organization.*

7. **megalopolis** (meg · a · lop′ o · lis) *n. The area between Boston and Washington, D.C., is considered one **megalopolis** because of the high density of population between these two cities.*

8. **ambidextrous** (am · bi · dex · trous) (am · bē · dek′ strǿus) *adj. Some **ambidextrous** people use their left hands for writing and their right hands for everything else.*

9. **vociferous** (vo · cif · er · ous) (vō · sif′ er · ǿus) *adj. The couple in the apartment above us were so **vociferous** that the neighbors called the police to complain about the noise.*

10. **convocation** (con · vo · ca · tion) (kon · vo · kā′ shun) *n. At the beginning of the college year, a **convocation** is held, at which time the president of the college gives his welcoming address.*

11. **avocation** (av · o · ca · tion) (av · o · kā′ shun) *n. Stamp collecting is my father's **avocation**.*

12. **irrevocable** (ir · rev · o · ca · ble) (iŕ · rev′ o · ka · bul) *adj. My boss said that his decision to fire my friend was an **irrevocable** one.*

13. **detention** (de · ten · tion) (de · ten′ shun) *n. The accused person was held in **detention** until bail was raised for him.*

14. **detente** (de · tente) (dā · tantǿ′) *n. The President said that **detente** between the two nations would continue if each country lived up to its agreements.*

STOP. Check answers at the end of Chapter Six (p. 247).

Practice for Additional Words Derived from Combining Forms

Directions: Match each word with the *best* definition.

_____ 1. postmortem	a. a group of people called together
_____ 2. posterity	b. easing of strained relations
_____ 3. posterior	c. one very large city
_____ 4. provoke	d. an autopsy
_____ 5. pacifist	e. one who is against war
_____ 6. ambidextrous	f. confinement; a keeping back
_____ 7. convocation	g. not to be recalled
_____ 8. detente	h. after death
_____ 9. vociferous	i. future generations
_____ 10. posthumously	j. to stir up; irritate
_____ 11. detention	k. able to use both hands equally well
_____ 12. megalopolis	l. hobby
_____ 13. avocation	m. clamorous
_____ 14. irrevocable	n. in the rear

STOP. Check answers at the end of Chapter Six (p. 247).

EXERCISE 14

Step I. Combining Forms

A. Directions: A list of combining forms with their meanings follows. Look at
the combining forms and their meanings. Concentrate on learning each combining form and its meaning. Cover the meanings,
read the combining forms, and state the meanings to yourself.
Check to see if you are correct. Now cover the combining forms,
read the meanings, and state the combining forms to yourself.
Check to see if you are correct.

Combining Forms	*Meanings*
1. luc, lum	light; clear
2. err	wander
3. soph	wise

208

4. sist, sta	stand
5. nov	new
6. dorm	sleep
7. peri	around
8. hyper	over; above; excessive (very much)
9. ego	I; me; the self

B. Directions: Cover the preceding meanings. Write the meanings of the following combining forms.

Combining Forms	Meanings
1. luc, lum	_____
2. err	_____
3. soph	_____
4. sist, sta	_____
5. nov	_____
6. dorm	_____
7. peri	_____
8. hyper	_____
9. ego	_____

Step II. Words Derived from Combining Forms

1. **lucid** (lu • cid) (lū' sid) *adj.* Clear; easily understood; bright; shining. *When I ask a question about something I don't understand, I like to receive a **lucid** explanation.*

2. **translucent** (trans • lu • cent) (trans • lū' sent) *adj.* Permitting light to go through but not permitting a clear view of any object. *We had a **translucent** screen on our window that allowed light to go through, but persons looking through the screen would not get a clear view of what was in the room.*

3. **error** (er' ŗor) *n.* A mistake; something done, said, or believed incorrectly; a wandering from what is correct. *The **error** in judgment seemed like a very small mistake, but it caused a great deal of suffering for others.*

4. **sophisticated** (so • phis • ti • cat • ed) (so • fis' ti • kāt • id) *adj.* Not in a simple, natural, or pure state; worldly-wise; not naive; cultured; highly complicated; complex; experienced. *Because she has traveled quite a lot and is very cultured, she always acts in a **sophisticated** manner.*

5. **sophomore** (soph · o · more) (sof′ o · moṛé) *n.* A second-year student in American high schools or colleges; an immature person; one who thinks he or she knows more than is the case. *As a college **sophomore**, I have two more years to go before I graduate.*

6. **philosophy** (phi · los · o · phy) (fi · los′ o · fē) *n.* (*pl.* **phies**) The study of human knowledge; the love of wisdom and the search for it; a search for the general laws that give a reasonable explanation of something. *Students of **philosophy** seek to understand various ideas better.*

7. **circumstance** (cir · cum · stance) (sir′ kum · stansé) *n.* Something connected with an act, an event, or a condition; (*often pl.*): the conditions, influences, and so on surrounding and influencing persons or actions; formal display, as in *pomp and circumstance.* *The **circumstances** of the suicide were so suspicious that a full-scale investigation was started.*

8. **substitute** (sub′ sti · tūté) *v.* To put in place of another person or thing. *n.* One who takes the place of another person; something that is put in place of something else or is available for use instead of something else. *When our teacher was absent, a **substitute** took her place.*

9. **consist** (con · sist) (kon · sist′) *v.* To be made up of. *I know what the plan **consists** of because I made it up myself.*

10. **assist** (as · sist′) *v.* To give help to. *n.* An act of helping. *John **assisted** his friend because his friend had always helped him.*

11. **distant** (dis′ tant) *adj.* Separated or apart by space and/or time; away from; far apart; not closely related. *A **distant** relative came to visit us, but I had never met her before because I am not closely related to her.*

12. **obstacle** (ob · sta · cle) (ob′ sta · kul) *n.* Something that stands in the way or opposes; something that stops progress; an obstruction. *There were many **obstacles** that stood in the way of my going to college, but I was able to overcome each of them.*

13. **persist** (per · sist′) *v.* To continue in some course or action even though it is difficult. *Even though she knew that it would be difficult to become an actress, she **persisted** in trying.*

14. **innovation** (in · no · va · tion) (in · n̸o · vā′ shun) *n.* Something newly introduced; a new method; something new. *The man's **innovation** saved his company millions of dollars because his new method made it possible to manufacture the product cheaper.*

15. **novel** (nov′ el) *n.* A work of fiction of some length. *adj.* New; strange; unusual. *It takes some people a while to get used to **novel** ideas because they do not like anything new or different.*

16. **dormitory** (dor · mi · to · ry) (dor′ mi · tor · ē) *n.* (*pl.* **ries**) A large room in which many persons sleep; a building providing sleeping and living quarters, especially at a school, college, or resort (summer or winter hotel). *Our college **dormitory** houses one hundred students.*

17. **dormant** (dor′ mant) *adj.* Asleep or as if asleep; not active. *Bears are **dormant** during the winter.*

18. **period** (pe · ri · od) (pir′ ē · od) *n.* A portion of time; a portion of time into which something is divided; a punctuation mark that signals a full stop at the end of a sentence, also used after abbreviations. *In high school, the school day was divided into seven class **periods.***

19. **periodical** (pe · ri · od · i · cal) (pir · ē · od′ i · kul) *adj.* Referring to publications, such as magazines, that appear at fixed time intervals. *n.* A periodical publication. *I have a subscription to a **periodical** that is published every month.*

20. **hypertension** (hy · per · ten · sion) (hī · per · ten′ shun) *n.* High blood pressure. *When someone is diagnosed as having **hypertension**, he or she should have his or her blood pressure checked frequently to make sure that it doesn't get too high.*

21. **egocentric** (e · go · cen · tric) (ē · gō · sen′ trik) *adj.* Self-centered; relating everything to oneself. *He is so **egocentric** that everything he says seems to start with* I, me, *or* my.

Special Note

Hyper, meaning "over," "above," "excessive" (very much), is placed at the beginning of a great number of words. For example:

1. *Hypersensitive* —oversensitive.

2. *Hyperactive* —overactive.

3. *Hyperproductive* —overproductive.

Check your dictionary for more words with *hyper.*

Step III. Practice

A. Directions: A number of sentences with missing words follows. Choose the word that *best* fits the sentence from the following words, and write it in the blank.

Word List

translucent, assist, lucid, circumstance, persist, error, philosophy, distant, substitute, dormitory, sophomore, obstacle, novel, sophisticated, consist, innovation, dormant, hypertension, period, egocentric, periodical.

1. I make the most _____s when I am very excited about something because I don't stop to think.

2. He was not very _____ when he spoke; so we still do not know what took place.

3. I like the _____ glass we have in our living room because it allows light to come in, but people can't see clearly inside the room.

4. Some scientists may take courses in _____ because they are interested in general laws that give reasonable explanations that apply to the whole field of science.

5. Under what _____s would you consider taking this job?

6. Now that I'm a(n) _____, I have only two more years after this one to graduation.

7. Doctors have more _____equipment today, which helps them to diagnose illnesses better.

8. We had a(n) _____in our geometry class because our regular teacher was out ill.

9. The man needed a(n) _____ to get his car started, but no one seemed to want to stop to help.

10. In the not too _____ future, I intend to become a geologist.

11. Although I will probably meet many_____s in my life, I intend to overcome them.

12. I want to know what the medicine_____ s of because I am allergic to some drugs.

13. In the past four decades, many_____ s have been developed by man that were never dreamed possible a century ago.

14. Ms. Smith uses_____ approaches in teaching her course because she finds that students enjoy new ways of learning.

15. The doctor said that the disease was_____ at the moment, but it could become active at any time.

16. We have both males and females living in our college_____.

17. I am the kind of person who will_____until I achieve what I started out to achieve.

18. Some people are so _____ that they talk only about themselves.

19. The doctor's prognosis for Nancy's mother was not too good because her mother suffers from _____ and has already had one stroke.

212

20. If this _____ of drought does not end, the farmers will not be able to produce the crops that are needed.

21. I receive a few _____ s every month, but I don't always have time to read all the articles in them.

STOP. Check answers at the end of Chapter Six (p. 247).

B. Directions: In the Word Square there are seventeen words from Exercise 14. Find the words in the square and match them with their correct meanings. Note that there are more meanings than words. If there is no word in the square for a meaning, write *none,* and give the word.

WORD SQUARE

I	N	N	O	V	A	T	I	O	N	P	T	S
I	S	P	E	R	S	I	S	T	O	H	R	Q
D	O	D	I	S	T	A	N	T	V	I	A	W
O	P	O	B	S	T	A	C	L	E	L	N	K
R	H	R	L	U	S	S	O	E	L	O	S	T
M	O	M	O	B	Y	S	N	R	I	S	L	D
A	M	I	O	S	N	I	S	R	N	O	U	L
N	O	T	M	T	O	S	I	O	G	P	C	Y
T	R	O	E	I	N	T	S	R	S	H	E	H
R	E	R	R	T	Y	O	T	E	E	Y	N	W
O	L	Y	R	U	L	U	C	I	D	E	T	N
P	M	Y	O	T	O	D	U	E	E	O	R	A
H	O	M	P	E	R	I	O	D	I	C	A	L

Meanings   *Words*

1. Clear; easily understood   _____

2. Permitting light to go through   _____

3. A mistake   _____

4. Worldly-wise   _____

5. Second-year student   _____

213

6. The study of human knowledge   _____

7. Conditions or influences connected
   with an act or event   _____

8. To put in place of   _____

9. To be made up of   _____

10. Give help to   _____

11. Separated or apart by space and/or time   _____

12. Something in the way of   _____

13. Continue in some course even
    though it's difficult   _____

14. A new idea   _____

15. Strange; unusual; long work of fiction   _____

16. Large room in which many people sleep   _____

17. Asleep; not active   _____

18. Portion of time   _____

19. Referring to a publication that
    is put out at regular intervals   _____

20. High blood pressure   _____

21. Self-centered   _____

STOP. Check answers at the end of Chapter Six (pp. 247–248).

C. Directions: In the following sentences, give the meaning that *best* fits the underlined word.

1. We were able to view a distant star through the telescope. _____

2. The dormant volcano had been inactive for so long that no one expected it to erupt when it did. _____.

3. Under what circumstances do you feel we should allow such things to take place? _____

4. The light that shone through the translucent glass made different designs in our room, depending on the time of day. _____

5. Your error in auditing the books is so serious that the mistake could cost you your job. _____

214

6. Jean was not very <u>lucid</u> when she awakened after having been attacked; so we had to wait until she could be clearer about what had happened.
_____

7. Because I don't know what that travel package <u>consists</u> of, I'd like you to tell me exactly what is included._____

8. I took a course in <u>philosophy</u> because I love to examine ideas and deal with such questions as "What is good?" and "What is truth?"
_____

9. At college some persons live off campus rather than in a <u>dormitory</u>.
_____

10. What picture will you <u>substitute</u> to take the place of the one you took out?
_____

11. It gives me a good feeling to be able to <u>assist</u> people when they need help.
_____

12. Whenever an <u>obstacle</u> is put in my way that makes things difficult for me, I try to think of ways to remove it. _____

13. The doctors were hoping that the <u>innovations</u> in heart surgery that had just been introduced at the hospital would help to save patients' lives.
_____

14. I will <u>persist</u> in doing my work this way, even though it is more difficult, because I know that it is the correct way. _____

15. I always forget to put a <u>period</u> after abbreviations._____

16. When my <u>periodical</u> did not arrive for three months in a row, I wrote to the magazine publisher's office to complain. _____

17. <u>Hypertension</u> is called the "silent killer" because many people are not aware that they have high blood pressure. _____

18. It is difficult to carry on a dialogue with an <u>egocentric</u> person because he always seems to be interested only in himself. _____
_____

19. Whenever someone says that I'm behaving like a <u>sophomore</u>, I know that he or she is not giving me a compliment. _____

20. I like to go out with <u>sophisticated</u> people because they are cultured and know how to behave properly. _____

21. I enjoy reading books with <u>novel</u> plots because I like strange or unusual stories. _____

STOP. Check answers at the end of Chapter Six (p. 248).

> **inter.** Between; among. When *inter* comes at the
> beginning of a word, it means "between" or "among."
> *Do not* confuse *inter* with *intra.* For example: *inter-
> departmental*—between departments; *interdependent*—
> dependent upon one another; *interstate*—between
> states; *intercollegiate*—between colleges.
>
> **intra.** Within; inside of. *Intra* comes at the begin-
> ning of a word. It means "within." Do not
> confuse *intra* with *inter.* For example: *intradepart-
> mental*—within the department; *intracollegiate*—with-
> in the college; *intramural*—within a school or an
> institution. Can you supply more words beginning
> with *inter* and *intra?* Check your dictionary for a
> large list of such words.

Additional Words Derived from Combining Forms

From your knowledge of combining forms, can you define the following words?

1. **perimeter** (pe · rim′ e · ter) *n.* *The **perimeter** of a circle would be its circumference.*

   _____

2. **periphery** (pe · riph · er · y) (pe · rif′ er · ē) *n.* (*pl.* **eries**) **Periphery** *and*
perimeter *are synonyms.*

   _____

3. **periscope** (per · i · scope) (per′ i · skōpé) *n.* *The sailor in the submarine
used the **periscope** to view the approaching destroyer.*

   _____

4. **hyperbole** (hy · per · bo · le) (hī · per′ bo · lē) *n.* *When Sharon said that
she had walked a million miles today, she was using **hyperbole.***

   _____

5. **illuminate** (il · lū′ · mi · naté) *v.* *The lights so **illuminated** the room that
everything could be seen clearly.*

   _____

216

6. **egotistic** (e • go • tis • tic) (ē • gō • tis′ tik) *adj. I do not enjoy being in the company of **egotistic** people because they are too concerned with themselves.*

_____

7. **novice** (nov • ice) (nov′ isȼ) *n. Everyone thought that he was an expert rather than a **novice** because of the way he handled himself on the tennis court.*

_____

8. **stamina** (stam′ i • na) *n. Professional athletes need a lot of **stamina** in order to keep playing.*

_____

9. **obstinate** (ob • sti • nate) (ob′ sti • nit) *adj. My friend is so **obstinate** that once he makes up his mind, he will never change it.*

_____

10. **sophistry** (soph • ist • ry) (sof′ ist • rē) *n. (pl. ies) Some persons are so clever in presenting their illogical arguments that it is difficult to recognize that the arguments are filled with **sophistry**.*

_____

11. **erratic** (er • rat • ic) (erȼ • rat′ ik) *adj. Her behavior was so **erratic** that we wondered if she was mentally ill.*

_____

12. **periodic** (pe • ri • od • ic) (pir • ē • od′ ik) *adj. The phases of the moon are periodic.*

_____

STOP. Check answers at the end of Chapter Six (pp. 248–249).

Practice for Additional Words Derived from Combining Forms

Directions: Match each word with the *best* definition.

_____ 1. perimeter   a. to give light to

_____ 2. periphery   b. a beginner

_____ 3. periscope   c. staying power

_____ 4. hyperbole   d. faulty reasoning

_____ 5. egotistic   e. the outer part or boundary
                                            of something
_____ 6. illuminate

_____ 7. novice   f. conceited

_____ 8. erratic   g. great exaggeration

_____ 9. obstinate

_____ 10. stamina

_____ 11. sophistry

_____ 12. periodic

h. an instrument used by a submarine to see all around

i. a measure of the outer part of
a closed plane figure

j. not regular; not stable

k. stubborn

l. taking place at regular intervals

STOP. Check answers at the end of Chapter Six (p. 249).

EXERCISE 15

Step I. Combining Forms

A. Directions: A list of combining forms with their meanings follows. Look
at the combining forms and their meanings. Concentrate on
learning each combining form and its meaning. Cover the
meanings, read the combining forms, and state the meanings to
yourself. Check to see if you are correct. Now cover the combining forms, read the meanings, and state the combining forms
to yourself. Check to see if you are correct.

Combining Forms	*Meanings*
1. miss, mitt	send
2. pon, pos	place; set
3. anima, animus	spirit; mind; soul
4. magna	great; large
5. hypn, hypno	sleep
6. feder, fid, fide	trust; faith
7. nasc, nat	born
8. equi	equal
9. pop	people

B. Directions: Cover the preceding meanings. Write the meanings of the following combining forms.

Combining Forms	*Meanings*
1. miss, mitt	_____

218

2. pon, pos   _____

3. anima, animus   _____

4. magna   _____

5. hypn, hypno   _____

6. feder, fid, fide   _____

7. nasc, nat   _____

8. equi   _____

9. pop   _____

Step II. Words Derived from Combining Forms

1. **mission** (mis · sion) (mish′ un) *n.* Group or team of persons sent some place to perform some work; the task, business, or responsibility that a person is assigned; the place where missionaries carry out their work; a place where poor people may go for assistance. *The astronauts were sent on a special mission to try to locate a missing spaceship.*

2. **permission** (per · mis · sion) (per · mish′ un) *n.* Act of allowing the doing of something; a consent. *I received permission from the instructor to audit her class.*

3. **dismiss** (dis · miss′) *v.* To tell or allow to go; to discharge, as from a job; to get rid of; to have done with quickly; to reject. *The class was dismissed when the period was over.*

4. **admission** (ad · mis · sion) (ad · mish′ un) *n.* Act of allowing to enter; entrance fee; a price charged or paid to be admitted; acknowledgment; a confession, as to a crime. *We did not know we had to pay admission to enter the fair.*

5. **submit** (sub · mit′) *v.* To give in to another; to surrender; to concede; to present for consideration or approval; to present as one's opinion. *I will submit my manuscript to a publisher for possible publication.*

6. **transmit** (trans · mit′) *v.* To send from one place to another; to pass on by heredity; to transfer; to pass or communicate news, information, and so on. *Certain diseases are transmitted from the parent to the child through heredity.*

7. **intermission** (in · ter · mis · sion) (in · ter · mish′ un) *n.* Time between events; recess. *The intermissions between acts in the play were each fifteen minutes long.*

8. **position** (po · si · tion) (po · zish′ un) *n.* An act of placing or arranging; the manner in which a thing is placed; the way the body is placed, as in *sitting position*; the place occupied by a person or thing; the proper or appropriate place, as *in position*; job; a feeling or stand; social standing.

219

*He had been sitting in that **position** for so long that, if he hadn't moved a little, his legs would have fallen asleep.*

9. **postpone** (pōst · pōng′) *v.* To put off to a future time; to delay *They had to **postpone** their annual reading convention for another month because many members could not come at the scheduled time.*

10. **positive** (pos · i · tive) (poz′ i · tiv̸) *adj.* Being directly found to be so or true; real; actual; sure of something; definitely set; confident. *She was **positive** that she could describe the men who kidnapped her because they hadn't bothered to blindfold her.*

11. **posture** (pos · ture) (pos′ chur) *n.* The placing or carriage of the body or parts of the body; a mental position or frame of mind. *His sitting **posture** is so poor that after a while it may cause him to have back problems.*

12. **post** (pōst) *n.* A position or employment, usually in government service; an assigned beat; a piece of wood or other material to be used as a support; a place occupied by troops. *v.* To inform; to put up (as on a wall); to mail (as a letter). *Do you like the **post** you have with the government?*

13. **proposal** (pro · po · sal) (pro · pō′ zul) *n.* An offer put forth to be accepted or adopted; an offer of marriage; a plan. *As the governor's **proposal** for a tax plan was not acceptable to the people, the legislators voted against it.*

14. **animosity** (an · i · mos · i · ty) (an · i · mos′ i · tē) *n.* (*pl.* **ties**) Hatred; resentment. *She felt great **animosity** toward the persons who attacked her father and beat him so badly that he had to go to the hospital.*

15. **magnanimous** (mag · nan′ i · møus) *adj.* Forgiving of insults or injuries; high-minded; great of soul. *The speaker was very **magnanimous** to overlook the insults that were yelled at him.*

16. **magnify** (mag · ni · fy) (mag′ ni · fī) *v.* To increase the size of; to make larger. *The microscope **magnifies** very small objects so that they can be viewed easily.*

17. **magnificent** (mag · nif · i · cent) (mag · nif′ i · sent) *adj.* Splendid; beautiful; superb. *The palace was so **magnificent** that it was difficult to find words to describe its splendor.*

18. **hypnosis** (hyp · no · sis) (hip · nō′ sis) *n.* (*pl.* **ses; sēz**) A sleeplike trance that is artifically brought about. *I can't believe that I was put in a state of **hypnosis** and did all those silly things, because I do not remember anything that took place.*

19. **federal** (fed′ er · al) *adj.* Of or formed by a compact relating to or formed by an agreement between two or more states, groups, and so on; relating to a union of states, groups, and so on in which central authority in common affairs is established by consent of its members. *All the states in the*

220

*United States joined to form a **federal** government in which common affairs, such as foreign policy, defense, and interstate commerce, are controlled by the government.*

20. **confide** (con · fīde′) *v.* To tell in trust; to tell secrets trustingly. *If you do not want others to know your secrets, **confide** only in people you can trust.*

21. **innate** (iṇ · nāte′) *adj.* Inborn; born with; not acquired from the environment; belonging to the fundamental nature of something; beginning in; coming from. *Innate characteristics are those that cannot be acquired after birth.*

22. **postnatal** (post · nat · al) (pōst · nāt′ ul) *adj.* Occurring after birth. *It is important that all infants receive good **postnatal** care.*

23. **prenatal** (prē · nāt′ ul) *adj.* Being or taking place before birth. *A pregnant woman should take good care of herself so that her unborn child will be receiving good **prenatal** care.*

24. **nature** (na · ture) (nā′ chur) *n.* The necessary quality or qualities of something; sort; kind; wild state of existence; uncivilized way of life; overall pattern or system; basic characteristic of a person; inborn quality; the sum total of all creation; the whole physical universe. *It seems to be his **nature** to behave in such a friendly manner all the time.*

25. **popular** (pop · u · lar) (pop′ yu · lar) *adj.* Referring to the common people or the general public; approved of; admired; liked by most people. *Jack and Herb were voted the most **popular** boys in their class because they were liked by the most people.*

26. **population** (pop · u · la · tion)(pop · yu · lā′ shun) *n.* Total number of people living in a country, city, or any area. *According to the census figures, the **population** in the United States is about 220,000,000 people.*

27. **equivalent** (e · quiv · a · lent) (e · kwiv′ a · lent) *adj.* Equal in value, meaning, force, and so on. *The amounts were **equivalent**, so that each person had exactly the same number.*

Special Notes

1. Do not confuse the word *post*, meaning "a position or employment," "a support for a sign," "to inform," and so on, with the combining form *post* meaning "after." The word *post* comes from the combining form *pos, pon*, meaning "place" or "set."

2. The word *innate* meaning "born with" refers to characteristics or qualities with which you are born. You cannot acquire these after birth. The term *innate* can also be applied to things about which you say that something is such an important part of the thing in question that it is necessarily a part of

221

it. For example: the *innate* weakness of certain kinds of government. Note that "innate weakness" does not mean "inborn weakness." *Inborn* can apply only to living beings.

3. When the term *federal* is spelled with a capital letter, it means "relating to or supporting the central government of the United States" or "relating to or loyal to the Union cause in the American Civil War of 1861–1865."
   a. The *Federal* Bureau of Investigation is an agency of the United States that investigates violations of *federal* criminal laws.
   b. The *Federal* soldiers were those who fought for the Union cause in the Civil War.

Step III. Practice

A. Directions: A number of sentences with missing words follows. Choose the word that *best* fits the sentence. Put the word in the blank. Each word is used only once.

Word List

dismiss, mission, population, popular, submit, animosity, equivalent, intermission, admission, transmit, positive, post, magnify, position, prenatal, postnatal, proposal, postpone, posture, magnanimous, confide, federal, magnificent, hypnosis, nature, innate, permission.

1. Tom has to _____ his report to his advisor for approval.

2. The _____ in some cities is so large that there are not enough jobs for all the people.

3. A misanthrope would have _____ toward all people because he or she is a hater of mankind.

4. The men are going on such a secret_____that even they do not yet know what they are supposed to accomplish.

5. It appears that our jobs are _____ because we have the same duties to perform, and we're getting paid the same.

6. I wonder how it feels to be the most _____ person in school and be admired by practically everyone?

7. Have you gained _____ to the school you want to go to in the fall?

8. Did you know that the company will have to_____ a number of persons because it is not as productive as it was?

9. Tonight the network is going to_____the television program from England to the United States.

222

10. Will the _____ between events be long or short?

11. Try to _____ the conference for as long as you can so that we can gather more information.

12. The politician running for office was presenting his _____ on the issue of school busing.

13. If you always sit slouched over and never stand up straight, you will have bad _____ .

14. I am _____ that the capital of the United States is Washington, D.C.

15. She has been employed in a very important _____ in government service for the past decade.

16. When Ms. Smith was pregnant, she visited her obstetrician every month to make sure that she was receiving proper _____ care.

17. When Jim's third _____ of marriage was turned down, he began to wonder whether there was something wrong with him.

18. Babies who are born prematurely need special _____ care.

19. _____ people are so great of spirit that they can overlook many things that others of us may not be able to overlook.

20. Some people _____ their errors so that they seem larger than they are.

21. One of the wealthiest men in the world built himself the most _____ mansion that has ever been seen.

22. While under the spell of _____ , I did some very embarrassing things that I would not have done if I had been awake.

23. As she was born with that defect, it is _____ .

24. When we went on our camping trip, we went to a place that was away from all civilization, and we lived in a state of _____ .

25. I _____ only in people I know I can trust.

26. Although in a(n) _____ government all states must obey laws that are common to all, each state does have control of its own internal affairs.

27. In many states you need your parents' _____ in order to be allowed to marry under the age of eighteen.

STOP. Check answers at the end of Chapter Six (p. 249).

B. Directions: A list of definitions follows. Give the word that *best* fits the definition. Try to relate the definition to the meanings of the combining forms

Word List

dismiss, admission, submit, transmit, intermission, position, postpone, positive, posture, post, proposal, magnanimous, permission, magnify, magnificent, hypnosis, federal, confide, innate, postnatal, prenatal, nature, popular, population, equivalent, animosity, mission.

1. To send from one place to another _____
2. Sure of something _____
3. A piece of wood or other material to be used as a support _____
4. The manner in which a thing is placed _____
5. Forgiving of insults or injuries _____
6. The placing or carriage of the body _____
7. Time between events _____
8. A sleeplike trance that is artificially brought about _____
9. Splendid _____
10. An offer put forth to be accepted or adopted _____
11. Being before birth _____
12. Born with _____
13. Occurring after birth _____
14. The necessary qualities of something _____
15. Relating to or formed by an agreement among two or more states _____
16. To reveal in trust _____
17. To enlarge _____
18. Hatred _____
19. Total number of people living in a country _____
20. Entrance fee _____
21. Task or responsibility _____
22. Equal in value, meaning, and so on _____
23. Liked by most people _____
24. To delay _____

25. To tell or allow to go _____

26. To give in to another _____

27. A consent _____

STOP. Check answers at the end of Chapter Six (p. 249).

C. Directions: Sentences containing the meaning of vocabulary presented in Exercise 15 follow. Choose the word that *best* fits the meaning of the word or phrase underlined in the sentence.

Word List

admission, dismissed, popular, position, mission, submit, intermission, equivalent, magnanimous, posts, positive, posture, innate, nature, prenatal, postnatal, magnify, magnificent, postpone, transmit, hypnosis, federal, population, confide, animosity, proposal, permission.

1. Because I did not have the entrance fee, I could not enter the park.

   _____

2. I refuse to give in to that group of people's way of doing things.

   _____

3. After working there for a decade, I was told that I was going to be let go.

   _____

4. I am certain that this is the correct way to put that together. _____

5. The city we visited was exceptionally impressive. _____

6. Could you please put off going on that trip for another two weeks?

   _____

7. Your carriage is so poor when you walk. Can't you straighten up?

   _____

8. We used strong timber to hold up our birdhouse. _____

9. Will there be a break between the acts in the show? _____

10. All week the newsreporters had to pass on information about the floods so that people would know when they could return to their homes.

    _____

11. It's rare to meet someone who can turn the other check and be so forgiving of insults. _____

12. I need something that will increase the size of this print so that I can see it better. _____

13. The doctor gave me <u>suggestions to induce a sleeplike trance</u> so that he could try to cure me of my phobia of heights. _____

14. Have you read my <u>plan</u> in full? _____

15. Children need good <u>after birth</u> care. _____

16. It's difficult to determine <u>the basic characteristic</u> of a person. _____

17. The color of your eyes is determined by your genes and is an <u>inborn</u> characteristic. _____

18. I always try to give the twins <u>equal</u> attention. _____

19. I am shocked at what my best friend will <u>reveal</u> to me <u>in trust</u>. _____

20. In order to have a good start in life, a child needs good <u>before birth</u> care. _____

21. What type of government are we talking about when we say "<u>relating to a union of states in which central authority in common affairs is established by consent of its members</u>"? _____

22. Some leaders tend to be more <u>admired</u> than others. _____

23. Do you know <u>the total number of people</u> in your community?

_____

24. The government would not give its <u>consent</u> to some aliens to remain in this country when it was found out that the aliens had criminal records in their own countries. _____

25. Do you have a <u>special task</u> that you must accomplish? _____

26. Is this <u>the proper place</u> for the chair? _____

27. <u>The hatred</u> that the people felt for the demagogue who attempted to deceive them was evident in their faces. _____

STOP. Check answers at the end of Chapter Six (p. 249).

EXTRA WORD
POWER

> **mal.** Bad; ill; evil; wrong; not perfect. *Mal* is found at the beginning of a great number of words. Examples: *malfunction*—to function badly; *malnourished*—badly nourished; *malformed*—abnormally formed; *maltreated*—treated badly. How many more words with *mal* can you supply? Check your dictionary for a list of words beginning with *mal*.
>
> **semi.** Half; not fully; partly; occurring twice in a

period. *Semi* is found at the beginning of a great number of words. For example: *semiblind*—partly blind; *semicircle*—half circle; *semiannual*—twice in a year, every half year; *semistarved*—partly starved; *semiwild*—partly wild. How many more words with *semi* can you supply? Check your dictionary for a long list of words beginning with *semi*.

PEANUTS •   **By Charles M. Schulz**

© 1960 United Feature Syndicate, Inc.

Additional Words Derived from Combining Forms

From your knowledge of combining forms, can you define the following words?

1. **equivocate** (e · quiv · o · cate) (e · kwiv′ o · cāte) *v. He always seems to equivocate when he does not want to commit himself to giving an exact answer.*

   _____

2. **missile** (mis′ sile) *n. That big stone, which he used as a missile, hit its target.*

   _____

3. **remission** (re · mis · sion) (re · mish′ un) *n. The doctors were delighted that the disease had reached a state of remission and was now dormant.*

   _____

4. **emissary** (em · is · sa · ry) (em′ is · sa · rē) *n. Usually, an emissary is sent to another country to try to learn about the other country's plans and to try to influence the plans.*

   _____

5. **intermittent** (in · ter · mit′ tent) *adj. Because the pain was intermittent, he had some pain-free moments.*

   _____

6. **intercede** (in · ter · cede) (in · ter · sēde′) *v. The company's trouble-shooter was called upon to intercede in the dispute that had hurt relations between the company and the town.*

   _____

227

7. **intervene** (in · ter · vēnǥ´) *v. Because the strike had been going on for so long, the courts decided to* **intervene** *by asking for a "cooling off" period for both sides.*

---

8. **proposition** (prop · o · si · tion) (prop · o · zish´ un) *n. His* **proposition** *sounded like a very sophisticated plan; so we decided to consider it at our next conference.*

---

9. **disposition** (dis · po · si · tion) (dis · po · zish´ un) *n. Because he has such a good* **disposition**, *I'm sure that he will be very nice to you.*

---

10. **depose** (de · pose) (de · pōzǥ´) *v. After some monarchs have been* **deposed**, *they have been executed.*

---

11. **expound** (ex · pound) (ik · spound´) *v. As the class had difficulty understanding the concept of intelligence, the professor* **expounded** *further on it.*

---

12. **infidelity** (in · fi · del · i · ty) (in · fi · del´ i · tē) *n. Both spouses were suing for divorce on the grounds of* **infidelity** *because each had found that the other had been unfaithful.*

13. **perfidious** (per · fid · i · ous) (per · fid´ ē · ǥus) *adj. I did not know that I had a* **perfidious** *friend until I heard from others that my secrets had all been told.*

---

14. **magnate** (mag´ nātǥ) *n. Howard Hughes, a* **magnate** *of considerable wealth, lived in seclusion the last years of his life.*

---

15. **malediction** (mal · e · dic · tion) (mal · e · dik´ shun) *n. The words* **malediction** *and* benediction *are antonyms.*

---

16. **malefactor** (mal · e · fac · tor) (mal´ e · fak · tor) *n. When a* **malefactor** *is caught by the police, he usually is sent to jail for his crimes.*

---

17. **animate** (an´ i · mātǥ) *v. When Arthur tells a story, he becomes so* **animated** *that every part of him is alive and active.*

STOP. Check answers at the end of Chapter Six (p. 250).

Practice for Additional Words Derived from Combining Forms

Directions: Match each word with the *best* definition.

_____ 1. equivocate

_____ 2. missile

_____ 3. remission

_____ 4. proposition

_____ 5. disposition

_____ 6. animate

_____ 7. malediction

_____ 8. infidelity

_____ 9. malefactor

_____ 10. intervene

_____ 11. intercede

_____ 12. intermittent

_____ 13. emissary

_____ 14. perfidious

_____ 15. depose

_____ 16. expound

_____ 17. magnate

a. a criminal; one who does something bad

b. breach of trust; adultery

c. a speaking badly of someone

d. to come between

e. starting or stopping again

f. a person sent on a special mission

g. a temporary stopping of a disease

h. to remove from a throne or other high position

i. to come between

j. to use ambiguous language on purpose

k. a very important or influential person

l. a plan put forth for consideration

m. one's usual frame of mind

n. to state in detail

o. to make alive

p. a weapon intended to be thrown

q. treacherous

STOP. Check answers at the end of Chapter Six (p. 250).

CROSSWORD PUZZLE 5

Directions: The meanings of many of the combining forms from Exercises 13–15 follow. Your knowledge of these combining forms will help you to solve this crossword puzzle. Note that *combining form* is abbreviated as *comb. f.*

Across

1. Slang for a large crowd
3. A musical syllable
5. Same as #4 Down
6. Comb. f. for *equal*
7. Comb. f. for *out of; from; lacking*
8. Abbreviation of *mail*
9. Comb. f. for *sleep*
11. A friend
12. Ready to eat

Down

1. Way of saying *mother*
2. Comb. f. for *war*
3. Comb. f. for *faith*
4. Comb. f. for *without*
7. Comb. f. for *wander*
8. Meaning of *homo*
10. Comb. f. for *wrong*
11. Comb. f. for *peace*
13. Comb. f. for *after*

230

15. Comb. f. for *spirit; mind*
19. You feel this way when you ache
21. Abbreviation of *masculine*
24. An insect
25. Antonym of *happy*
26. Comb. f. for *I; me*
27. An insect
29. Rhymes with *hat*
30. Antonym of *bottom*
31. Meaning of *mono* and *uni*
32. Comb. f. for *one who*
34. Same as #32 Across
35. Eighth letter of the alphabet
36. Antonym of *actress*
37. Comb. f. for *new*
39. Sixteenth letter of the alphabet
40. Same as #7 Across
41. Meaning of *hyper*
44. Meaning of *dorm*
48. Meaning of *cura*
49. On a nice day it shines
50. Antonym of *off*
52. Third letter of the alphabet
53. A number rhyming with *fine*
55. The highest card is an ____
56. Another word for *clear*
58. Comb. f. for *one who*
59. Eighteenth letter of the alphabet
60. Thirteenth letter of the alphabet
61. Meaning of *en; em*
62. Same as #38 Down
64. Pronoun referring to *us*
65. Twenty-fifth letter of the alphabet
66. Antonym of *no*
67. Same as #61 Across
68. Same as #18 Down

14. Time period
16. Comb. f. for *large*
17. Not required
18. Comb. f. for *stand*
20. Ending added to form past tense of regular verbs
21. A subway in Paris
22. Something that happened long____
23. Comb. f. for *wise*
28. Homonym of *two*
29. Same as #4 Down
33. Abbreviation of *railroad*
34. Antonym of *off*
38. Comb. f. for *voice*
39. Comb. f. for *around*
42. A truck for moving
43. When you take the same books out of the library, you____them
45. Comb. f. for *clear; light*
46. Antonym of *friend*
47. Comb. f. for *city*
51. A woman who lives in a convent
52. Comb. f. for *citizen*
54. Poetic way of saying *before*
57. Contraction for *do not*
63. Same as #52 Across

STOP. Check answers at the end of Chapter Six (p. 251).

WORD SCRAMBLE 5

Directions: Word Scramble 5 is based on words from Exercises 13-15. The meanings are your clues to arranging the letters in correct order. Write the correct word in the blank.

Meanings

1. netttaino   ————————   mental concentration

2. stneoin   ————————   mental strain

3. gllieeebtnr   ————————   warlike

4. aciliinv   ————————   one not in the military

5. vlcii   ————————   polite

6. tiocispl   ————————   the science or art of government

7. locav   ————————   referring to voice

8. tocovain   ————————   a person's work

9. goubumais   ————————   having two or more meanings

10. cayfip   ————————   to quiet

11. cludi   ————————   clear

12. rerro   ————————   mistake

13. phosreomo   ————————   second-year student

14. crmuctinecas   ————————   something connected with an act

15. bistttuues   ————————   to put in place of

16. tasiss   ————————   aid

17. blaceost   ————————   something in the way

18. stpresi   ————————   to continue in some course

19. loven   ————————   new

20. mordtan   ————————   inactive

21. rediop   ————————   a portion of time

22. tegrccineo   ————————   self-centered

23. ismnosi   ————————   the task or responsibility a person is assigned

24. smissid   ————————   to tell to go

25. dimsonias   ————————   entrance

26. tusbim   ————————   to give in to another

27. trinessimnoi   ————————   time between events

28. tenoospp   ————————   to put off

29. sitviope   ————————   definitely set; sure

232

30. stop   _____ to inform; piece of timber

31. sloprpao   _____ an offer

32. gaimyfn   _____ to enlarge

33. nosyhpsi   _____ sleeplike trance artificially brought on

34. nodifec   _____ to reveal in trust

35. tanine   _____ born with

36. ratneu   _____ necessary qualities of something

37. luoppra   _____ liked by most people

38. quelineavt   _____ equal to

39. timanysio   _____ hatred

STOP. Check answers at the end of Chapter Six (p. 251).

ANALOGIES 5

Directions: Find the word from the following list that *best* completes each analogy. There are more words in the list than you need.

Word List

avocation, vocation, vacation, civilian, persist, polite, malediction, convocation, infidelity, tense, intention, novel, malefactor, active, peace, lucid, impolite, intense, expert, novice, inactive, innate, nature, aid, magnificent, dismiss, confide, animosity, oral, vocabulary, civilization, knowledge, proposal, politics, politician, attorney, stubborn, visage, consequence, sequence, affect, cyclone, decimate, fertilization, fertile, agnostic, concession, procession, antitoxin, contemporary, toxicologist, content.

1. Credible : incredible :: benediction :_____.

2. Uniform : same :: criminal : _____.

3. Hyper : hypo :: ambiguous :_____.

4. Admit : deny :: civil :_____.

5. Independent : dependent :: veteran :_____.

6. Intention : aim :: assembly : _____.

7. Quiet : vociferous :: relaxed :_____.

8. Entrance : exit :: dormant : _____.

9. Shy : bashful :: tenacious : _____.

10. Magnify : enlarge :: unfaithfulness : _____.

11. Belligerent : war :: pacifist : _____.

12. Content : dissatisfied :: love : _____.

13. Pine : tree :: banking : _____.

14. Infinite : finite :: military : _____.

15. Unpopular : popular :: weak : _____.

16. Error : mistake :: assist : _____.

17. Monotonous : changeless :: continue : _____.

18. Provoke : irritate :: unusual : _____.

19. Astronomer : stars :: philosopher : _____.

20. Position : post :: vocal : _____.

STOP. Check answers at the end of Chapter Six (pp. 251–252).

MULTIPLE-CHOICE VOCABULARY TEST 5

Directions: This is a test on words in Exercises 13–15. Words are presented according to exercises. *Do all exercises before checking answers.* Underline the meaning that *best* fits the word.

Exercise 13

1. attention
   a. aim
   b. mental strain
   c. mental concentration
   d. very strong

2. intention
   a. mental concentration
   b. extreme force
   c. mental strain
   d. aim

3. tension
   a. mental strain
   b. aim
   c. mental concentration
   d. very strong

4. intense
   a. mental strain
   b. very strong
   c. mental concentration
   d. aim

5. belligerent
   a. aim
   b. very strong
   c. hatred
   d. warlike

6. civilian
   a. polite
   b. a state of human society
   c. refers to citizenship
   d. person not in the military

7. civics
   a. cultural development
   b. not in uniform
   c. polite
   d. the study of the rights and responsibilities of citizenship

8. civilization
   a. dealing with citizens
   b. polite
   c. cultural development, as of a people
   d. not in the military

9. civil
   a. not in uniform
   b. polite
   c. cultural development
   d. the study of the rights and responsibilities of citizens

10. politics
    a. science or art of government
    b. cultural development
    c. rule by people
    d. refers to a city

11. politician
    a. science or art of government
    b. refers to citizens
    c. refers to a city
    d. person engaged in the science or art of government

12. metropolitan
    a. surrounding area of a city
    b. a person involved in city government
    c. city government
    d. referring to a major city center and its surrounding area

13. vocal
    a. manner of speaking
    b. referring to the voice
    c. referring to a person's work
    d. referring to peace

14. vocabulary
    a. refers to work
    b. refers to the voice
    c. refers to new words
    d. list of words that are defined

15. vocation
    a. one's work
    b. voice
    c. outspoken
    d. list of words

16. ambiguous
    a. referring to two
    b. having two or more meanings
    c. referring to many words
    d. referring to words with the same meanings

17. postscript
    a. a letter
    b. something written
    c. a signature
    d. something added to a letter after the writer's signature

18. pacify
    a. an agreement
    b. to calm
    c. to help
    d. to work with

Exercise 14

19. lucid
    - a. a light
    - b. clear
    - c. permitting light to go through
    - d. to view

20. translucent
    - a. a clear view
    - b. light
    - c. permitting light to go through but not allowing a clear view
    - d. light can go through and permits a clear view

21. error
    - a. to walk around
    - b. to wander off walking
    - c. a mistake
    - d. to lie

22. sophisticated
    - a. worldly-wise
    - b. very knowledgeable
    - c. not clever
    - d. to know how to dress

23. sophomore
    - a. third-year student
    - b. immature person
    - c. someone who is knowledgeable
    - d. someone not too smart

24. philosophy
    - a. refers to knowledge
    - b. wise man
    - c. the study of human knowledge
    - d. charity

25. circumstances
    - a. the conditions surrounding an act
    - b. the acts
    - c. the events
    - d. aims

26. substitute
    - a. to put in place of
    - b. to place
    - c. to set
    - d. to take

27. consist
    - a. to place
    - b. to stand
    - c. to put together
    - d. to be made up of

28. assist
    - a. to stand by
    - b. to stand off
    - c. to help
    - d. to place

29. distant
    - a. separated by time and/or space
    - b. a relation
    - c. refers to space
    - d. to stand by

30. obstacle
    - a. something helpful
    - b. something harmful
    - c. something that stands in the way
    - d. a large rock

31. persist
    - a. to stand around
    - b. to move on
    - c. to stand for
    - d. to continue in some course even when it is difficult

32. innovation
    a. a book
    b. a strange idea
    c. something newly introduced
    d. an immunization

33. novel
    a. refers to a nonfiction book
    b. new
    c. something done over
    d. refers to a biography

34. dormitory
    a. a house
    b. a room
    c. a resort
    d. a building providing sleeping and living quarters at a school

35. dormant
    a. active
    b. inactive
    c. awake
    d. referring to door

36. period
    a. a circle
    b. time
    c. portion of time
    d. portion of something

37. hypertension
    a. mental strain
    b. very strong force
    c. very tired
    d. high blood pressure

38. egocentric
    a. not concerned with self
    b. self-centered
    c. self-sufficient
    d. able to help self

Exercise 15

39. mission
    a. the task or responsibility a person is assigned
    b. a vacation trip
    c. a house
    d. atomic particles

40. permission
    a. weekly allowance
    b. a consent
    c. to give in to
    d. to give

41. dismiss
    a. to leave
    b. to let alone
    c. to tell to go
    d. to go

42. admission
    a. act of allowing to enter
    b. allow to do
    c. refers to money
    d. an allowance

43. submit
    a. to allow to do
    b. to let go
    c. to give in to
    d. to help

44. transmit
    a. to send away
    b. to give in
    c. to let go
    d. to send from one place to another

45. intermission
   a. a space
   b. time period
   c. a responsibility
   d. time between events

46. position
   a. place occupied by a thing
   b. to put off
   c. something proper
   d. to put away

47. postpone
   a. to mail
   b. to delay
   c. to put away
   d. to stay

48. positive
   a. the manner of sitting
   b. to put off
   c. sure of
   d. not confident

49. posture
   a. a place
   b. a setting
   c. the manner of carrying the body
   d. mental strain

50. post
   a. a government job
   b. government
   c. to put off
   d. to serve

51. proposal
   a. to put off
   b. to send away
   c. an acceptance
   d. an offer

52. magnanimous
   a. large
   b. highly spirited
   c. forgiving of insults
   d. splendid

53. magnify
   a. to see from
   b. something large
   c. to help
   d. to enlarge

54. magnificent
   a. forgiving of insults
   b. large of spirit
   c. splendid
   d. large

55. animosity
   a. full of spirit
   b. refers to the mind
   c. hatred
   d. large of soul

56. hypnosis
   a. sleep
   b. put to sleep
   c. a sleeplike trance artificially brought on
   d. a drug

57. federal
   a. government
   b. relating to states
   c. faith in government
   d. relating to an agreement between two or more states to join into a union

58. confide
   a. faith in
   b. to tell in trust
   c. to tell everything
   d. to give information

59. innate
   a. not born
   b. acquired after birth
   c. birth
   d. born with

60. postnatal   a. refers to nose condition   c. born with
                 b. occurring before birth   d. occurring after birth

61. prenatal   a. refers to birth   c. occurring before birth
                 b. born with   d. occurring after birth

62. nature   a. outside   c. the necessary qualities of something
                 b. flowers   d. a person

63. popular   a. people   c. the number of people
                 b. approved of   d. lots of people

64. population   a. people   c. liked by people
                 b. total number of people living in an area   d. an area in which people live

65. equivalent   a. equal to   c. a comparison
                 b. unlike   d. a mathematical sign

TRUE/FALSE TEST 5

Directions: This is a true/false test on Exercises 13–15. Read each sentence carefully. Decide whether it is true or false. Put a *T* for *true* or an *F* for *false* in the blank. The number after the sentence tells you if the word is from Exercise 13, 14, or 15.

_____ 1. When you pay <u>attention</u> to something, you do not need to concentrate. 13

_____ 2. A <u>pacifist</u> is <u>belligerent</u>. 13

_____ 3. A <u>civilian</u> is a member of the armed forces. 13

_____ 4. *Intense* and *tension* are synonyms. 13

_____ 5. If you live in a <u>metropolitan</u> area, you are in or near a major city. 13

_____ 6. If you <u>postpone</u> something, you are putting it off. 15

_____ 7. A <u>proposal</u> is something you must accept. 15

_____ 8. All <u>intermissions</u> are at least ten minutes. 15

_____ 9. A <u>sophisticated</u> plan is a complex plan. 14

_____10. You can clearly see through something <u>translucent</u>. 14

_____11. Politics is the science of people. 13

_____12. Civilization can exist in the wilderness without people. 13

_____13. Your vocation is what you are called. 13

_____14. A postscript is the last paragraph of your essay. 13

_____15. When you are ambiguous, what you say can be taken two ways. 13

_____16. The way you dress would be due to innate factors. 15

_____17. *Equivalent* and *similar* are synonyms. 15

_____18. An egocentric person is concerned with himself or herself. 14

_____19. To persist in a course means you need an assist. 14

_____20. *Civil* and *rude* are antonyms. 13

_____21. An innovation is an archaic plan. 14

_____22. A dormant disease is in remission. 14, 15

_____23. To transmit information means that you send it from one place
to another. 15

_____24. *Hypnosis* and *dormant* are synonyms. 15, 14

_____25. *Animosity* and *love* are antonyms. 15

_____26. *Submit* and *concede* are synonyms. 15

_____27. A person who behaves like a sophomore is someone who is worldly-
wise. 14

_____28. Federal refers to all unions. 15

_____29. Only astronauts can go on missions. 15

_____30. A novel can be an autobiography. 14

STOP. Check answers for both tests at the end of Chapter Six (p. 252).

SCORING OF TESTS

Multiple-Choice Vocabulary Test		True/False Test	
Number Wrong	*Score*	*Number Wrong*	*Score*
0–4	Excellent	0–3	Excellent
5–10	Good	4–6	Good
11–14	Weak	7–9	Weak
Above 14	Poor	Above 9	Poor
Score _____		Score _____	

1. If you scored in the excellent or good range on *both tests,* you are doing well. Go on to Chapter Seven.

2. If you scored in the weak or poor range on either test, look below and follow directions for Additional Practice. Note that the words on the tests are arranged so that you can tell in which exercise to find them. This will help you if you need additional practice.

ADDITIONAL PRACTICE SETS

A. Directions: Write the words you missed on the tests from the three exercises in the space provided. Note that the tests are presented so that you can tell to which exercises the words belong.

Exercise 13 Words Missed

1. _____   6. _____
2. _____   7. _____
3. _____   8. _____
4. _____   9. _____
5. _____   10. _____

Exercise 14 Words Missed

1. _____   6. _____
2. _____   7. _____
3. _____   8. _____
4. _____   9. _____
5. _____   10. _____

Exercise 15 Words Missed

1. _____   6. _____
2. _____   7. _____
3. _____   8. _____
4. _____   9. _____
5. _____   10. _____

B. Directions: Restudy the words that you have written down on this page. Study the combining forms from which those words are derived.

Do Step I and Step II for those you missed. Note that Step I and Step II of the combining forms and vocabulary derived from these combining forms are on the following pages:

Exercise 13—pp. 199–202.

Exercise 14—pp. 208–211.

Exercise 15—pp. 218–222.

C. Directions: Do Additional Practice 1 on this page and the next if you missed words from Exercise 13. Do Additional Practice 2 on pp. 243–244 if you missed words from Exercise 14. Do Additional Practice 3 on pp. 244–246 if you missed words from Exercise 15. Now go on to Chapter Seven.

Additional Practice 1 for Exercise 13

A. Directions: The combining forms presented in Exercise 13 follow. Match the combining form with its meaning.

_____ 1. tend, tens, tent   a. war

_____ 2. bello, belli   b. city

_____ 3. civ, civis   c. stretch; strain

_____ 4. polis   d. after

_____ 5. pac, pax   e. both

_____ 6. voc, vox   f. peace

_____ 7. post   g. voice; call

_____ 8. ambi   h. citizen

STOP. Check answers at the end of Chapter Six (p. 252).

B. Directions: The words presented in Exercise 13 follow. Match the word with its meaning.

_____ 1. attention   a. aim

_____ 2. intention   b. person not in the military

_____ 3. tension   c. cultural development, as of a people

_____ 4. intense

_____ 5. belligerent   d. mental concentration

_____ 6. civilian   e. the science or art of government

_____ 7. civics   f. referring to a major city center and its surrounding area

242

_____ 8.	civilization	g. warlike
_____ 9.	civil	h. referring to the voice
_____ 10.	politics	i. job; profession
_____ 11.	politician	j. able to be taken two or more ways
_____ 12.	metropolitan	
_____ 13.	vocal	k. having extreme force
_____ 14.	vocabulary	l. person engaged in the science or art of government
_____ 15.	vocation	
_____ 16.	ambiguous	m. the study of the rights and responsibilities of citizenship
_____ 17.	postscript	
_____ 18.	pacify	n. to calm
		o. something written after signature
		p. polite; relating to ordinary community life
		q. a list of words with definitions
		r. mental strain

STOP. Check answers at the end of Chapter Six (p. 252).

Additional Practice 2 for Exercise 14

A. Directions: The combining forms presented in Exercise 14 follow. Match the combining form with its meaning.

_____ 1.	luc, lum	a. wise
_____ 2.	err	b. sleep
_____ 3.	soph	c. stand
_____ 4.	sist, sta	d. light; clear
_____ 5.	nov	e. I; me; the self
_____ 6.	dorm	f. over; above; excessive
_____ 7.	peri	g. wander
_____ 8.	hyper	h. around
_____ 9.	ego	i. new

STOP. Check answers at the end of Chapter Six (p. 253).

B. Directions: The words presented in Exercise 14 follow. Match the
word with its meaning.

_____ 1. lucid	a.	second-year student
_____ 2. translucent	b.	to put in place of
_____ 3. error	c.	separated by time and/or space
_____ 4. sophisticated	d.	work of fiction of some length
_____ 5. sophomore	e.	clear
_____ 6. philosophy	f.	something newly introduced
_____ 7. circumstances	g.	inactive
_____ 8. substitute	h.	to continue in some course even when it is difficult
_____ 9. assist	i.	the study of human knowledge
_____ 10. consist	j.	mistake
_____ 11. distant	k.	to help
_____ 12. obstacle	l.	worldly-wise
_____ 13. persist	m.	something in the way of
_____ 14. innovation	n.	something connected with an act
_____ 15. novel	o.	portion of time
_____ 16. dormitory	p.	self-centered
_____ 17. dormant	q.	permitting light to go through but not allowing a clear view
_____ 18. period	r.	high blood pressure
_____ 19. hypertension	s.	a building providing sleeping quarters
_____ 20. egocentric	t.	to be made up of

STOP. Check answers at the end of Chapter Six (p. 253).

Additional Practice 3 for Exercise 15

A. Directions: The combining forms presented in Exercise 15 follow.
Match the combining form with its meaning.

_____ 1. miss, mitt   a. spirit; mind; soul

_____ 2. pon, pos   b. born

_____ 3. anima, animus   c. place; set

_____ 4. magna   d. people

_____ 5. hypn, hypno   e. trust; faith

_____ 6. feder, fid, fide   f. great; large

_____ 7. nasc, nat   g. equal

_____ 8. equi   h. sleep

_____ 9. pop   i. send

STOP. Check answers at the end of Chapter Six (p. 253).

B. Directions: The words presented in Exercise 15 follow. Match the word with its meaning.

_____ 1. mission   a. place occupied by a thing

_____ 2. dismiss   b. sure of

_____ 3. admission   c. time between events

_____ 4. permission   d. the manner of carrying the body

_____ 5. submit   e. to enlarge

_____ 6. transmit   f. referring to agreement of two or more states to join into a union

_____ 7. intermission

_____ 8. position   g. the task or responsibility of a person

_____ 9. postpone

_____ 10. positive   h. sleeplike trance artificially brought on

_____ 11. posture

_____ 12. post   i. occurring after birth

_____ 13. proposal   j. necessary qualities of something or someone

_____ 14. magnanimous

_____ 15. animosity   k. to give in to

_____ 16. magnify   l. to tell to go

_____ 17. magnificent   m. splendid

_____ 18. hypnosis   n. total number of people in an area

_____ 19. federal   o. occurring before birth

_____20. confide	p.	forgiving of insults
_____21. innate	q.	liked by many people
_____22. postnatal	r.	government job
_____23. prenatal	s.	act of allowing to enter
_____24. nature	t.	to send from one place to another
_____25. popular	u.	to tell in trust
_____26. population	v.	hatred
_____27. equivalent	w.	equal to
	x.	a consent
	y.	born with
	z.	to delay
	aa.	an offer

STOP. Check answers at the end of Chapter Six (p. 253).

ANSWERS: Chapter Six

Exercise 13 (pp. 199–208)

Practice A

(1) attention, (2) intention, (3) tension, (4) intense, (5) pacify, (6) belligerent, (7) civics, (8) civilian, (9) politics, (10) politician, (11) ambiguous, (12) vocation, (13) civilization, (14) civil, (15) vocal, (16) vocabulary, (17) postscript, (18) metropolitan.

Practice B

(1) c, (2) d, (3) b, (4) d, (5) c, (6) c, (7) b, (8) d, (9) c, (10) a, (11) d, (12) b, (13) d (14) b, (15) a, (16) a, (17) c, (18) d.

Practice C

(1) mental concentration, (2) aims, (3) mental strain, (4) very strong, (5) warlike, (6) one not in the military, (7) the part of political science dealing with the rights and responsibilities of citizens, (8) cultural development of a people, (9) the science or art of government, (10) polite, (11) one who is in politics, (12) referring to a major city center and surrounding area, (13) freely expressive of opinions, (14) stock of words, (15) work, (16) having two or more meanings, (17) addition to a letter after signature, (18) calm.

Additional Words Derived from Combining Forms (pp. 206–207)

1. **postmortem.** Happening or performed after death; pertaining to an examination of a human body after death; a postmortem examination; autopsy.

2. **posterior.** Located behind; in the rear; later; following after; coming after in order; succeeding; (sometimes *pl.*) the buttocks.

3. **posterity.** Future generations; all of one's descendants (offsprings).

4. **posthumously.** After death.

5. **provoke.** To stir up anger or resentment; to irritate.

6. **pacifist.** One who is against war.

7. **megalopolis.** One very large city made up of a number of cities; a vast, populous, continuously urban area.

8. **ambidextrous.** Able to use both hands equally well.

9. **vociferous.** Of forceful, aggressive, and loud speech; marked by a loud outcry; clamorous.

10. **convocation.** A group of people called together; an assembly.

11. **avocation.** Something one does in addition to his or her regular work, usually for enjoyment; a hobby.

12. **irrevocable.** Not to be recalled, withdrawn, or annulled; irreversible; not able to be changed.

13. **detention.** A keeping or holding back; confinement; the state of being detained in jail.

14. **detente.** Easing of strained relations, especially between nations.

Practice for Additional Words Derived from Combining Forms (p. 208)

(1) d, (2) i, (3) n, (4) j, (5) e, (6) k, (7) a, (8) b, (9) m, (10) h, (11) f, (12)c, (13) l, (14) g.

Exercise 14 (pp. 208–218)

Practice A

(1) error, (2) lucid, (3) translucent, (4) philosophy, (5) circumstance, (6) sophomore, (7) sophisticated, (8) substitute, (9) assist, (10) distant, (11) obstacle, (12) consist, (13) innovation, (14) novel, (15) dormant, (16) dormitory, (17) persist, (18) egocentric, (19) hypertension, (20) period, (21) periodical.

Practice B

(1) lucid, (2) translucent, (3) error, (4) none—sophisticated, (5) sophomore, (6) philosophy, (7) none—circumstances, (8) substitute, (9) consist, (10) assist,

(11) distant, (12) obstacle, (13) persist, (14) innovation, (15) novel, (16) dormitory, (17) dormant, (18) period, (19) periodical, (20) none—hypertension, (21) none—egocentric.

WORD SQUARE

I	N	N	O	V	A	T	I	O	N	P	T	S
I	S	P	E	R	S	I	S	T	O	H	R	Q
D	O	D	I	S	T	A	N	T	V	I	A	W
O	P	O	B	S	T	A	C	L	E	L	N	K
R	H	R	L	U	S	S	O	E	L	O	S	T
M	O	M	O	B	Y	S	N	R	I	S	L	D
A	M	I	O	S	N	I	S	R	N	O	U	L
N	O	T	M	T	O	S	I	O	G	P	C	Y
T	R	O	E	I	N	T	S	R	S	H	E	H
R	E	R	R	T	Y	O	T	E	E	Y	N	W
O	L	Y	R	U	L	U	C	I	D	E	T	N
P	M	Y	O	T	O	D	U	E	E	O	R	A
H	O	M	P	E	R	I	O	D	I	C	A	L

Practice C

(1) separated by distance, far away, (2) inactive, (3) conditions, (4) permitting light to go through, (5) mistake, (6) clear, (7) is made up of, (8) the study of human knowledge, (9) place that houses persons, (10) put in place of, (11) help, (12) obstruction, (13) new methods, (14) continue, (15) punctuation mark that signals a full stop, (16) publication issued at fixed time intervals, (17) high blood pressure, (18) self-centered, (19) immature person, (20) cultured, (21) unusual.

Additional Words Derived from Combining Forms (pp. 216–217)

1. **perimeter.** A measure of the outer part or boundary of a closed plane figure; boundary line of a closed plane figure.

2. **periphery.** The outer part or boundary of something.

3. **periscope.** An instrument used by a submarine to see all around.

4. **hyperbole.** Great exaggeration or overstatement.

5. **illuminate.** To give light to; light up; make clear.

6. **egotistic.** Conceited; very concerned with oneself; selfish; vain.

7. **novice.** Someone new at something; a rookie; a beginner.

8. **stamina.** Staying power; resistance to fatigue, illness, and the like.

9. **obstinate.** Stubborn; tenacious.

10. **sophistry.** Faulty reasoning; unsound or misleading but clever and plausible (appearing real) argument or reasoning.

11. **erratic.** Wandering; not regular; not stable.

12. **periodic.** Occurring or appearing at regular intervals.

Practice for Additional Words Derived from Combining Forms (pp. 217-218)

(1) i, (2) e, (3) h, (4) g, (5) f, (6) a, (7) b, (8) j, (9) k, (10) c, (11) d, (12) l.

Exercise 15 (pp. 218-229)

Practice A

(1) submit, (2) population, (3) animosity, (4) mission, (5) equivalent, (6) popular, (7) admission, (8) dismiss, (9) transmit, (10) intermission, (11) postpone, (12) position or proposal, (13) posture, (14) positive, (15) post or position, (16) prenatal, (17) proposal, (18) postnatal, (19) Magnanimous, (20) magnify, (21) magnificent, (22) hypnosis, (23) innate, (24) nature, (25) confide, (26) federal, (27) permission.

Practice B

(1) transmit, (2) positive, (3) post, (4) position, (5) magnanimous, (6) posture, (7) intermission, (8) hypnosis, (9) magnificent, (10) proposal, (11) prenatal, (12) innate, (13) postnatal, (14) nature, (15) federal, (16) confide, (17) magnify, (18) animosity, (19) population, (20) admission, (21) mission, (22) equivalent, (23) popular, (24) postpone, (25) dismiss, (26) submit, (27) permission.

Practice C

(1) admission, (2) submit, (3) dismissed, (4) positive, (5) magnificent, (6) postpone, (7) posture, (8) posts, (9) intermission, (10) transmit, (11) magnanimous, (12) magnify, (13) hypnosis, (14) proposal, (15) postnatal, (16) nature, (17) innate, (18) equivalent, (19) confide, (20) prenatal, (21) federal, (22) popular, (23) population, (24) permission, (25) mission, (26) position, (27) animosity.

Additional Words Derived from Combining Forms (pp. 227-228)

1. **equivocate.** To use ambiguous language on purpose.

2. **missile.** An object, especially a weapon, intended to be thrown or discharged, as a bullet, an arrow, a stone, and so on.

3. **remission.** A temporary stopping or lessening of a disease; a pardon.

4. **emissary.** A person or an agent sent on a specific mission.

5. **intermittent.** Starting or stopping again at intervals; not continuous; coming and going at intervals.

6. **intercede.** To come between; to come between as an influencing force; to intervene.

7. **intervene.** To come between; to act as an influencing force; to intercede.

8. **proposition.** A plan or something put forth for consideration or acceptance.

9. **disposition.** One's usual frame of mind or one's usual way of reacting; a natural tendency.

10. **depose.** To remove from a throne or other high position; to let fall.

11. **expound.** To state in detail; to set forth; to explain.

12. **infidelity.** Breach of trust; lack of faith in a religion; unfaithfulness of a marriage partner; adultery.

13. **perfidious.** Violating good trust; treacherous; deceitful; deliberately faithless.

14. **magnate.** A very important or influential person.

15. **malediction.** A speaking badly of someone; slander; a curse.

16. **malefactor.** Someone who does something bad; one who commits a crime; a criminal.

17. **animate.** To make alive; to move to action.

Practice for Additional Words Derived from Combining Forms (p. 229)

(1) j, (2) p, (3) g, (4) l, (5) m, (6) o, (7) c, (8) b, (9) a, (10) d, i, (11) i, d, (12) e, (13) f, (14) q, (15) h, (16) n, (17) k.

Crossword Puzzle 5 (pp. 230–231)

1.M	O	2.B			3.F	4.A		
5.A		6.E	Q	U	I		7.E	
	8.M	L			9.D	O	R	10.M
11.P	A	L				12.R	I	13.P 14.E
15.A	N	I	16.M 17.U 18.S			19.S	O	R 20.E
21.M 22.A 23.S	C		24.A	N	T		25.S	A D
26.E	G	O	27.G	N	A	28.T	29.A	T
30.T	O	P	31.O	N	E		32.O	33.R
34.O	R		35.H		36.A	C	T	O R
37.N	O	38.V		39.P		40.E		
	41.O 42.V	E	43.R		44.S 45.L 46.E	E	47.P	
48.C	A	R	E		49.S U N		50.O 51.N	52.C
	53.N	I	54.E		55.A C E		56.L U C I	57.D
	58.E	R		59.R 60.M		61.I	N	62.V O 63.C
	64.W	E		65.Y	66.Y	E	S	67.I N
								68.S T A

Word Scramble 5 (pp. 231–233)

(1) attention, (2) tension, (3) belligerent, (4) civilian, (5) civil, (6) politics, (7) vocal, (8) vocation, (9) ambiguous, (10) pacify, (11) lucid, (12) error, (13) sophomore, (14) circumstance, (15) substitute, (16) assist, (17) obstacle, (18) persist, (19) novel, (20) dormant, (21) period, (22) egocentric, (23) mission, (24) dismiss, (25) admission, (26) submit, (27) intermission, (28) postpone, (29) positive, (30) post, (31) proposal, (32) magnify, (33) hypnosis, (34) confide, (35) innate, (36) nature, (37) popular, (38) equivalent, (39) animosity.

Analogies 5 (pp. 233–234)

(1) malediction, (2) malefactor, (3) lucid, (4) impolite, (5) novice, (6) convocation, (7) tense, (8) active, (9) stubborn, (10) infidelity, (11) peace, (12) animosity,

(13) vocation,[1] (14) civilian, (15) intense, (16) aid, (17) persist, (18) novel, (19) knowledge, (20) oral.

Multiple-Choice Vocabulary Test 5 (pp. 234-239)

Exercise 13

(1) c, (2) d, (3) a, (4) b, (5) d, (6) d, (7) d, (8) c, (9) b, (10) a, (11) d, (12) d, (13) b, (14) d, (15) a, (16) b, (17) d, (18) b.

Exercise 14

(19) b, (20) c, (21) c, (22) a, (23) b, (24) c, (25) a, (26) a, (27) d, (28) c, (29) a, (30) c, (31) d, (32) c, (33) b, (34) d, (35) b, (36) c, (37) d, (38) b.

Exercise 15

(39) a, (40) b, (41) c, (42) a, (43) c, (44) d, (45) d, (46) a, (47) b, (48) c, (49) c, (50) a, (51) d, (52) c, (53) d, (54) c, (55) c, (56) c, (57) d, (58) b, (59) d, (60) d, (61) c (62) c, (63) b, (64) b, (65) a.

True/False Test 5 (pp. 239-240)

(1) F, (2) F, (3) F, (4) F, (5) T, (6) T, (7) F, (8) F, (9) T, (10) F, (11) F, (12) F, (13) F, (14) F, (15) T, (16) F, (17) T, (18) T, (19) F, (20) T, (21) F, (22) T, (23) T, (24) F,[2] (25) T, (26) T, (27) F, (28) F, (29) F, (30) F.

STOP. Turn to page 240 for the scoring of the tests.

Additional Practice Sets (pp. 241-246)

Additional Practice 1

A. (1) c, (2) a, (3) h, (4) b, (5) f, (6) g, (7) d, (8) e.
B. (1) d, (2) a, (3) r, (4) k, (5) g, (6) b, (7) m, (8) c, (9) p, (10) e, (11) l, (12) f, (13) h, (14) q, (15) i, (16) j, (17) o, (18) n.

---

[1] *Vocation* is the answer because the relationship between *pine* and *tree* is one of *classification.*
[2] Persons can be active while under *hypnosis.* Also, *hypnosis* is a noun and *dormant* is an adjective.

Additional Practice 2

A. (1) d, (2) g, (3) a, (4) c, (5) i, (6) b, (7) h, (8) f, (9) e.

B. (1) e, (2) q, (3) j, (4) l, (5) a, (6) i, (7) n, (8) b, (9) k, (10) t, (11) c, (12) m, (13) h, (14) f, (15) d, (16) s, (17) g, (18) o, (19) r, (20) p.

Additional Practice 3

A. (1) i, (2) c, (3) a, (4) f, (5) h, (6) e, (7) b, (8) g, (9) d.

B. (1) g, (2) l, (3) s, (4) x, (5) k, (6) t, (7) c, (8) a, (9) z, (10) b, (11) d, (12) r, (13) aa, (14) p, (15) v, (16) e, (17) m, (18) h, (19) f, (20) u, (21) y, (22) i, (23) o, (24) j, (25) q, (26) n, (27) w.

©1974 by NEA, Inc. Reprinted by permission of NEA, Inc.

CHAPTER SEVEN

EXERCISE 16

Step I. Combining Forms

A. Directions: A list of combining forms with their meanings follows. Look at the combining forms and their meanings. Concentrate on learning each combining form and its meaning. Cover the meanings, read the combining forms, and state the meanings to yourself. Check to see if you are correct. Now cover the combining forms, read the meanings, and state the combining forms to yourself. Check to see if you are correct.

Combining Forms	*Meanings*
1. pater, patri	father
2. phil, phile, philo	love
3. psych, psyche, psycho	spirit; mind; soul
4. se	apart
5. greg	flock

B. Directions: Cover the preceding meanings. Write the meanings of the following combining forms.

255

Combining Forms	*Meanings*
1. pater, patri	_____
2. phil, phile, philo	_____
3. psych, psyche, psycho	_____
4. se	_____
5. greg	_____

Step II. Words Derived from Combining Forms

1. **paternal** (pa · ter′ nal) *adj.* Of or like a father; fatherly; related on the father's side of the family; inherited or received from the father. *My girlfriend resented her boyfriend's behaving in such a **paternal** manner toward her.*

2. **paternity** (pa · ter · ni · ty) (pa · ter′ ni · tē) *n.* Fatherhood; state of being a father; origin or descent from a father; provides for citizenship of the child born out of wedlock if fatherhood is established. *The court would try to determine the **paternity** of the child.*

3. **paternalism** (pa · ter · nal · ism) (pa · ter′ nal · iz · um) *n.* The principle or practice of managing the affairs of a country or group of employees as a father manages the affairs of children. *The employees resented the **paternalism** of their employer.*

4. **patricide** (pat · ri · cide) (pat′ ri · sīd¢) *n.* The murder of one's own father. *The crime was an especially horrible one because it concerned **patricide**; however, when the jurors learned all the circumstances of the crime and how the father had mistreated his children, the crime became more understandable.*

5. **patriotic** (pa · tri · ot · ic) (pā′ trē · ot · ik) *adj.* Characteristic of a person who loves his or her country; loving one's country; showing support and loyalty of one's country. *Many **patriotic** people were aroused to anger when they saw the American flag being dragged through the mud.*

6. **patron** (pā′ tron) *n.* A person who buys regularly at a given store or who goes regularly to a given restaurant, resort, and so on; a regular customer; a wealthy or influential supporter of an artist or writer; one who gives one's wealth or influence to aid an institution, an individual, or a cause; a guardian saint or god. *I have been a **patron** of that restaurant for several years.*

7. **philanthropist** (phi · lan · thro · pist) (fi · lan′ thro · pist) *n.* A person who shows love toward one's fellow human beings by active efforts to promote their welfare; one who shows goodwill toward others by practical

kindness and helpfulness. *The **philanthropist** contributed a great amount of money to the community for worthy causes.*

8. **psychology** (psy · chol · o · gy) (p̸sī · kol′ o · jē) *n.* The science of the mind; the science that studies the behavior of humans and other animals; the mental or behavioral characteristics of a person or persons. *We took a course in **psychology** because we wanted to learn more about people's behavior and why they act as they do.*

9. **psychiatrist** (psy · chi · a · trist) (p̸sī · kī′ a · trist) *n.* A doctor who specializes in the treatment of persons with mental, emotional, or behavioral disorders. *The court requested that a **psychiatrist** examine the defendant to determine whether he was legally sane and able to stand trial.*

10. **psychotic** (psy · chot · ic) (p̸sī · kot′ ik) *adj.* Having to do with or caused by serious mental disease; insane. *The psychiatrist said that the defendant was **psychotic** and should not stand trial because he was criminally insane.*

11. **gregarious** (gre · gar · i · ous) (gre · gar′ ē ȯus) *adj.* Tending to live in a flock, herd, or community rather than alone; marked by a fondness to be with others than alone; outgoing; sociable. *Jane, who is shy, is the opposite of her **gregarious** husband, who can't stand being alone.*

12. **congregate** (con · gre · gate) (kon′ gre · gāt̸) *v.* To come together into a group, crowd, or assembly; to assemble; to come together or collect in a particular place or locality. *Everyone **congregated** around the famous actor and tried to get his autograph.*

13. **aggregate** (ag · gre · gate) (ag′ ȼre · git) *n.* A mass of separate things joined together; the whole sum or amount; the total. *adj.* Formed by the collection of units or particles into a body, mass, or amount; total. *v.* To amount to; to come to; to total; to come together in a mass or group; to collect; unite; accumulate. *Taken separately, the amount was not very much, but in the **aggregate**, it was very high.*

14. **segregate** (seg′ re · gāt̸) *v.* To set apart from others; to separate. *Try not to **segregate** yourself from others at the party; be more sociable.*

15. **seclusion** (se · clu · sion) (se · klū′ zhun) *n.* The act of keeping apart from others; the act of confining in a place hard to find; the act of segregating or hiding; the act of isolating oneself; isolation. *The writer said that she was going into **seclusion** to finish writing her novel because she needed complete quiet and solitude to finish her work.*

16. **seduce** (se · duce) (se · dūs̸′) *v.* To tempt to wrongdoing; to persuade into disobedience; to persuade or entice (lead on by exciting desire) into partnership in sexual intercourse. *In the film the older man tried to **seduce** the young girl, but she did not allow herself to be enticed by the older man's charm and money.*

257

17. **sedition** (se · di · tion (se · dish′ un) *n.* Conduct consisting of speaking, writing, or acting against an established government or seeking to overthrow it by unlawful means; incitement to rebellion or discontent. *Anyone found guilty of sedition can be severely punished by the government, especially in times of war.*

Special Note

Note that the word *philosophy* appears in Exercise 14. *Philosophy* is derived from the combining form *philo* as well as *soph.*

Step III. Practice

A. Directions: Define the underlined word in each of the following sentences.

1. My paternal grandfather died of a heart attack at an early age, so my father feels that his chances of having one are pretty high. _____

2. The company I work for operates on the principles of paternalism, but many of us resent the company's attitude of always knowing what is best for us. _____

3. I read a book recently in which there was so much hatred between the father and his sons that it actually led to patricide. _____

4. I feel that I am as patriotic as the next person, but I don't like to march in parades or wave flags to prove my patriotism. _____

5. At the dance the boys segregated themselves in the left corner of the room, and the girls segregated themselves in the right corner of the room.
_____

6. At the trial the lawyer was trying to prove that his client had not seduced the young girl but that she had been a willing partner and that she had in fact seduced his client. _____

7. The money the charity ball amassed aggregated one hundred thousand dollars. _____

8. After the death of her famous husband, she went into seclusion and refused to see or speak to anyone. _____

9. I have been a patron of this restaurant for a long time, but after my treatment today I will no longer frequent this restaurant. _____

10. Today many more fathers are taking paternity more seriously, and in a number of situations fathers rather than mothers are raising the children.
_____

11. The well-known philanthropist donated his fortune to his university and to a cat. _____

12. Because John is such a gregarious person, you almost never find him alone.
_____

258

13. When my friend kept having the same nightmare for weeks and weeks, and she became ill from lack of sleep, we suggested that she seek help from a psychiatrist. _____

14. At our school the students seem to congregate at the student center. _____

15. Pat majored in psychology at college because she wanted to be a psychologist. _____

16. We knew that the man was peculiar because of his odd behavior, but we didn't realize that he was psychotic until he went on a wild rampage and tried to kill many people. _____

17. In the United States, as well as in other countries, sedition against the government is a serious crime. _____

STOP. Check answers at the end of Chapter Seven (p. 295).

B. Directions: Match each word with the best definition.

_____ 1. paternal	a. one who shows goodwill by giving practical help
_____ 2. patron	b. insane
_____ 3. psychology	c. to come together in a group
_____ 4. psychiatrist	d. a wealthy supporter of an artist
_____ 5. paternity	e. tending to live in a flock
_____ 6. psychotic	f. fatherhood
_____ 7. philanthropist	g. fatherly
_____ 8. patriotic	h. the total
_____ 9. segregate	i. to tempt to wrongdoing
_____ 10. congregate	j. the murder of one's own father
_____ 11. aggregate	k. the science of the mind
_____ 12. sedition	l. the act of keeping apart from others
_____ 13. seduce	m. incitement to rebellion
_____ 14. patricide	n. to separate
_____ 15. paternalism	o. loving one's country
_____ 16. gregarious	p. a specialist in the disorders of the mind
_____ 17. seclusion	q. the practice of managing a company in a fatherly way

STOP. Check answers at the end of Chapter Seven (p. 295).

C. Directions: A number of sentences with missing words follow. Choose the word that *best* fits the sentence. All the words are used.

Word List

paternal, patron, psychology, psychiatrist, paternity, psychotic, philanthropist, patriotic, segregate, congregate, seclusion, gregarious, paternalism, patricide, aggregate, sedition, seduce.

1. Looking at the _____ of my past experiences with the firm, I should have known better and not trusted them.

2. The _____ said that she could not help me unless I trusted her and told her everything that bothered me and all my feelings.

3. My brother has always behaved in a(n) _____ manner toward me because there is a fifteen-year age span between us.

4. Dennis is taking a lot of _____ courses at school because he is interested in learning about the behavior of persons.

5. During the Renaissance, many artists were fortunate to have a person who acted as a(n) _____ to them.

6. A person who is _____ should be confined in a mental institution.

7. My _____ friend is never alone.

8. My friends tend to _____ at my house.

9. There is one group of people at school who tend to _____ themselves from all the other students.

10. Because Joseph is an outgoing person, he does not like _____.

11. No one can _____ me into doing anything I do not want to do.

12. It is difficult to determine the _____ of a child with one hundred percent accuracy.

13. Congress is responsible for passing laws against the crime of

    _____.

14. _____ is a horrible crime.

15. Some countries govern based on a policy of _____.

16. The _____ man said that he had fought for his country before and that he was ready to fight for it again.

17. There is a(n) _____ in our town who has helped many persons and who can always be counted on to give to needy causes.

STOP. Check answers at the end of Chapter Seven (p. 295).

ous. Full of; having. **Ous** is found at the end of a
great number of adjectives. For example: *wondrous—*
full of wonder; *joyous—*full of joy; *monogamous—*
having to do with monogamy.

ize. To cause to be or become; to be like; to be formed
into. *Ize* is found at the end of many verbs. For example: *unionize—*to form into a union; *Americanize—*
to become an American; *liquidize—*to cause to be
liquid.

Additional Words Derived from Combining Forms

From your knowledge of combining forms, can you define the following words?

1. **expatriate** (ex · pa · tri · ate) (eks · pā′ trē · āt¢) *v.* (eks · pā′ trē · it) *n.*
*A number of Russians have **expatriated** themselves from Russia and fled
to the United States.*

_____

2. **bibliophile** (bib · li · o · phile) (bib′ lē · o · fīl¢) *n. My brother, who is a
bibliophile, spends all his time reading or taking out books from the library.*

_____

3. **philanthrope** (phil · an · thrope) (fil′ an · thrōp¢) *n. It seems incredible
that in the same family you can have a person who is a misanthrope and
another who is a **philanthrope**.*

_____

4. **philanderer** (phi · lan · der · er) (fi · lan′ der · er) *n. Jane will not marry
Jim because she wants to marry someone whom she can trust rather than
a **philanderer**.*

_____

5. **psychosis** (psy · cho · sis) (p̸sī · kō′ sis) *n.* (*pl.* **ses**) *The psychiatrist said
that Jim's behavior indicated that he had some form of **psychosis** and that
he would have to be hospitalized.*

_____

6. **psychopath** (psy · cho · path) (p̸sī′ ko · path) *n. The police felt that the
horrible murders were being committed by a **psychopath**.*

_____

7. **psychic** (psy · chic) (p̸sī′ kik) *n. adj. My friend went to a psychic because
he felt that the **psychic** could help him communicate with his dead fiancée.*

_____

8. **egregious** (e · gre · gious) (e · grē′ jus) *adj.* *The doctor's **egregious** mistake may cost him the life of his patient.*

STOP. Check answers at the end of Chapter Seven (pp. 295–296).

Practice for Additional Words Derived from Combining Forms

Directions: Match each word with the *best* definition.

_____ 1. expatriate

_____ 2. bibliophile

_____ 3. philanthropist

_____ 4. philanderer

_____ 5. psychosis

_____ 6. psychopath

_____ 7. psychic

_____ 8. egregious

a. a mentally ill person

b. a mental disorder characterized by lost contact with reality

c. conspicuously bad

d. a lover of books

e. a person sensitive to nonphysical forces

f. a person who has many love affairs with no intention of marriage

g. one who has renounced his or her native country

h. a person who shows his or her love to mankind by helpfulness to mankind

STOP. Check answers at the end of Chapter Seven (p. 296).

EXERCISE 17

Step I. Combining Forms

A. Directions: A list of combining forms with their meanings follows. Look at the combining forms and their meanings. Concentrate on learning each combining form and its meaning. Cover the meanings, read the combining forms, and state the meanings to yourself. Check to see if you are correct. Now cover the combining forms, read the meanings, and state the combining forms to yourself. Check to see if you are correct.

Combining Forms	*Meanings*
1. matr, matri, matro	mother
2. juris, jus	law

3. di   two

4. vers, vert   turn

5. rog   ask; beg

B. Directions: Cover the preceding meanings. Write the meanings of the following combining forms.

Combining Forms	Meanings
1. matr, matri, matro	_____
2. juris, jur	_____
3. di	_____
4. vers, vert	_____
5. rog	_____

Step II. Words Derived from Combining Forms

1. **maternal** (ma · ter′ nal) *adj.* Motherly; having to do with a mother; inherited or derived from a mother; related on the mother's side of the family. *My friend behaves in a **maternal** manner toward her boyfriend, but he seems to like it.*

2. **maternity** (ma · ter · ni · ty) (ma · ter′ ni · tē) *n.* The state of being a mother; motherhood; a hospital or section of a hospital designated for the care of women immediately before and during childbirth and for the care of newborn babies. *adj.* Pertaining to or associated with the period in which a woman is pregnant, and with childbirth. *When my sister started to have labor pains, her husband rushed her to the **maternity** ward in the hospital.*

3. **matrimony** (mat · ri · mo · ny) (mat′ ri · mō · nē) *n.* The act or state of being married; the union of man and woman as husband and wife; marriage. ***Matrimony** is something that should not be gone into lightly.*

4. **justice** (jus · tice) (jus′ tis¢) *n.* The maintenance of what is reasonable and well founded; the assignment of deserved rewards or punishments; the quality or characteristic of being fair and impartial; rightfulness; correctness. *The man said with all **justice** that he had not been treated fairly.*

5. **justification** (jus · ti · fi · ca · tion) (jus · ti · fi · kā′ shun) *n.* A reason, circumstance, explanation, or fact that justifies or defends; good reason. *Everyone felt that the defendant had great **justification** to do what she did; however, she shouldn't have because it was against the law.*

6. **juror** (ju′ ror) *n.* One of a group of persons sworn to deliver a verdict in a case submitted to them; member of a jury. *The jury was deadlocked because one **juror** kept voting differently from the other **jurors**.*

7. **divorce** (di • vorce) (di • vorsȼ') *n.* A legal dissolvement of a marriage relation usually by a court or other body having the authority; the legal ending
of a marriage. *v.* To end legally a marriage; separate; disunite. *Even though
the rate of divorce seems to be increasing each year, the institution of
marriage is still respected.*

8. **dilemma** (di • lem' ma) *n.* Any situation that necessitates a choice between
equally unfavorable or equally unpleasant alternatives; an argument that
presents two equally unfavorable alternatives. *Jane has a dilemma because
she didn't study for her exam. If she takes the exam, she will fail it, but
if she doesn't take the exam, her instructor will give her an automatic "F."*

9. **divide** (di • vīdȼ') *v.* To separate into parts. *We were trying to figure out
how to divide the pie when our dog jumped on the table and ate it all up.*

10. **divert** (dī • vert') *v.* To turn aside or from a path or course; to draw off to
a different course, purpose, and so on. *The police were trying to divert the
robbers' attention so that they could sneak to the back of the bank.*

11. **versatile** (ver' sa • tilȼ) *adj.* Capable of turning from one subject, task, or
occupation to another; able to do many things well; many-sided; changeable; variable. *The versatile actor has played many different types of roles.*

12. **converse** (con • verse) (kon' versȼ) *n.* A thing, especially a statement, that
is turned around, usually producing a different idea or meaning; something
that is opposite or contrary. *adj.* Opposite; contrary; turned about. *The
converse of "all persons are animals" would not be correct.*

13. **reversible** (re • vers • ible) (re • ver' si • bul) *adj.* Capable of being opposite
or contrary to a previous position; having two finished or usable sides (of a
fabric, and so on). *I have a reversible jacket that I wear a lot, but someone
thought that I had two different jackets because the sides are so different.*

14. **adverse** (ad • versȼ') or (ad' versȼ) *adj.* Hostile; contrary to one's interest
or welfare; unfavorable. *Her adverse remarks made us realize how hostile
she was to our position on the issue.*

15. **controversy** (con • tro • ver • sy) (kon' tro • ver • sē) *n.* (*pl.* **sies**) A dispute,
especially a lengthy and public one, between sides holding opposing views;
a quarrel; debate; argument. *The controversy that has been raging for so
long between the two opponents may be settled soon.*

16. **advertise** (ad • ver • tise) (ad' ver • tīzȼ) *v.* To give public notice of in
newspapers, on radio, on television, and so on; to praise the good qualities
of a product, service, and so on; to call attention to; to notify, inform.
*Sponsors advertise their products because they feel that this helps to sell
them.*

17. **interrogate** (in • ter' ro • gātȼ) *n.* To ask questions of formally; to examine
by questioning. *The police said that everyone in the room would be*

interrogated and that no one could leave because the answer to the mystery was contained in that room.

18. **arrogant** (ar' to • gant) *adj.* Full of pride and self-importance; overbearing; haughty. *The **arrogant** man made me feel very uncomfortable because I do not like persons who are overbearing and impressed with their own importance.*

19. **derogatory** (de • rog • a • to • ry) (de • rog' a • tor • ē) *adj.* Tending to make less well regarded; tending to belittle someone or something; disparaging; belittling. *When the hostess kept making **derogatory** remarks about everyone, Sharon stood up, got her hat and coat, and left.*

Special Note

The term *converse* (kon • versé') can also be a verb meaning "to talk informally together." This definition is not presented in this lesson.

Step III. Practice

A. Directions: A list of definitions follow. Choose the word from the word list that *best* fits the definition.

Word List

maternal, maternity, matrimony, justice, justification, juror, divorce, dilemma, divide, divert, versatile, converse, reversible, adverse, controversy, advertise, interrogate, arrogant, derogatory.

1. good reason   _____

2. member of a jury   _____

3. the state of being a mother   _____

4. the maintenance of what is
   reasonable   _____

5. to ask questions formally   _____

6. tending to belittle someone   _____

7. to end legally a marriage   _____

8. overbearing   _____

9. the act of being married   _____

10. having two usable sides   _____

11. to draw off to a different
    course   _____

265

12. an argument that presents two
    equally unfavorable alternatives   _____

13. something that is opposite or
    contrary   _____

14. a dispute   _____

15. hostile   _____

16. to praise the good qualities of   _____

17. motherly   _____

18. to separate into parts   _____

19. changeable   _____

STOP. Check answers at the end of Chapter Seven (p. 296).

B. Directions: A few paragraphs with missing words follow. Fill in the blanks
                with the word that *best* fits. Words may be used more than
                once.

Word List

*maternal, maternity, matrimony, justice, justification, juror, divorce, dilemma,
divide, divert, versatile, converse, reversible, adverse, controversy, advertise,
interrogated, arrogant, derogatory.*

   My best friend was the first of our group to get a(n) 1_____ .
After having been married for two years, he decided that 2_____
was not for him. He told us that his wife behaved in a very 3_____
manner to him and if he wanted someone 4_____ he could
go back home to his mother. His wife, on the other hand, did not want a(n)
5_____ . She felt that there was no 6_____ for
one. She wanted them to go to a marriage counselor, but my friend didn't
want to. In all 7_____ , I should say that my friend is a(n)
8_____ person, who thinks a lot of himself, and that his
wife would probably be better off without him. He has always made
9_____ remarks about his wife, so we didn't know why he
married her in the first place. When we 10_____ my friend
about this, he said that he had met her when he was a(n) 11_____ .
She, too, was a(n) 12_____ . It seems that the case was a very
complicated one, and they spent a lot of time together. She had a strong sense
of 13_____ , and during the trial she tried to see to it that
14_____ would triumph. The case concerned a(n)
15_____ that had been going on for a long time and that
finally ended in violence. However bitter the 16_____ , there
was no 17_____ for the violence. One 18_____

always tried to 19 _____ the others from their purpose, but his wife always got them back on the track. She helped the others to see the 20 _____ that the defendant had and how he felt that he had no choice. My friend said that he fell in love with her then and wanted to marry her. Interestingly, she did not want to enter 21 _____ with him at that time. She is a nurse who works in the 22 _____ ward and she didn't feel that she was ready for marriage. My friend pursued her. He actually said that he would 23 _____ his love for her in the papers if she didn't marry him. We were surprised to hear this since, as I've said, my friend is such a(n) 24 _____ fellow. It seemed incredible to me that his position was in the 25 _____ now and that he had such 26 _____ feelings toward his wife. My friend said that he did indeed love his wife when they were married, but he doesn't now. She treats him as if he were an infant in the 27 _____ ward. She is not very 28 _____, so she is not able to change her role from being a nurse to being a wife. He felt that she would not change, so he decided to get a(n) 29 _____.

My friend did get the 30 _____, but to this day they haven't decided how to 31 _____ their property because she has refused to discuss it with him or the lawyers.

STOP. Check answers at the end of Chapter Seven (p. 296).

C. Directions: Define the underlined word in each of the following sentences.

1. Jim Sloan must believe in <u>matrimony</u> because he has been married about thirteen times. _____

2. Jim Sloan must be an expert on <u>divorce</u> because of his many marriages. _____

3. Psychologists claim that a woman does not automatically have <u>maternal</u> instincts and these must be learned. _____

4. There is no <u>justification</u> for child abuse. _____

5. The boxer knew that he had a <u>dilemma</u> because he would lose whatever his choice. _____

6. A <u>reversible</u> coat serves dual purposes. _____

7. Please refrain from making <u>derogatory</u> remarks about my friends. _____

8. We were in a state of shock when the police stopped our car and said that they were taking us to the police station to <u>interrogate</u> us about a recent robbery. We knew that it was a case of mistaken identity, but how could we prove it? _____

9. The <u>arrogant</u> man talked about his ancestors all evening long.
   _____

10. No one wanted to say anything <u>adverse</u> to him about his friend, but we felt that he should know that his friend was ridiculing him behind his back.
    _____

11. My sister bought some beautiful <u>maternity</u> clothes._____

12. When the baby wanted something that we didn't want her to have we tried to <u>divert</u> her attention away from it. _____

13. How should we <u>divide</u> the monies that we made?_____

14. I feel that the more <u>versatile</u> you are, the better able you are to survive in our society._____

15. The <u>controversy</u> between the two different factions at our plant is threatening our production. _____

16. It seems to me that the <u>converse</u> of that statement is true.
    _____

17. More work needs to be done on this before we <u>advertise</u> its virtues.
    _____

18. The <u>juror</u> said that he could not make up his mind about the guilt of the defendant. _____

19. We felt that <u>justice</u> had been served when the man who had murdered innocent bystanders was himself murdered by one of his partners.
    _____

STOP. Check answers at the end of Chapter Seven (p. 296).

EXTRA WORD POWER

> **tude.** Condition of; state of. *Tude* is found at the end of a great number of nouns. For example: *gratitude*—the state of being grateful; *solitude*—the state of being alone; *exactitude*—the state of being exact.
>
> **ness.** Quality of; state of. *Ness* is found at the end of many nouns. For example: *happiness*—the state of being happy; *goodness*—the state of being good; *preparedness*—the state of being prepared or ready.

Additional Words Derived from Combining Forms

From your knowledge of combining forms, can you define the following words?

1. **matriarch** (ma · tri · arch) (mā′ trē · ark) *n.* *In the novel the main character was a **matriarch** who ruled her family with an iron hand, and no one dared to defy her.*

2. **matricide** (ma · tri · cide) (mā′ tri · sīd¢) *n.* *In the novel one of the sons commits the horrible crime of **matricide** because he hates his mother so much.*

3. **jurisdiction** (ju · ris · dic · tion) (jur · is · dik′ shun) *n.* *The police chief said that he could not help us because he did not have **jurisdiction** in the next county, but he did tell us whom to speak to in the next county.*

4. **jurisprudence** (ju · ris · pru · dence) (jur · is · prū′ dens¢) *n.* *If one were to study the course of court decisions in the United States, one would see that many times **jurisprudence** is influenced by social and economic factors.*

5. **dichotomy** (di · chot · o · my) (dī · kot′ o · mē) *n.* *(pl.* **mies***) The psychiatrist said that the psychopath had been living with the **dichotomy** of good and evil within him.*

6. **adversity** (ad · ver · si · ty) (ad · ver′ si · tē) *n.* *From the day that Jill left school, **adversity** seemed to be her constant companion, even though she tried hard to escape from all the misfortunes.*

7. **pervert** (per · vert′) *v.* (per′ vert) *n.* *It seems inconceivable that a teacher would try to **pervert** young people, but in last night's newspaper it was stated that a teacher was arrested for trying to engage young children in pornographic films.*

8. **aversion** (a · ver · sion) (a · ver′ zhun) *n.* *My friend avoids going to seafood restaurants because she has an **aversion** to fish.*

9. **subversion** (sub · ver · sion) (sub · ver′ zhun) *n.* *When the heads of government found out that a group of persons were attempting the **subversion** of the government, the persons were arrested and thrown into jail.*

10. **introvert** (in'. tro • vert) *n.* (in • tro • vert') *v. Jim is an **introvert**, yet his friends are outgoing persons.*

---

11. **abrogate** (ab' ro • gāte) *v. The student council passed some new bylaws that **abrogated** some former ones, which were outdated.*

---

12. **prerogative** (pre • rog' a • tivé) *n. Because Marie is a gifted person, she has the **prerogative** to go to any school that she wants to.*

---

13. **surrogate** (sur' ţo • gāté) *n. The court appointed a **surrogate** to act in legal matters for the two children whose parents had recently died.*

STOP. Check answers at the end of Chapter Seven (p. 297).

Practice for Additional Words

Directions: Match each word with the *best* definition.

_____ 1. matriarch	a. a substitute
_____ 2. matricide	b. a person drawn inward toward himself or herself
_____ 3. jurisdiction	c. a strong dislike
_____ 4. dichotomy	d. the killing of a mother by a son or daughter
_____ 5. jurisprudence	e. a systematic attempt to overthrow a government
_____ 6. adversity	f. a mother who is ruler of her family
_____ 7. pervert	g. an exclusive or special right or privilege
_____ 8. aversion	h. the limits in which authority may be exercised
_____ 9. subversion	i. to cause to turn away from what is right
_____ 10. abrogate	j. the course of court decisions
_____ 11. prerogative	k. to invalidate
_____ 12. surrogate	l. division into two parts
_____ 13. introvert	m. a hardship

STOP. Check answers at the end of Chapter Seven (p. 297).

EXERCISE 18

Step I. Combining Forms

A. Directions: A list of combining forms with their meanings follows. Look at the combining forms and their meanings. Concentrate on learning each combining form and its meaning. Cover the meanings, read the combining forms, and state the meanings to yourself. Check to see if you are correct. Now cover the combining forms, read the meanings, and state the combining forms to yourself. Check to see if you are correct.

Combining Forms	Meanings
1. sphere	ball
2. therm, thermo	heat
3. techni, techno	arts and crafts (especially industrial arts); method; system; skill
4. hydr, hydra, hydro	water
5. fort	strong
6. tract	draw; pull

B. Directions: Cover the preceding meanings. Write the meanings of the following combining forms.

Combining Forms	Meanings
1. sphere	_____
2. therm, thermo	_____
3. techni, techno	_____
4. hydr, hydra, hydro	_____
5. fort	_____
6. tract	_____

Step II. Words Derived from Combining Forms

1. **sphere** (sfir) *n.* A round geometrical body whose surface is equally distant at all points from the center; any rounded body; a globe, a ball; any of the stars or planets; the place or surroundings in which a person exists, works, lives, and so on. *The United States's* **sphere** *of influence extends across the world.*

2. **hemisphere** (hem · i · sphere) (hem · i · sfir′) *n.* A half sphere or globe; half the earth's surface (either the northern or southern half of the earth as divided by the equator or the eastern or western half as divided by a meridian) *The United States is in the Northern* **Hemisphere.**

3. **atmosphere** (at · mos · phere) (at′ mo · sfir) *n.* The air that surrounds the earth; the mass of gases that surrounds the earth and is held to it by the force of gravity; the air in any given place; a mental or moral environment; surrounding influence; the feeling or coloring that surrounds a work of art. *A heavy* **atmosphere** *seemed to fill the room after Mary spoke to her mother in such harsh and bitter tones.*

4. **thermometer** (ther · mom′ e · ter) *n.* An instrument for measuring the temperature of a body or of space, especially one consisting of a graduated glass tube with a bulb, usually mercury, that expands and rises in the tube as the temperature increases. *We didn't need our outdoor* **thermometer** *to tell us that it was 100 degrees outside; we knew it immediately when we stepped out of the house.*

5. **thermostat** (ther′ mo · stat) *n.* An automatic device for regulating temperature; any device that automatically responds to temperature changes and activates switches controlling equipment such as furnaces, refrigerators, and air conditioners. *We knew that our* **thermostat** *for regulating heat was broken because we were freezing, yet the thermostat was set at 68 degrees.*

6. **thermal** (ther′ mal) *adj.* Pertaining to, using, or causing heat. *In the winter when Jack goes skiing, he wears* **thermal** *underwear to keep warm.*

7. **technical** (tech · ni · cal) (tek′ ni · kal) *adj.* Having to do with an art, science, discipline, or profession; having to do with industrial arts, applied sciences, mechanical trades or crafts; marked by specialization; meaningful or of interest to persons of specialized knowledge rather than to laypersons; marked by a strict legal interpretation. *The document was written in such* **technical** *language that not one of us understood it, so we had to bring it to a lawyer.*

8. **technique** (tech · nique) (tek · nēk′) *n.* The manner in which a scientific or complex task is accomplished; the degree of skill or command of fundamentals shown in any performance. *The doctors claimed that they had perfected a new surgical* **technique** *that should save many lives.*

9. **technician** (tech · ni · cian) (tek · nish′ un) *n.* A specialist in the details of a subject or skill, especially a mechanical one; any artist, musician, and so on with skilled technique. *The lab* **technician** *said that my contact lenses would be ready shortly.*

10. **technology** (tech · nol · o · gy) (tek · nol′ o · jē) *n.* Applied science; a technical method of achieving a practical purpose; the totality of the means employed to provide objects necessary for human existence and

comfort. *Life in a world of **technology** has many, many advantages, but there are some drawbacks too, and people must weigh the drawbacks against the advantages in future endeavors.*

11. **hydrant** (hy · drant) (hī′ drant) *n.* An upright pipe or street fixture with a valve for drawing water directly from a water main; fireplug. *The firefighters said that the pressure from the water **hydrant** was too low and that would make it difficult to put out the fire.*

12. **dehydrate** (de · hy · drate) (dē · hī′ drāt¢) *v.* To remove water from; to lose water or moisture; dry. *After being lost in the desert for a few days with nothing to drink, the three men were **dehydrated**.*

13. **fortress** (for · tress) (for′ tris) *n.* A large place strengthened against attack; a fort or group of forts, often including a town; any place of security; a stronghold. *Some very wealthy persons build homes that are like **fortresses** to protect themselves from thieves.*

14. **fortify** (for · ti · fy) (for′ ti · fī) *v.* To strengthen against attack; to surround with defenses; to strengthen and secure (as a town) by forts; to give physical strength and courage to; to add mental or moral strength to. *In films many persons **fortify** themselves with a drink before they attack some problem.*

15. **fortitude** (for′ ti · tūd¢) *n.* Strength of mind that enables persons to bear pain or encounter danger with courage. *The passerby showed great **fortitude** when he tried to help the man who was being mugged.*

16. **contract** (con · tract) (kon′ trakt) *n.* A binding agreement between two or more persons or parties; a covenant. *After we signed the **contract**, we shook hands.*

17. **contract** (con · tract) (kon · trakt′) *v.* To draw together; to make smaller; shrink; shorten; to shorten a word by omitting one or more sounds or letters; to bring on oneself as an obligation or debt; to get. *The doctor isolated the patient who had a contagious disease because he didn't want the other patients to **contract** it.*

18. **detract** (de · tract) (de · trakt′) *v.* To draw away or divert; to take away a part, as from quality, value, or reputation. *The speaker's mannerisms were so annoying that they **detracted** from what she was saying*

19. **retract** (re · tract) (re · trakt′) *v.* To draw back; to take back; to withdraw. *The politician apologized and said that he wanted to **retract** his earlier statements in which he had criticized the mayor of the town.*

20. **traction** (trac · tion) (trak′ shun) *n.* The act of drawing; the state of being drawn; the force exerted in drawing; friction; in medicine, a pulling or drawing of a muscle, organ, and so on for healing a fracture, dislocation, and so on. *My friend's doctor had to be put in **traction** because he had a slipped disk.*

21. **abstract** (ab • stract) (ab' strakt) *adj.* Thought of apart from any specific object; disassociated from any particular instance; difficult to understand; theoretical; not concrete. *n.* A short statement giving the main points of a book, article, or research paper. *Our professor asked us to write an* **abstract** *of three research articles.*

22. **abstract** (ab • stract) (ab • strakt') *v.* To take away or remove; to withdraw; to take away secretly, slyly, or dishonestly; to divert; to make an abstraction. *The company spy was able to* **abstract** *the information that she wanted without anyone knowing about it.*

Special Notes

1. Note that the words *contract* (kon' trakt) *n.* and *contract* (kon • tract') *v.* are spelled identically but are pronounced differently and have different meanings. Most of the words that you have met have had more than one meaning; however, they were usually pronounced the same. Because the words *contract* (kon' trakt) *n.* and contract (kon • trakt') *v.* are usually pronounced differently (pronunciations vary from region to region) and each word has meanings different from those of the other, they are presented separately. The same holds for the words *abstract* (ab' strakt) *adj.*, *n.* and *abstract* (ab • strakt') *v.*, which are presented in the main part of the exercise, and for the words *forte* (forté) *n.* and forte (for' ta) *adj.*, *adv.*, which are presented in the Additional Words section.

2. The word *hydrophobia,* which is derived from the combining forms *hydro* and *phob,* is presented in Exercise 3.

3. The word *subtraction,* which is derived from the combining forms *sub, ion,* and *tract,* is presented in the Extra Word Power section of Exercise 12.

A. Directions: A number of sentences with missing words follow. Choose the word that *best* fits the sentence. Put the word in the blank. Notice that two words are presented twice because they are used twice.

Word List

sphere, hemisphere, atmosphere, thermometer, thermostat, thermal, technical, technique, technician, technology, hydrant, dehydrate, fortress, fortify, fortitude, contract, detract, retract, traction, abstract, abstract, contract.

1. When the three men in trench coats walked into the diner, the _____ seemed to change.

2. The coach said that the only thing I need to _____ me against my opponent is the knowledge that I am better than he and that I will win the match.

3. Herbert was afraid that Jane's outlandish costume would _____ from what she had to say.

4. When the speaker realized that he had made an error, he said that he wanted to _____ his former statement.

5. The author said that she was in a state of ecstasy when she signed her first _____ to write a book.

6. The victims of the fire said that they didn't think that they had the _____ to continue after their house and all their belongings were burned to ashes, but they did.

7. We knew that we were in serious trouble when the concrete for the foundation of our house began to _____ from the cold.

8. When the _____ read 104 degrees, we thought it was broken, but the doctor said that the reading was correct and that our friend had pneumonia.

9. The athlete was in terrible pain from a pulled muscle, so the doctor put him in _____ .

10. In what _____ is Canada?

11. The students protested that the _____ was set too low in the dormitory and that the students were freezing.

12. Many people sleep with a(n) _____ blanket in the winter to keep warm.

13. That is too _____ for me; I need something more concrete.

14. The report is too _____ for me to understand; put it in plain language.

15. Her _____ for making jam earned her a fortune.

16. My brother is a(n) _____ in an electronics plant.

17. The twenty-first century will be known for even more _____ than the twentieth century.

18. The doctor was concerned that his patient with the very high fever would _____ unless he was put into the hospital and given special care.

19. Jennifer couldn't _____ the information she needed from the various journals.

20. When it is very hot, the city usually allows one _____ in each area to be opened so that the children can run in the water and cool off.

21. The police said that the gangster's home was a(n) _____ that was filled with machine guns and other weapons.

22. The architect designed a house that looked like a(n) _____.

STOP. Check answers at the end of Chapter Seven (p. 298).

B. Directions: Match each word with the *best* definition.

_____ 1. abstract
_____ 2. abstract
_____ 3. contract
_____ 4. contract
_____ 5. technical
_____ 6. technique
_____ 7. fortify
_____ 8. hydrant
_____ 9. sphere
_____ 10. thermostat
11. atmosphere
_____ 12. technology
_____ 13. hemisphere
_____ 14. detract
_____ 15. dehydrate
_____ 16. retract
_____ 17. fortitude
_____ 18. traction
_____ 19. thermometer
_____ 20. thermal
_____ 21. technician
_____ 22. fortress

a. applied science
b. an upright pipe for drawing water from a water main
c. any place of security
d. a specialist in the details of a skill
e. to remove water from
f. strength of mind that enables persons to bear pain
g. having to do with an art, science, discipline, or profession
h. the air that surrounds the earth
i. causing heat
j. the manner in which a complex task is accomplished
k. an automatic device for regulating temperature
l. to strengthen against attack
m. the act of drawing
n. to draw together
o. to take away secretly
p. a globe
q. half the earth's surface
r. a binding agreement
s. a short statement giving the main points of an article
t. an instrument for measuring temperature
u. to take away a part, as from quality
v. to take back

STOP. Check answers at the end of Chapter Seven (p. 298).

C. Directions: In the Word Square there are fourteen words from Exercise 18. Find the words in the square and match them with their correct meanings. Note that there are more meanings than words. If there is no word in the square for a meaning, write *none* and give the word. (If a word in the square is used for two meanings, it is counted as appearing twice in the square.)

WORD SQUARE →

D	E	H	Y	D	R	A	T	E	T
H	E	M	I	S	P	H	E	R	E
Y	C	O	N	T	R	A	C	T	C
D	E	T	R	A	C	T	H	A	H
R	E	T	R	A	C	T	N	O	N
A	B	S	T	R	A	C	T	O	I
N	T	H	E	R	M	A	L	U	C
T	A	R	U	N	K	O	O	S	A
F	O	R	T	I	F	Y	E	R	L
T	E	C	H	N	O	L	O	G	Y

Meanings   *Words*

  1. to strengthen against attack   _____

  2. the act of drawing   _____

  3. having to do with an art or profession   _____

  4. to draw back   _____

  5. to divert   _____

  6. an instrument for measuring temperature   _____

  7. a globe   _____

  8. half the earth's surface   _____

  9. the air that surrounds the earth   _____

10. to take away secretly   _____

11. a binding agreement between two or
    more persons

    _____

12. a short statement giving the main points
    of an article

    _____

13. causing heat

    _____

14. the manner in which a complex task
    is accomplished

    _____

15. an automatic device for regulating
    temperature

    _____

16. to draw together

    _____

17. applied science

    _____

18. strength of mind that enables persons
    to bear pain

    _____

19. to remove water from

    _____

20. any place of security

    _____

21. an upright pipe for drawing water

    _____

22. a specialist in the details of a skill

    _____

STOP. Check answers at the end of Chapter Seven (p. 298).

Check answers at the end of Chapter Seven (p. 298).

EXTRA WORD
POWER

> **fy.** Make; cause to be; change into; become. *Fy* is
> found at the end of a number of verbs. For example:
> *fortify*—to make strong; *simplify*— to make easier;
> *beautify*—to make beautiful; *modify*—to change
> slightly or make minor changes in character, form,
> and so on; to change or alter; *verify*—to affirm.
>
> **an, ian.** Native of; belonging to. *An* or *ian* is found
> at the end of words that express some kind of con-
> nection with a place, person, doctrine, and so on.
> For example: *American*—a native of America;
> *Asian*—a native of Asia; *Mohammedan*—believing
> in the principles of Mohammed; *Christian*—believing
> in the Christian religion.

Additional Words Derived from Combining Forms

From your knowledge of combining forms, can you define the following
words?

1. **thermophilic** (ther • mo • phil • ic) (ther • mō • fil′ ik) *adj.* *The scientists were studying the **thermophilic** organisms to try to determine why they flourish in heat.*

---

2. **thermography** (ther • mog • ra • phy) (ther • mog′ ra • fē) *n.* *Doctors are using **thermography** to detect certain diseases or abnormalities in the body.*

---

3. **technocracy** (tech • noc • ra • cy) (tek • nok′ ra • sē) *n.* *In the science fiction film the government, which was a **technocracy**, was run by the technical experts and anything that did not have a useful function was not supported by the government.*

---

4. **hydraulics** (hy • drau • lics) (hī • drau′ liks) *n.* *My brother is studying **hydraulics** in engineering because he is interested in the practical uses of water and other liquids.*

---

5. **hydrotherapy** (hy • dro • ther • a • py) (hī • drō • ther′ a • pē) *n.* *Many doctors use **hydrotherapy** to treat their patients who have certain diseases.*

---

6. **forte** (fortę) *n.* *After listening to her speech, we knew that public speaking was not her **forte**.*

---

7. **forte** (for • te) (for′ tā) *adj., adv.* *The musician played the passage **forte**.*

---

8. **tractable** (trac • ta • ble) (trak′ ta • bul) *adj.* *The dangerous animal was so **tractable**, it had to have been tranquilized.*

---

9. **protract** (pro • tract) (prō • trakt′) *v.* *The lawyers tried to **protract** the case so that they would have more time to prepare an adequate defense.*

STOP. Check answers at the end of Chapter Seven (p. 299).

Practice for Additional Words

Directions: Match each word with the best definition.

_____	1. thermophilic	a. one's strong point
_____	2. thermography	b. in a loud and forceful manner
_____	3. technocracy	c. to prolong in time
_____	4. hydraulics	d. easily controlled
_____	5. hydrotherapy	e. a technique for measuring variations of heat in the body to detect disease
_____	6. forte	f. the use of water to treat disease
_____	7. forte (for′ tā)	g. a branch of science dealing with the practical uses of liquid in motion
_____	8. tractable	h. government ruled by technical experts
_____	9. protract	i. growing at a high temperature

STOP. Check answers at the end of Chapter Seven (p. 299).

CROSSWORD PUZZLE 6

Directions: The meanings of many of the combining forms from Exercises 16–18 follow. Your knowledge of these combining forms will help you to solve this crossword puzzle. Note that *combining form* is abbreviated as *comb. f.*

1. A person sworn to deliver a verdict in a case
6. Draws away or diverts
14. Same as #2 Down
15. A broad sash worn with a Japanese kimono
16. Castigate
17. Forms the plural of many words
18. To lose firmness
20. Grassland
22. A stain
23. To strike lightly
25. Comb. f. for *away*
26. Abbreviation for *central standard time*
28. A pronoun
29. Abbreviation for *horsepower*
31. Motherly
36. Roman numeral for *one hundred*
37. A time period
39. A way of saying "mother"
40. A girl's name
41. Mistake
43. Same as #19 Down
44. Frigid
46. Having little importance
48. You do this to lose weight
49. Abbreviation for East Indies
50. Perform
51. Comb. f. for *two*
53. Abbreviation for military government
54. Abbreviation for *Nevada*
55. Same as #28 Across
56. Comb. f. for *peace*
58. Abbreviation for *not applicable*
60. Same as #19 Down
61. Same as #25 Down
62. Same as #28 Across
63. Comb. f. for *see*
65. Persons who frequent a place
68. A binding agreement
70. To go out of

1. Fairness
2. Comb. f. for *not*
3. Symbol used by motion picture industry
4. An interjection
5. Comb. f. for *ask*
6. A choice between equally unfavorable alternatives
7. Comb. f. for *out of*
8. Comb. f. for *draw, pull*
9. Comb. f. for *again, back*
10. Not concrete
11. You can drink out of this
12. Abbreviation for *technical knockout*
13. To establish
18. Comb. f. for *ball*
19. Comb. f. for *without*
21. Same as #7 Down
24. Same as #19 Down
25. Roman numeral for *five hundred*
27. To separate
30. To extend
32. Abbreviation for *Alcoholics Anonymous*
33. The egg of a louse
34. A foreigner
35. Abbreviation for *liter*
38. An occupation requiring skill
42. Abbreviation for *railway post office*
44. Goal or intention
45. Comb. f. for *citizen*
47. Abbreviation for *yard*
48. Same as #25 Down
50. A round, flat, thin object
52. Antonym of *out*
56. You write with this
57. Abbreviation for *center*
59. Suitable
61. Slang for *to kill* (two words)
64. Abbreviation for *post office*

71. Abbreviation for *number*

66. Symbol used at the beginning of a medical prescription
67. Abbreviation for *New Testament*

STOP. Check answers at the end of Chapter Seven (p. 299).

WORD SCRAMBLE

Directions: Word Scramble 6 is based on words from Exercises 16–18. The meanings are your clues to arranging the letters in correct order. Write the correct word in the blank.

Meanings

1. alpanret   _____ fatherly
2. itynretap   _____ fatherhood
3. iicdpater   _____ the murder of one's own father
4. ciiaopttr   _____ loving one's country
5. roaptn   _____ a wealthy supporter of an artist
6. ooyspchygl   _____ the science of the mind
7. ccoiyspht   _____ insane
8. gateeesgr   _____ to isolate
9. aeiouggrrs   _____ tending to live in a flock
10. gatenocgre   _____ to come together in a group
11. gateggare   _____ the whole sum or amount
12. eesdcu   _____ to tempt to wrongdoing
13. itymatren   _____ motherhood
14. cietsuj   _____ rightfulness
15. orujr   _____ member of a jury
16. cedvior   _____ legal dissolvement of a marriage
17. mmaidel   _____ an argument that presents two equally unfavorable alternatives
18. trevid   _____ to turn from a path
19. eeiltasrv   _____ changeable
20. noceesrv   _____ opposite

21. eservda   _____   hostile

22. rraganto   _____   haughty

23. torydeogra   _____   belittling

24. eerhps   _____   a ball

25. hterlam   _____   pertaining to heat

26. euqinhetc   _____   the manner in which a complex task is accomplished

27. ssefrotr   _____   any place of security

28. yfitrof   _____   to strengthen against attack

29. tratcer   _____   to take back

30. batsacrt   _____   not concrete

STOP. Check answers at the end of Chapter Seven (p. 300).

ANALOGIES 6

Directions: Find the word from the following list that *best* completes each analogy. There are more words in the list than you need.

Word List

hydrophobia, phobia, claustrophobia, contract, thermal, technical, technique, abstract, body, limbs, feet, error, impediment, arrogant, psychic, psychotic, psychology, psychiatrist, murder, mother, ruler, flock, gregarious, isolate, injustice, philanthrope, fairness, atmosphere, dollar, half, hemisphere, sphere, adversity, dehydrated, attract, divert, shorten, separate, fort, forte, protect, hide.

1. paternal : father :: maternal : _____.

2. Foot : podiatrist :: mind : _____.

3. Sophisticated : naive :: concrete : _____.

4. Height : acrophobia :: water : _____.

5. Tense : calm :: congregate : _____.

6. Attitude : posture :: medium : _____.

7. Uniform : same :: justice : _____.

8. Full : satiated :: dry : _____.

9. Dime : nickel :: sphere : _____.

283

10. Deportment : behavior :: detract : _____ .

11. Life : biology :: mind : _____ .

12. Healthy : well :: insane : _____ .

13. Marriage : unite :: divorce : _____ .

14. Retract : withdraw :: contract : _____ .

15. Plump : corpulent :: proud : _____ .

16. Shy : introverted :: outgoing : _____ .

17. Siren : warn :: fortress : _____ .

18. Lucid : ambiguous :: misanthrope : _____ .

19. Following : subsequent :: misfortune : _____ .

20. Heart : defect :: speech : _____ .

STOP. Check answers at the end of Chapter Seven (p. 300).

MULTIPLE-CHOICE VOCABULARY TEST 6

Directions: This is a test on words in Exercises 16–18. Words are presented according to exercises. *Do all exercises before checking answers.* Underline the meaning that *best* fits the word.

Exercise 16

1. paternal
   a. a father
   b. loving a father
   c. fatherhood
   d. related on the father's side

2. paternity
   a. fatherly
   b. fatherhood
   c. a father
   d. ruling like a father

3. paternalism
   a. fatherly
   b. managing a company
   c. fatherhood
   d. the practice of managing a country as a father

4. patricide
   a. hatred of a father
   b. murder of one's father
   c. murder of a father
   d. a horrible murder

5. patriotic
   a. loyal to one's country
   b. marching in parades
   c. fighting in a war
   d. a soldier

6. patron
   a. a frequent moviegoer
   b. a regular customer
   c. a person who goes to lots of different places
   d. an irregular customer

284

7. philanthropist
   a. a lover of mankind
   b. a helper
   c. a person who shows love of mankind by practical helpfulness
   d. a person who participates in public life

8. psychology
   a. a healing science
   b. a helping science
   c. science of life
   d. science of the mind

9. psychiatrist
   a. a specialist
   b. a doctor who specializes in the treatment of mental disorders
   c. a doctor
   d. a doctor who specializes in the treatment of nerves

10. psychotic
    a. ill
    b. confined to a mental institution
    c. mentally ill
    d. a murderer

11. gregarious
    a. a follower of others
    b. a fondness of noise
    c. a fondness for company
    d. an animal lover

12. congregate
    a. a fondness for company
    b. to join
    c. to bring
    d. to collect in a particular place

13. aggregate
    a. to separate
    b. to collect into a whole
    c. to collect
    d. to form

14. segregate
    a. to collect together
    b. to separate
    c. to divide
    d. to total

15. seclusion
    a. isolation
    b. the act of storing
    c. the act of hiding something illegal
    d. a hard place to find

16. seduce
    a. to deceive
    b. to lie
    c. to entice into wrongdoing
    d. to bring charges against

17. sedition
    a. an illegal act
    b. an insult leveled at the government
    c. a crime
    d. an act seeking to incite persons to overthrow the government

Exercise 17

18. maternal
    a. motherhood
    b. like a mother
    c. loving a mother
    d. a mother

19. maternity

    a. giving birth
    b. a home for mothers
    c. referring to a special place
    d. motherhood

20. matrimony

    a. the act of being married
    b. motherhood
    c. a marriage proposal
    d. the marriage ceremony

21. justice

    a. the court system
    b. the act of making a judgment
    c. the judge and jury
    d. fairness

22. justification

    a. good reason
    b. the act of justice
    c. the act of reasoning
    d. something done according to law

23. juror

    a. a person
    b. a person sworn to deliver a verdict
    c. a person appointed by the judge
    d. a person sworn to be a witness

24. divorce

    a. a separation
    b. a decision to separate
    c. a legal ending of a marriage
    d. a court decision

25. dilemma

    a. something confusing
    b. a choice
    c. an argument that is difficult to settle
    d. a choice between two equally difficult alternatives

26. divide

    a. to separate into two parts
    b. to separate into many parts
    c. to isolate
    d. to separate into parts

27. divert

    a. to separate
    b. to turn from a course
    c. to turn toward a course
    d. to turn around

28. versatile

    a. a changeable person
    b. able to do a few things well
    c. many-sided
    d. able to act

29. converse

    a. opposite
    b. to turn toward
    c. to turn away
    d. to turn back

30. reversible

    a. able to be the same
    b. something equally good
    c. able to be opposite to a previous position
    d. able to be removed

31. adverse
 a. turned toward   c. unfavorable
 b. turned away   d. turned in

32. controversy
 a. a minor quarrel   c. a lengthy dispute
 b. an argument that is d. a difficult decision
  never settled

33. advertise
 a. to call attention to c. to make judgments
 b. to discuss   about
           d. to please

34. interrogate
 a. to spy   c. to speak to
 b. to informally question d. to formally question

35. arrogant
 a. questioning   c. overbearing
 b. important   d. distrustful

36. derogatory
 a. questioning in a rude c. coarse
  manner   d. belittling
 b. prying

Exercise 18

37. sphere
 a. something found in c. any rounded body
  the sky   d. a special planet
 b. something without air

38. hemisphere
 a. North America   c. the earth
 b. a half globe   d. two bodies that are
           round

39. atmosphere
 a. outer space   c. the air that surrounds
 b. gases   the earth
           d. the vacuum that exists
            when there is no air

40. thermometer
 a. an instrument de- c. a measuring
  signed to measure   instrument
  air pressure   d. an instrument to mea-
 b. an instrument de-   sure the temperature
  signed to measure   of a body or of space
  fever of a person

41. thermostat
 a. a measuring device c. a heat regulator
 b. an automatic device d. a device for controlling
  for regulating   the temperature of
  temperature   gases

42. thermal
 a. refers to underwear c. causing heat
 b. causing control of heat d. causing fever

43. technical
   a. meaningful to lay-persons
   b. marked by common knowledge
   c. marked by specialization
   d. marked by common interpretation

44. technique
   a. the manner in which a task is accomplished
   b. hard work
   c. proper manner to accomplish a difficult task
   d. a technician's work

45. technician
   a. a specialist
   b. a specialist in a certain field
   c. a worker
   d. a specialist in the details of a skill

46. technology
   a. a technical skill
   b. the production of goods
   c. the providing of comfort
   d. applied science

47. hydrant
   a. a water main
   b. a street fixture with a valve for drawing water
   c. a water faucet
   d. an upright cylinder

48. dehydrate
   a. to take water from
   b. to squeeze
   c. to give water to
   d. to squeeze thoroughly

49. fortress
   a. a large place
   b. a hideout
   c. any place of security
   d. a place of seclusion

50. fortify
   a. to surround
   b. to help
   c. to strengthen against attack
   d. to surround a town

51. fortitude
   a. help against pain
   b. strength of mind
   c. help against danger
   d. any place of security

52. contract
   a. to draw apart
   b. to draw back
   c. to shrink
   d. to make something

53. detract
   a. to draw to
   b. to take in
   c. to draw away
   d. to shorten

54. retract
   a. to draw out
   b. to withdraw
   c. to draw
   d. to use friction to draw away something

55. traction
   a. the act of drawing
   b. the act of drawing back
   c. the act of staying still
   d. the act of drawing away

56. abstract
   a. concrete
   b. difficult to understand
   c. confusing story
   d. associated with a particular instance

TRUE/FALSE TEST 6

Directions: This is a true/false test on Exercise 16–18. Read each sentence carefully. Decide whether it is true or false. Put a *T* for *true* or an *F* for *false* in the blank. The number after the sentence tells you if the word is from Exercise 16, 17, or 18.

_____ 1. Psychology is only concerned with animal behavior. 16

_____ 2. Patricide is the killing of a father only by a son. 16

_____ 3. A patron does not regularly buy at the same place. 16

_____ 4. Something technical is usually easily understood by anyone 18

_____ 5. When something contracts, it gets smaller 18

_____ 6. *Divorce* and *divide* are synonyms. 17

_____ 7. An introvert would not be gregarious. 17, 16

_____ 8. Something easily understood would not be abstract. 18

_____ 9. When someone has an aversion to something, he or she likes it. 17

_____ 10. All patriotic persons are heroes. 16

_____ 11. A psychiatrist is a specialist who treats mentally healthy persons. 16

_____ 12. A philanderer is prone to propose matrimony. 16, 17

_____ 13. A fortress is a stronghold. 18

_____ 14. A matriarch is an absolute ruler of a country. 17

_____ 15. A prune is a dehydrated fruit. 18

_____ 16. Thermophilic organisms thrive in the heat. 18

_____ 17. *Divert* and *detract* are synonyms. 17, 18

_____ 18. An expatriate lives in his or her native land. 16

_____ 19. A psychic is a mentally ill person. 16

_____ 20. When you have something in the aggregate, you have the whole amount. 16

STOP. Check answers for both tests at the end of Chapter Seven (p. 300).

SCORING OF TESTS

Multiple-Choice Vocabulary Test		True/False Test	
Number Wrong	*Score*	*Number Wrong*	*Score*
0–3	Excellent	0–1	Excellent
4–6	Good	2–3	Good
7–9	Weak	4–5	Weak
Above 9	Poor	Above 5	Poor
Score _____		Score _____	

1. If you scored in the excellent or good range on *both tests,* you are doing well. You have now completed the work in this text.

2. If you scored in the weak or poor range on either test, look below and follow directions for Additional Practice. Note that the words on the tests are arranged so that you can tell in which exercise to find them. This will help you if you need additional practice.

ADDITIONAL PRACTICE SETS

A. Directions: Write the words you missed on the tests from the three exercises in the space provided. Note that the tests are presented so that you can tell to which exercises the words belong.

Exercise 16 Words Missed

1. _____   6. _____
2. _____   7. _____
3. _____   8. _____
4. _____   9. _____
5. _____   10. _____

Exercise 17 Words Missed

1. _____   6. _____
2. _____   7. _____
3. _____   8. _____
4. _____   9. _____
5. _____   10. _____

Exercise 18 Words Missed

1. _____   6. _____

2. _____   7. _____

3. _____   8. _____

4. _____   9. _____

5. _____   10. _____

B. Directions: Restudy the words that you have written down on p. 290 and this page. Study the combining forms from which those words are derived. Do Step I and Step II for those you missed. Note that Step I and Step II of the combining forms and vocabulary derived from those combining forms are on the following pages:

Exercise 16—pp. 255–258

Exercise 17—pp. 262–265

Exercise 18—pp. 271–274

C. Directions: Do Additional Practice 1 on this page and the next if you missed words from Exercise 16. Do Additional Practice 2 on pp. 292–293 if you missed words from Exercise 17. Do Additional Practice 3 on pp. 294–295 if you missed words from Exercise 18.

Additional Practice 1 for Exercise 16

A. Directions: The combining forms presented in Exercise 16 follow. Match the combining form with its meaning.

_____ 1. pater, patr   a. flock

_____ 2. phil, phile, philo   b. spirit; mind; soul

_____ 3. greg   c. father

_____ 4. se   d. love

_____ 5. psych, psyche, psycho e. apart

STOP. Check answers at the end of Chapter Seven (p. 301).

B. Directions: The words presented in Exercise 16 follow. Match the word with its meaning.

_____ 1. paternal   a. an influential supporter of an artist

_____ 2. paternity   b. one who shows goodwill by helping others

_____ 3. paternalism   c. insane

_____ 4. patricide   d. the science of the mind

_____ 5. patriotic   e. marked by a fondness for being with others

_____ 6. patron   f. incitement to rebellion

_____ 7. philanthropist   g. to come together in a group

_____ 8. psychology   h. fatherhood

_____ 9. psychiatrist   i. loving one's country

_____ 10. psychotic   j. fatherly

_____ 11. gregarious   k. the murder of one's father

_____ 12. congregate   l. to tempt to wrongdoing

_____ 13. aggregate   m. the act of isolating oneself

_____ 14. segregate   n. the practice of managing a business as a father

_____ 15. seclusion   o. a doctor who specializes in treatment of the mentally ill

_____ 16. seduce   p. total

_____ 17. sedition   q. to separate

STOP. Check answers at the end of Chapter Seven (p. 301).

Additional Practice 2 for Exercise 17

A. Directions: The combining forms presented in Exercise 17 follow. Match the combining form with its meaning.

Combining Forms	Meanings
1. matr, matri, matro	a. turn
2. juris, jus	b. ask; beg

3. di

c. mother

4. vers, vert

d. law

5. rog

e. two

STOP. Check answers at the end of Chapter Seven (p. 301).

B. Directions: The words presented in Exercise 17 follow. Match the word
with its meaning.

_____ 1. maternal

a. good reason

_____ 2. maternity

b. to end a marriage legally

_____ 3. matrimony

c. hostile

_____ 4. justice

d. to turn from a path

_____ 5. justification

e. a person sworn to deliver a
verdict

_____ 6. juror

f. motherly

_____ 7. divorce

g. belittling

_____ 8. dilemma

h. having two usable sides

_____ 9. divide

i. rightfulness

_____ 10. divert

j. many-sided

_____ 11. versatile

k. haughty

_____ 12. converse

l. to ask questions formally

_____ 13. reversible

m. motherhood

_____ 14. adverse

n. the state of being married

_____ 15. controversy

o. to separate into parts

_____ 16. advertise

p. an argument that presents
two equally unfavorable
alternatives

_____ 17. interrogate

q. a statement that is turned
around

_____ 18. arrogant

r. a dispute

_____ 19. derogatory

s. to praise the good qualities of
a product

STOP. Check answers at the end of Chapter Seven (p. 301).

A. Directions: The combining forms presented in Exercise 18 follow.
Match the combining form with its meaning.

_____ 1. sphere   a. strong

_____ 2. therm, thermo   b. water

_____ 3. techni, techno   c. draw; pull

_____ 4. hydr, hydra, hydro   d. ball

_____ 5. fort   e. heat

_____ 6. tract   f. arts and crafts (especially
industrial arts); method;
system; skill

STOP. Check answers at the end of Chapter Seven (p. 301).

B. Directions: The words presented in Exercise 18 follow. Match the word
with its meaning.

_____ 1. sphere   a. causing heat

_____ 2. hemisphere   b. the act of drawing

_____ 3. atmosphere   c. to divert

_____ 4. thermometer   d. to make smaller

_____ 5. thermostat   e. to strengthen against attack

_____ 6. thermal   f. a half globe

_____ 7. technical   g. a street fixture for drawing
water from a water main

_____ 8. technique   h. the air that surrounds the earth

_____ 9. technician   i. theoretical

_____ 10. technology   j. an instrument for measuring
temperature

_____ 11. hydrant   k. the degree of skill shown in a
performance

_____ 12. dehydrate   l. having to do with applied
science

_____ 13. fortress   m. strength of mind

_____ 14. fortify   n. an automatic device for
regulating temperature

_____ 15. fortitude

_____ 16. contract

_____ 17. detract

_____ 18. retract

_____ 19. traction

_____ 20. abstract

o. a ball

p. a specialist in the details of a skill

q. to remove water from

r. a stronghold

s. to withdraw

t. applied science

STOP. Check answers at the end of Chapter Seven (p. 301).

ANSWERS: Chapter Seven

Exercise 16 (pp. 255-262)

Practice A

(1) related on the father's side, (2) the practice of managing the affairs of a company like a father, (3) the killing of a father by his son or daughter, (4) loving of one's country, (5) separated, (6) tempted into wrongdoing, (7) totaled, (8) isolation, (9) regular customer, (10) fatherhood, (11) person who shows goodwill toward his or her fellow human beings by practical kindness, (12) outgoing, (13) a doctor who specializes in mental disorders, (14) assemble, (15) the study of the mind, (16) insane, (17) incitement to rebellion.

Practice B

(1) g, (2) d, (3) k, (4) p, (5) f, (6) b, (7) a, (8) o, (9) n, (10) c, (11) h, (12) m, (13) i, (14) j, (15) q, (16) e, (17) l.

Practice C

(1) aggregate, (2) psychiatrist, (3) paternal, (4) psychology, (5) patron, (6) psychotic, (7) gregarious, (8) congregate, (9) segregate, (10) seclusion, (11) seduce, (12) paternity, (13) sedition, (14) Patricide, (15) paternalism, (16) patriotic, (17) philanthropist.

Additional Words Derived from Combining Forms (pp. 261-262)

1. **expatriate.** To banish; exile; to withdraw oneself from one's native country; to renounce one's citizenship; an exile; an expatriated person. (The term *expatriated* is an adjective.)

2. **bibliophile.** A lover of books; a book collector.

3. **philanthrope.** A lover of mankind; a philanthropist; a humanitarian.

4. **philanderer.** A person who makes love without serious intentions; a person who flirts; a person who has many love affairs; a person who has many love affairs without intentions of marriage.

5. **psychosis.** Any severe form of mental disturbance or disease that has far-reaching and deep disorders of behavior; mental derangement by defective or lost contact with reality.

6. **psychopath.** A person suffering from mental disease.

7. **psychic.** A person sensitive to nonphysical forces; a medium (a person thought to have powers of communicating with the spirits of the dead); lying outside the sphere of physical science or knowledge; immaterial or spiritual in origin or force; marked by extraordinary or mysterious sensitivity, perception, or understanding.

8. **egregious.** Remarkably bad; conspicuously bad; outrageous; flagrant.

Practice for Additional Words Derived from Combining Forms (p. 262)

(1) g, (2) d, (3) h, (4) f, (5) b, (6) a, (7) e, (8) c.

Exercise 17 (pp. 262-270)

Practice A

(1) justification, (2) juror, (3) maternity, (4) justice, (5) interrogate, (6) derogatory, (7) divorce, (8) arrogant, (9) matrimony, (10) reversible, (11) divert, (12) dilemma, (13) converse, (14) controversy, (15) adverse, (16) advertise, (17) maternal, (18) divide, (19) versatile.

Practice B

(1) divorce, (2) matrimony, (3) maternal, (4) maternal, (5) divorce, (6) justification, (7) justice, (8) arrogant, (9) derogatory, (10) interrogated, (11) juror, (12) juror, (13) justice, (14) justice, (15) controversy, (16) controversy, (17) justification, (18) juror, (19) divert, (20) dilemma, (21) matrimony, (22) maternity, (23) advertise, (24) arrogant, (25) converse (26) adverse, (27) maternity, (28) versatile, (29) divorce, (30) divorce, (31) divide.

Practice C

(1) the state of marriage, (2) the legal ending of a marriage, (3) motherly, (4) explanation, (5) a situation that necessitates a choice between two equally unfavorable alternatives, (6) having two usable sides, (7) belittling, (8) formally question, (9) haughty, (10) unfavorable, (11) relating to a pregnant woman, (12) draw, (13) separate, (14) able to do many things well, (15) dispute, (16) opposite, (17) call attention to, (18) member of a jury, (19) assignment of deserved rewards and punishments.

296

Additional Words Derived from Combining Forms (pp. 268–270)

1. **matriarch.** A mother who is the ruler of a family or tribe; a woman who is ruler of a family, group, or state.

2. **matricide.** The murder of a mother by her son or daughter.

3. **jurisdiction.** The right or power of administering justice or law; authority; power; control; the extent of authority; the territory over which such authority extends; the limits in which authority may be exercised.

4. **jurisprudence.** A system or body of law; the course of court decisions; the science or philosophy of law; a branch of law.

5. **dichotomy.** Division into two parts, especially mutually exclusive or contradictory parts; division into two parts, kinds, and so on; a schism.

6. **adversity.** A condition marked by unhappiness, misfortune, or distress; a stroke of misfortune; an unfavorable or harmful event; a hardship.

7. **pervert.** To lead astray; to turn or lead from the right way; to corrupt; a person who has been led astray; a person who practices sexual perversion, that is, one who deviates from the normal in sexual habits.

8. **aversion.** A strong dislike; a fixed dislike; a feeling of distaste toward something with a desire to avoid it or turn from it.

9. **subversion.** A systematic attempt to overthrow or undermine a government or political system by persons working secretly within the country involved; anything that tends to overthrow.

10. **introvert.** A person who directs his or her thoughts inward; a person who is more interested in his or her own thoughts and feelings than in what is going on around him or her; *informal*: a shy person.

11. **abrogate.** To abolish a law, custom, and so on, by an authoritative act; to repeal; to do away with; to invalidate.

12. **prerogative.** The right or privilege that no one else has; special superiority or privilege that one may get from an official position, office, and so on.

13. **surrogate.** A substitute; a deputy; a person appointed to act in the place of another; something that serves as a substitute.

Practice for Additional Words Derived from Combining Forms (p. 270)

(1) f, (2) d, (3) h, (4) l, (5) j, (6) m, (7) i, (8) c, (9) e, (10) k, (11) g, (12) a, (13) b.

Practice A

(1) atmosphere, (2) fortify, (3) detract, (4) retract, (5) contract, (6) fortitude, (7) contract, (8) thermometer, (9) traction, (10) hemisphere, (11) thermostat, (12) thermal, (13) abstract, (14) technical, (15) technique, (16) technician, (17) technology, (18) dehydrate, (19) abstract, (20) hydrant, (21) fortress, (22) sphere.

Practice B

(1) o, s, (2) o, s, (3) n, r, (4) n, r, (5) g, (6) j, (7) l, (8) b, (9) p, (10) k, (11) h, (12) a, (13) q, (14) u, (15) e, (16) v, (17) f, (18) m, (19) t, (20) i, (21) d, (22) c.

Practice C

(1) fortify, (2) none—traction, (3) technical, (4) retract, (5) detract, (6) none—thermometer, (7) sphere, (8) hemisphere, (9) none—atmosphere, (10) abstract, (11) contract, (12) abstract, (13) thermal, (14) none—technique, (15) none—thermostat, (16) contract, (17) technology, (18) none—fortitude, (19) dehydrate, (20) none—fortress, (21) hydrant, (22) none—technician.

WORD SQUARE

D	E	H	Y	D	R	A	T	E	T
H	E	M	I	S	P	H	E	R	E
Y	C	O	N	T	R	A	C	T	C
D	E	T	R	A	C	T	H	A	H
R	E	T	R	A	C	T	N	O	N
A	B	S	T	R	A	C	T	O	I
N	T	H	E	R	M	A	L	U	C
T	A	R	U	N	K	O	O	S	A
F	O	R	T	I	F	Y	E	R	L
T	E	C	H	N	O	L	O	G	Y

Additional Words Derived from Combining Forms (pp. 278–279)

1. **thermophilic.** Growing at a high temperature; requiring high temperature for development.

2. **thermography.** A process of writing or printing involving the use of heat; a technique for detecting and measuring variations of heat emitted by various regions of the body and transforming them into signals that can be recorded photographically—used to diagnose abnormal or diseased underlying conditions.

3. **technocracy.** Government by technical experts.

4. **hydraulics.** The science dealing with water and other liquids in motion, their uses in engineering, the laws of their actions, and so on.

5. **hydrotherapy.** The treatment of disease by the use of water.

6. **forte.** Something a person does very well; a strong point.

7. **forte** (for′ tā). Loud; strong; in a loud and forceful manner; loudly; strongly.

8. **tractable.** Easily managed or controlled; easy to deal with; obedient.

9. **protract.** To draw out; lengthen in time; to extend forward or outward; to prolong in time.

Practice for Additional Words Derived from Combining Forms (p. 280)

(1) i, (2) e, (3) h, (4) g, (5) f, (6) a, (7) b, (8) d, (9) c.

Crossword Puzzle 6 (pp. 280–282)

1 J	2 U	3 R	4 O	5 R	■	6 D	7 E	8 T	9 R	10 A	11 C	12 T	13 S
14 U	N	■	15 O	B	I	■	16 R	E	B	U	K	E	
17 S	■	18 S	19 A	G	■	20 L	21 E	A	■	22 S	P	O	T
23 T	24 A	P	■	25 D	E	■	26 C	27 S	T	■	■	■	
28 I	■	29 H	30 P	■	31 M	32 A	T	E	R	33 N	34 A	35 L	
36 C	■	37 E	R	38 A	■	39 M	A	■	40 G	A	I	L	■
41 E	42 R	R	O	R	■	43 A	■	44 A	R	C	T	I	45 C
■	46 P	E	T	T	47 Y	■	48 D	I	E	T	■	49 E	I
50 D	O	■	R	■	51 D	52 I	■	53 M	G	■	54 N	V	
55 I	■	56 P	A	57 C	■	58 N	59 A	■	60 A	■	61 D	■	62 I
63 S	64 P	E	C	T	■	65 P	A	T	66 R	O	67 N	S	
68 C	O	N	T	R	69 A	C	T	■	70 E	X	I	T	
									71 N				

Word Scramble 6 (pp. 282–283)

(1) paternal, (2) paternity, (3) patricide, (4) patriotic, (5) patron, (6) psychology, (7) psychotic, (8) segregate, (9) gregarious, (10) congregate, (11) aggregate, (12) seduce, (13) maternity, (14) justice, (15) juror, (16) divorce, (17) dilemma, (18) divert, (19) versatile, (20) converse, (21) adverse, (22) arrogant, (23) derogatory, (24) sphere, (25) thermal, (26) technique, (27) fortress, (28) fortify, (29) retract, (30) abstract.

Analogies 6 (pp. 283–284)

(1) mother, (2) psychiatrist, (3) abstract, (4) hydrophobia, (5) isolate, (6) psychic, (7) fairness, (8) dehydrated, (9) hemisphere, (10) divert, (11) psychology, (12) psychotic, (13) separate, (14) shorten, (15) arrogant, (16) gregarious, (17) protect, (18) philanthrope, (19) adversity, (20) impediment.

Multiple-Choice Test 6 (pp. 284–288)

Exercise 16

(1) d, (2) b, (3) d, (4) b,[1] (5) a, (6) b, (7) c, (8) d, (9) b, (10) c, (11) c, (12) d, (13) b, (14) b, (15) a, (16) c, (17) d.

Exercise 17

(18) b, (19) d, (20) a, (21) d, (22) a, (23) b, (24) c, (25) d, (26) d, (27) b, (28) c, (29) a, (30) c, (31) c, (32) c, (33) a, (34) d, (35) c, (36) d.

Execise 18

(37) c, (38) b, (39) c, (40) d, (41) b, (42) c, (43) c, (44) a, (45) d, (46) d, (47) b, (48) a, (49) c, (50) c, (51) b, (52) c, (53) c, (54) b, (55) a, (56) b.

True/False Test 6 (p. 289)

(1) F, (2) F, (3) F, (4) F, (5) T, (6) F, (7) T, (8) T, (9) F, (10) F, (11) F, (12) F, (13) T, (14) F, (15) T, (16) T, (17) T, (18) F, (19) F, (20) T.

STOP. Turn to page 290 for the scoring of the tests.

---

[1]The answer *b* is better than *c* because the *murder of a father* could refer to the murder of any person who is a father, not necessarily one's own father.

Additional Practice 1

A. (1) c, (2) d, (3) a, (4) e, (5) b.
B. (1) j, (2) h, (3) n, (4) k, (5) i, (6) a, (7) b, (8) d, (9) o, (10) c, (11) e, (12) g, (13) p, (14) q, (15) m, (16) l, (17) f.

Additional Practice 2

A. (1) c, (2) d, (3) e, (4) a, (5) b.
B. (1) f, (2) m, (3) n, (4) i, (5) a, (6) e, (7) b, (8) p, (9) o, (10) d, (11) j, (12) q, (13) h, (14) c, (15) r, (16) s, (17) l, (18) k, (19) g.

Additional Practice 3

A. (1) d, (2) e, (3) f, (4) b, (5) a, (6) c.
B. (1) o, (2) f, (3) h, (4) j, (5) n, (6) a, (7) l, (8) k, (9) p, (10) t, (11) g, (12) q, (13) r, (14) e, (15) m, (16) d, (17) c, (18) s, (19) b, (20) i.

APPENDIXES

APPENDIX A: THE DICTIONARY

The dictionary, which is an important reference book for all persons, is filled with information about individual words, as well as other useful information. Even though the dictionary is a necessary tool, with which all students should be familiar, it should not be used as a crutch; that is, every time you meet a word whose meaning is unknown to you, you should first try to use your knowledge of combining forms and context clues to unlock the meaning. If these techniques do not help, and the word is essential for understanding the passage, then you should look up the meaning.

To use the dictionary effectively, you should know that the purpose of dictionaries is not to prescribe or make rules about word meanings and pronunciations, but only to describe. Lexicographers use various methods to compile the words in the dictionary. One important method is based on citations of usage and research consulting older dictionaries. Another method involves choosing a group of people and recording the ways in which these subjects pronounce and use words. These then are recorded as the accepted standard spellings, definitions, and word usage.

Difficulties exist concerning pronunciation because persons in different parts of the country often pronounce words differently. Pronunciation in the East is often different from that in the South or Midwest. As a result, pronunciation of a word as given in the dictionary may not be in accord with your region's pronunciation of it.

Also, to compound this problem, different dictionaries may use different pronunciation keys. The pronunciation key is composed of words with diacritical marks. To know how to pronounce a word in a particular dictionary, you must familiarize yourself with the pronunciation key in that dictionary. For example, look at the way that five different dictionaries present a few similar words.

Word	Webster's New Twentieth Century Dictionary	Webster's Third New International Dictionary	Random House Dictionary of the English Language	The American Heritage Dictionary of the English Language	Funk & Wagnalls Standard College Dictionary
1. coupon	cou′pon	′k(y)ü, pän	ko͞o′pon	ko͞o′pŏn	ko͞o′pon
2. courage	cour′age	′kər · ij	kûr′ij	kûr′ĭj	kûr′ij
3. covet	cov′ĕt	′kəvət	kuv′it	kŭv′ĭt	kuv′it

If you had no knowledge of the pronunciation key of the specific dictionary, you would have difficulty in pronouncing the word. (See p. 307 for the Guide to Pronunciation in *Webster's New Twentieth Century Dictionary*.) Pronunciation guides are generally found at the beginning of dictionaries. Many dictionaries also have a simplified pronunciation key at the bottom of every page. (See pp. 308–309 for two pages from *Webster's New Twentieth Century Dictionary*.)

Because this text will be used in various parts of the country, this book uses a simplified pronunciation key, which is presented in Chapter One.

Before reading any further, list in the following space all the uses that you can think of for the dictionary.

USES OF THE DICTIONARY

_____

_____

_____

_____

_____

_____

_____

Now compare your list with the following:

I. *Uses of the Dictionary*

    A. *Information Concerning a Word*

        1. Spelling.

        2. Definitions.

        3. Correct usage.

        4. Pronunciation.

        5. Syllabication.

        6. Antonyms.

        7. Synonyms.

        8. Parts of speech.

9. Idiomatic phrases.

10. Etymology —the history of the word.

11. Semantics —the analysis of the word's meanings.

B. *Other Useful Information*

1. Biographical entries.

2. Lists of foreign countries, provinces, and cities with their population figures.

3. Charts of other geographical data.

4. Air distances between principal cities.

5. Listing of foreign words and phrases.

6. Complete listing of abbreviations in common use.

7. Tables of weights and measures.

8. Signs and symbols.

9. Forms of address.

Most persons do not realize what an abundance of information can be gained from the dictionary. (The kind of information presented varies according to the dictionary.)

Using your dictionary, answer the following questions:

1. In what countries do centaurs live? _____

2. Where is Mount Everest? _____

3. Was Prometheus the goddess of fire? _____

4. Is a songstress a man who writes songs? _____

5. Is *Miss.* an abbreviation for *Missus*? _____

6. Is haiku a Hawaiian mountain? _____

7. Did Andrew Jackson fight in the Civil War? _____

8. Is a statute a work of art? _____

9. Is a quadruped an extinct animal? _____

10. Is a centipede a unit of measurement in the metric system? _____

Using the given dictionary page (see p. 308), see how well you can answer the following questions. Answers are on the next page.

1. Would the word *Porphyrio* be found on this page? _____

2. Between what two words would you find *porose?* _____

3. How many definitions are given for *pore?* _____

4. What parts of speech can *pore* be? _____

5. In what seas do you find porcupine fish? _____

6. What was *pork* originally? _____

7. What is the slang meaning of *pork barrel?* _____

8. Is there such a thing as porcupine grass? _____

9. What is the Latin for *pore?* _____

10. What is *Populus alba?* _____

11. How many syllables does the word *poriferous* have? _____

12. Which syllable is accented in *porism?* _____

13. Which syllable is accented in *porismatic?* _____

14. According to the pronunciation key at the bottom of the page, *ā* sounds like *a* in what word? _____

15. The *c* in the word *porotic* sounds like _____ in the word _____ in the pronunciation key at the bottom of the page.

16. The *c* in the word *porcelain* sounds like _____ in the word _____ in the pronunciation key.

ANSWERS

1. no, *porphyrine* is the last word—*rio* would be after *rine*
2. *Porosa* and *porosity*
3. six
4. noun and verb
5. tropical
6. pig or hog
7. government appropriations for political patronage
8. yes
9. *porus*
10. the European white poplar
11. four
12. first
13. third
14. fate
15. c; cat or chord
16. *c*; ace

GUIDE TO PRONUNCIATION

PRONUNCIATION in this dictionary is indicated directly on the entry word by a system of symbols, or diacritical marks. Thus, the symbol c̦ is used to indicate the sound of the hard c in cat, and the word is entered in the vocabulary as c̦at. The Key to Pronunciation printed below gives a complete description of the symbols used and the sounds they represent. The modified sounds are unmarked, as the e in cent, the a in apply, the i in pin, the u in tub, the o in on, and the y in myth.

When two vowels stand together, only the one which indicates the sound of the word is marked, as in strēak, brāin, mōat. The clusters ae and oe ending a syllable are pronounced as ē; when followed by a consonant in the same syllable they are pronounced as e in met.

In a few instances it is impossible to indicate the pronunciation on the word itself; in such cases the word, or part of it, is respelled

in parentheses immediately following the entry. The word is respelled phonetically, that is, according to its sound, regardless of the letters that compose it. Examples of respelling are eight (āt); guide (gīd); heir (ār); and här'le-quin (-kin or -kwin).

The accents are indicated thus: primary ', secondary ". The secondary accent or subordinate stress·is normally indicated only when it falls at an irregular interval from the primary or main stress, that is, at an interval other than two syllables.

Although full vowel quality is indicated in all syllables, it should be understood that in totally unstressed syllables the vowel quality is variously reduced, or weakened, in colloquial speech to a more or less neutral sound. To avoid the confusion of excessive diacritical marks, sounds in non-English words are indicated by the English sounds most nearly approximating these.

KEY TO PRONUNCIATION

ā	as in	fāte, āle, ā'corn, be-rāte', nat''u-ral-i-zā'tion.
ă	" "	fär, fä'ther, ärch, mär'shal, cär-toon'; also as in whät, wänt.
ȧ	" "	fȧst, glȧss, a-lȧs'; also as in so'dȧ, ȧ-dapt'ȧ-ble.
ȧ	" "	fȧll, pȧw, ȧw'ful, ap-plȧud'.
ă	" "	fi'năl, sea'măn, tol'er-ănt, men'ăce.
ã	" "	cãre, ãir, mil'i-tãr-y, de-clãre'.
a	" "	at, ac-cord', com-par'i-son, car'ry.
ē	" "	ēve, mēte, hē, Ē'den, in-ter-vēne'; also as in hēre, drēar'y.
ẹ	" "	prẹy, eight, o-bẹy'.
ẽ	" "	hẽr, vẽrse, sẽr'vice, in-tẽr'.
e	" "	met, ebb, en-dorse', mon'e-tar-y, dis-tend'.
ee	" "	feed, pro-ceed', lee'way.
ī	" "	pīne, I-de'a, Ice'berg, de-cīde', al-lī'ance.
ĭ	" "	clĭque, ma-rĭne'; also as in Mar-tĭ'ni.
ĩ	" "	bĩrd, stĩr, ex'tĩr-pate, fĩrm'a-ment.
i	" "	it, hit, re-mit', cit'y; also as in pos'si-ble, grav'i-ty, pu'pil.
ō	" "	nōte, ōat, sō, ō'pen, hel-lō'; also as in ren'ō-vate, prō-pel'.
ŏ	" "	mŏve, prŏve, tŏmb.
ọ	" "	lọng, crọss, ọff, ọrb, fọr-bid', dọr'mer.
ô	" "	at'ôm, plôv'er; also as in ac'tôr, wôrd, wôrk.
o	" "	not, for'est, non'sense; also as in dog, broth, cost; also as in con-fess', con-cur'.
ọọ	" "	mọọn, cọọ, fọọd, brọọd'er.
oo	" "	book, hood, foot, look, cook'y.
ū	" "	ūse, fūse, ū-til'i-ty, fū'tile, im-mūne'.
ụ	" "	bụll, pụt, fụl-fil', boun'ti-fụl.
ü	" "	brüte, jü'ry; also used for the German ü.
ũ	" "	tũrn, fũr, bũr-lesque', de-mũr'.
u	" "	up, rub, sun'set, in-sult'.
ỹ	" "	crỹ, eỹe.
y	" "	myth, cit'y.
c̦	" "	c̦at, to-bac̦'c̦o.
ç	" "	ma-çhine'.
c	" "	ace, ce'dar.
ch	" "	church.
çh	" "	çhord.

g̣	as in	g̣em.
ñ	" "	añ'ger, sphiñx.
ṅ	" "	French boṅ.
ng	" "	ring.
ṣ	" "	mi'ṣer, aṣ.
th	" "	this.
th	" "	thin.
ẓ	" "	aẓure.
au	" "	umlaut.
aw	" "	straw.
ou	" "	out.
oi	" "	oil.
oy	" "	boy.
ew	" "	new, few.
ow	" "	now.
-tūre	as -chēr (in picture).	
-tion } -sion	as -shun (in nation, tension).	
-ciăn } -tiăn } -siăn	as -shun (in Martian, Melanesian, mortician).	
-ṣiăn } -ṣion	as -zhun (in Persian, fusion).	
-liŏn	as -lyun or -yun (in million).	
-ceous } -(s)cious	as -shus (in cretaceous, delicious, conscious).	
qu	as kw (in queen).	
-ous	as -us (in porous).	
ph-	as f- (in phone, etc.).	
-le	as -l (at end of syllable, as in able, cycle, etc.).	
-iȧ	as -yȧ (in pharmacopoeia).	
wh-	as hw- in whale, etc.	
kh	as in German doch (dokh).	

xii

Material on this page and that on pp. 308–309 is reprinted with permission from *Webster's New Twentieth Century Dictionary*, 2nd ed. (New York: William Collins and World Publishing Co., Inc., 1975). Copyright ©1975 by William Collins and World Publishing Co., Inc.

pop'ū·lāte, *v t.*; populated, *pt., pp.*; populating, *ppr.* [from ML. *populatus*, pp. of *populare*, to populate, from L. *populus*, the people.]
1. to be or become the inhabitants of; to inhabit.
2. to people; to furnish with people or inhabitants, either by natural increase or by immigration or colonization.

pop'ū·lāte, *v.i.* to propagate; to increase. [Obs.]

pop·ū·lā'tion, *n.* [LL. *populatio*.]
1. all the people in a country, region, etc.
2. the number of these.
3. a (specified) part of the people in a given area; as, the Japanese *population* of Hawaii.
4. a populating or being populated.
5. in biology, all the organisms living in a given area.
6. in statistics, a group of items or individuals.
population explosion; the very great and continuing increase in human population in modern times.

pop'ū·lā·tŏr, *n.* one who populates or peoples.

pop'ū·lin, *n.* [L. *populus*, poplar, and *-in*.] a crystallizable substance found in the bark, root, and leaves of the *Populus tremula*, or aspen, along with salicin.

Pop'ū·lism, *n.* [from L. *populus*, the people; and *-ism*.]
1. the theory and policies of Populists.
2. the Populistic movement.

Pop'ū·list, *n.* one belonging to the People's party.

Pop·ū·list'iç, *a.* same as *Populistic*.

Pop·ū·list'iç, *a.* 1. of Populists or their views.
2. having to do with the People's party.

pop'ū·lous, *a.* [L. *populosus*.] full of people; thickly populated.

pop'ū·lous·ly, *adv.* with many inhabitants in proportion to the extent of country.

pop'ū·lous·ness, *n.* the state of being populous.

Pop'ū·lus, *n.* [L., poplar.] a genus of trees which includes the common poplar. *Populus alba* is the European white poplar.

por'bēa"gle, *n.* [from Corn. dial.] any shark of the genus *Lamna*, especially *Lamna cornubica*, found in northern seas: it is large and fierce and brings forth living young rather than eggs.

por'çāte, por'çā·ted, *a.* [L. *porca*, a ridge.] ridged; formed in ridges.

pŏr'çe·lain (-lin), *n.* [so called from its resemblance to the Venus shell, which is, in It., *porcellana*, from *porcella*, a little pig, the upper surface of the shell resembling the curve of a pig's back.]
1. a fine, white, translucent, hard earthenware with a transparent glaze; china.
2. porcelain dishes or ornaments, collectively.

pŏr'çe·lain, *a.* made of porcelain.

pŏr'çe·lain çrab, a crab having a very smooth, polished shell, as *Porcellana platycheles*, the broad-clawed species.

pŏr'çe·lain·ized, *a.* altered by heating so as to resemble porcelain; in geology, metamorphosed so as to resemble white earthenware, as clays, shales, etc.

pŏr'çe·lain jas'pĕr, porcelanite.

pŏr·çe·lā'ne·ous, por·çel·lā'ne·ous, *a.* of or resembling porcelain.

por'çe·lā·nīte, por'çel·lā·nīte, *n.* a semi-vitrified clay or shale, somewhat resembling jasper.

por'çe·lā·nous, por'çel·lā·nous, *a.* same as *porcelaneous*.

pŏrch, *n.* [ME. and OFr. *porche*, from L. *porticus*, from *porta*, a gate, entrance, or passage.]
1. a covered entrance to a building, usually projecting from the wall and having a separate roof.
2. an open or enclosed gallery or room on the outside of a building; a veranda.
3. a portico; a covered walk. [Obs.]
the Porch; a portico in Athens where the Stoic philosopher Zeno taught his disciples.

pŏrch çlimb'ĕr (klim'), a burglar who gains entrance to a house by climbing the porch. [Slang.]

por'cine, *a.* [L. *porcinus*, from *porcus*, hog.] of or like pigs or hogs.

por'çū·pine, *n.*; *pl.* **por'çū·pines** or **por'çū·pine.** [ME. *porkepyn*, pork *despyne*; OFr. *porc espin*, the spinous hog, or spine hog; L. *porcus*, and *spina*, a spine or thorn.] any of a number of related gnawing animals; specifically, **(a)** the old-world porcupine,

Hystrix cristata, of the family *Hystricidæ*, bearing long, stiff, erectile spines sometimes a foot in length; **(b)** the North American porcupine, of the family *Erethisontidae*, which is armed with short, sharp quills or spines that may be easily detached from the body. The two species of this porcupine are *Erethizon dorsatus* of the eastern part of the United States and Canada, and *Erethizon epixanthus* of the West.

PORCUPINE

por'çū·pine ant'ēat·ĕr, an echidna, an ant-eating mammal resembling a porcupine.

por'çū·pine çrab, a Japanese crab having long spines on its carapace and limbs; the *Lithodes hystrix*.

por'çū·pine fish, a fish of the tropical seas, *Diodon hystrix*, which is covered with spines or prickles capable of being erected by its inflating the body; also, any fish with similarly erectile spines.

por'çū·pine gráss, the common prairie grass, *Stipa spartea*, of the United States.

por'çū·pine wood, the outer wood of the cocoanut palm, which, when cut horizontally, presents markings resembling porcupine quills.

pōre, *n.* [ME. *pore, poor*; L. *porus*; Gr. *poros*, a passage, a pore, from *perān*, to pierce.]
1. originally, a passage; a channel.
2. a tiny opening, usually microscopic, as in plant leaves, skin, etc., through which fluids may be absorbed or discharged.
3. a similar opening in rock or other substances.

pōre, *v.i.*; pored, *pt., pp.*; poring, *ppr.* [ME. *poren, pouren*.]
1. to gaze intently or steadily.
2. to look searchingly; to read carefully; to study minutely (with *over*); as, he *pored over* the book.
3. to think deeply and thoroughly; to ponder; meditate (with *on, upon*, or *over*); as, he *pored on* the wonders of science.

pōr'ĕr, *n.* one who pores.

por'gee, *n.* same as *porgy*.

por'gy (or -ji), *n.*; *pl.* **por'gies** or **por'gy,** [prob. var. of *pogy*.] any of a large number of salt-water food fishes having spiny fins and a wide body covered with large scales.

Pō·rif'e·rá, *n.pl.* [pore, and L. *ferre*, to bear.] in zoology, a phylum of invertebrates which includes sponges.

pō·rif'ĕr·ăn, *n.* any of the *Porifera*.

pō·rif'ĕr·ous, *a.* 1. having pores.
2. in zoology, of or related to the *Porifera*.

pō'ri·form, *a.* [L. *porus*, pore, and *form*.] resembling a pore.

pŏr'i·ness, *n.* the state of being porous, or having numerous pores.

pō'rism, *n.* [ME. *porysme*; ML. *porisma*; Gr. *porisma*, lit., a thing brought, from *porizein*, to bring.] in ancient mathematics, a geometrical proposition variously defined; specifically, (a) a proposition deduced from some other demonstrated proposition; a corollary; (b) a proposition that uncovers the possibility of finding such conditions as to make a specific problem capable of innumerable solutions.

pō·ris·mat'iç, *a.* pertaining to a porism; seeking to determine by what means and in how many ways a problem may be solved.

pō·ris·mat'iç·ăl, *a.* porismatic.

pō'rīte, *n.* a coral of the family *Poritidæ*, or of the genus *Porites*.

Pō·rī'tēs, *n.* [LL., from L. *porus*, pore.]
1. in zoology, a genus of perforate madreporarian corals, having small twelve-rayed calicles and a very porous structure.
2. a genus of millepores.

Pō·rit'i·dae, *n.pl.* a family of corals of which *Porites* is the type genus.

pŏrk, *n.* [ME. and OFr. *porc*; L. *porcus*, a pig.]
1. originally, a pig or hog.

2. the flesh of a pig or hog, used, fresh or cured, as food.

3. money, position, etc. received from the government through political patronage. [Slang.]

pŏrk bar'rel, government appropriations for political patronage, as for local improvements to please legislators' constituents. [Slang.]

pŏrk'ĕr, *n.* a hog, especially a young one, fattened for use as food.

pŏrk'et, *n.* a young hog. [Rare.]

pŏrk'fish, *n.*; *pl.* **pŏrk'fish·es** or **pŏrk'fish,** a black grunt, *Anisotremus virginicus*, with yellow stripes, of the West Indies.

pŏrk'i·ness, *n.* the state or quality of being porky.

pŏrk'ling, *n.* a young pig.

pŏrk pīe, 1. a meat pie made of chopped pork, usually eaten cold.
2. a soft hat with a round, flat crown, worn by men: now often *porkpie*.

pŏrk'pīe, *n.* same as *pork pie*, sense 2.

pŏrk'y, *a.*; *comp.* porkier; *superl.* porkiest,
1. of or like pork.
2. fat, as though overfed.
3. saucy, cocky, presumptuous, impertinent, or the like. [Slang.]

por'nŏ, *n.* pornography. [Slang.]

por'nŏ, *a.* pornographic. [Slang.]

por·noç'ra·cy, *n.* [Gr. *pornē*, prostitute, and *kratein*, to rule.] government by prostitutes; domination, sway, or influence of profligate women; specifically, the government of Rome in the early part of the tenth century.

por·nō·graph'iç, *a.* of, or having the nature of, pornography; obscene.

por·nog'ra·phy, *n.* [Gr. *pornē*, prostitute, and *graphein*, to write.]
1. originally, a description of prostitutes and their trade.
2. writings, pictures, etc. intended to arouse sexual desire.
3. the production of such writings, pictures, etc.

por·o·mĕr'iç, *n.* [arbitrary coinage, prob. from *porous*, and *polymeric*.] a synthetic, leather-like, porous material, often coated or impregnated with a polymer.

pō·rō·phyl'lous, *a.* [Gr. *poros*, pore, and *phyllon*, leaf.] in botany, having leaves covered with transparent points or dots.

Pō·rō'sá, *a.* [LL. *porosus*, full of pores.] same as *Perforata*.

pō·rōse', *a.* [LL. *porosus*, full of pores.]
1. porous.
2. of or pertaining to the *Porosa*.

pō·ros'i·ty, *n.*; *pl.* **pō·ros'i·ties,** [ME. *porositee*; ML. *porositas*, from *porosus*, from L. *porus*, a pore.]
1. the quality or state of being porous.
2. the ratio of the volume of a material's pores to that of its solid content.
3. anything porous.
4. a pore.

pō·rot'iç, *n.* [Gr. *pōros*, a callus.] any medicine which assists in the formation of callus.

pō'rous, *a.* [from *pore*.] full of pores, or tiny holes through which fluids, air, or light may pass; as, a *porous* skin; *porous* wood; *porous* earth.

pō'rous·ly, *adv.* in a porous manner.

pō'rous·ness, *n.* the quality or state of having pores; porosity; as, the *porousness* of the skin of an animal, or of wood.

por'pen·tine, *n.* porcupine. [Obs.]

por·phy·rā'çeous, *a.* same as *porphyritic*.

por'phyre, *n.* porphyry. [Obs.]

por'phy·rin, *n.* [from *hematoporphyrin*, from *hemato-*, and Gr. *porphyra*, purple, purple product of hemoglobin decomposition.] any of a group of pyrrole derivatives of hemoglobin and chlorophyll, containing no iron or magnesium.

por'phy·rine (-rēn), *n.* a chemical substance, colorless and uncrystallized, obtained from the bark of an Australian tree, *Alstonia constricta*.

fāte, fär, fàst, fạll, fĭnăl, cāre, at; mēte, prĕy, hēr, met; pīne, marine, bĭrd, pin; nōte, mōve, fọr, atŏm, not; mọọn, book;

Por·phyr'i·ŏ, *n.* [Gr. *porphyriōn,* the purple gallinule, from *porphyra,* purple.]
1. a genus of birds of the rail family, including *Porphyrio hyacinthinus,* the purple or hyacinthine gallinule, a bird found in Europe, Asia, and Africa, having a strong beak and long legs.
2. [p–] a bird of this genus.

PORPHYRIO

por'phy·rīte, *n.* any rock of a porphyritic nature.

por·phy·rit'iç, *a.* [ME. *porphiritike;* ML. *porphyriticus;* L. *porphyrites;* Gr. *porphyrītēs,* porphyry.]
1. composed of or pertaining to porphyry.
2. resembling porphyry; containing distinct crystals embedded in a fine-grained mass.

por''phy·ri·zā'tion, *n.* the act or process of porphyrizing, or the condition or quality of being porphyrized.

por'phy·rīze, *v.t.* to cause to resemble porphyry.

por'phy·rō·ğēne'', *a.* [Gr. *porphyra,* purple, and *gennān,* to beget.] born to the purple or of royal descent.

por''phy·rō·ğē·net'iç, *a.* [Gr. *porphyrītēs,* porphyry, and *gennān,* to beget.] of or relating to porphyrogenitism.

por''phy·rō·ğen'i·tism, *n.* the mode of succession in some royal families, notably the Byzantine, whereby a younger son, if born in the purple, that is, after the accession of his parents to the throne, was preferred to an older son, who was born before the parents' accession.

por''phy·rō·ğen'i·tus, *n.* [Gr. *porphyra,* purple, and *gennētos,* from *gennān,* to beget.] a son born to a sovereign, especially in the Byzantine Empire.

por'phy·roid, *n.* a rock that resembles, or has the structure of, porphyry.

por'phy·ry, *n.; pl.* **por'phy·rieş,** [ME. *purfire, porfire;* OFr. *porfire;* ML. *porphyreus,* from Gr. *porphyros,* purple.]
1. originally, a hard Egyptian rock having red and white feldspar crystals embedded in a fine-grained, dark-red or purplish ground-mass.
2. any igneous rock of similar texture.

por'phy·ry shell, a univalve shell of the genus *Murex;* also, a seashell, *Oliva porphyria,* that is spotted like porphyry.

Por'pi·tă, *n.* [Gr. *porpē,* brooch.] a genus of bright-colored, disk-shaped marine siphonophores.

por'poise (-pus), *n.; pl.* **por'pois·eş** or **por'poise,** [ME. *porcpisce, porpesse, porpese, porpus,* lit., swine fish, from L. *porcus,* a pig or swine, and *piscis,* a fish.]
1. any of a number of small, related cetaceans of the genus *Phocæna,* dark above and white below, with a triangle-shaped fin on the back, a blunt snout, and many teeth.

PORPOISE

2. a dolphin or any of several other small cetaceans.

por'pō·rāte, *a.* arrayed in purple or royal raiment.

por'pus, *n.* a porpoise. [Dial.]

por·rā'ceous, *a.* [L. *porraceus,* from *porrum,* a leek or onion.] greenish; resembling the leek in color.

por·rect', *a.* in zoology, denoting a part which extends forth horizontally.

por·rect', *v.t.* [L. *porrectus,* pp. of *porrigere,* to extend.] to extend horizontally.

por·rec'tion, *n.* [L. *porrectio,* from *porrigere; por,* for *pro,* forward, and *regere,* to direct.] the act of stretching forth.

por'ret, *n.* [It. *porretta;* L. *porrum,* a leek.] a scallion; a leek or small onion. [Now Dial.]

por'ridge, *n.* [altered from *pottage* by confusion with ME. *porrey;* OFr. *poree;* LL. *porrata,* leek broth, from L. *porrum,* leek.]
1. originally, pottage.
2. a soft food made of cereal or meal boiled in water or milk until thick. [Chiefly Brit.]

por'rin·ğer, *n.* [earlier *pottanger, pottager,* from Fr. *potager,* soup dish: altered by association with *porridge.*]
1. a small metal vessel for porridge, etc., especially one from which children are fed.
2. a headdress in the shape of a porringer. [Rare.]

pŏrt, *n.* [ME. *porte, port;* OFr. *porte;* L. *porta,* a door.]
1. a gateway; a portal. [Obs. except Scot.]
2. (a) a porthole; (b) the covering for this.
3. an opening, as in a cylinder face or valve face, for the passage of steam, gas, water, etc.
4. a mouthpiece of curved metal used in some bridle bits.

pŏrt, *v.t.* [ME. *porten;* OFr. *porter;* L. *portare* to carry.]
1. originally, to carry.
2. to carry, hold, or place (a rifle or sword) diagonally in front of one, crossing the left shoulder, as for inspection.

pŏrt, *n.* [ME. *porte;* OFr., from the v.]
1. the manner in which one carries oneself; carriage; deportment; demeanor.
2. the position of porting a weapon.
3. purport; meaning.
4. state; splendid or stately manner of living. [Obs.]
5. a piece of iron, somewhat in the shape of a horseshoe, fixed to the saddle or stirrup, and used to carry the lance when held upright. [Obs.]

pŏrt, *n.* [ME., from OFr. and AS. *port,* port, haven, harbor, from L. *portus,* a haven; akin to L. *porta,* gate; Gr. *poros,* a passage.]
1. a harbor; a haven; any bay, cove, inlet, or recess of the sea or of a lake, or the mouth of a river, which ships or vessels can enter, and where they can lie safe from injury by storms.
2. a city or town with a harbor where ships arrive and depart, and load or unload cargoes.
3. a port of entry.

pŏrt, *n.* [from *port* (harbor), with reference to the side opposite the steering oar.] the left-hand side of a ship or airplane as one faces forward, toward the bow; larboard: opposed to *starboard.*

pŏrt, *a.* of or on the port, or left-hand side.

pŏrt, *v.t.* and *v.i.* to move or turn (the helm) to the left.

pŏrt, *n.* [from *Oporto,* Portugal.] a fortified sweet wine, usually dark-red, originally from Portugal.

pŏr'tă, *n.; pl.* **pŏr'tae,** [L.] the entrance for nerves and ducts into an organ.

pŏrt·a·bil'i·ty, *n.* the condition or quality of being portable.

pŏrt'a·ble, *a.* [L. *portabilis.*]
1. that can be carried.
2. easily carried.
3. bearable; endurable. [Obs.]

pŏrt'a·ble, *n.* anything portable.

pŏrt'a·ble·ness, *n.* the quality or state of being portable.

pŏr'tăge, *n.* [ME.; OFr.; ML. *portaticum,* from *portare,* to carry.]
1. the act of transporting or carrying.
2. the cost or price of transporting or carrying.
3. capacity for carriage; tonnage; burden. [Obs.]
4. a carrying or transporting of boats and supplies overland between navigable rivers, lakes, etc., as during a canoe trip.
5. any place or route over which this is done.
6. a sailor's wages.

pŏr'tăge, *v.t.* and *v.i.;* portaged, *pt., pp.;* portaging, *ppr.* to carry or transport (boats, etc.) over a portage.

Pŏr'tăge for·mā'tion, a geological subdivision of the Upper Devonian of the United States. It is named after Portage township in New York State.

pŏr'tă·ğue, *n.* an obsolete Portuguese coin.

pŏr'tăl, *n.* [ME.; OFr.; ML. *portale,* orig. neut. of *portalis,* of a door, from L. *porta,* gate.]
1. a doorway or entrance, especially a large and imposing one.
2. in architecture, the lesser gate, where there are two gates of different dimensions.

3. formerly, a little square corner of a room, separated from the rest by a wainscot, and forming a short passage into a room.
4. any entrance: often figurative, as, the *portal* of wisdom. [Poetic.]
5. the portal vein.

pŏr'tăl, *a.* [ML. *portalis.*] designating, of, or like the vein carrying blood from the intestines, stomach, etc. to the liver.

pŏr'tăl-tö-pŏr'tăl pặy, wages for workers based on the total time spent from the moment of entering the mine, factory, etc. until the moment of leaving it.

pŏr·tă·men'tō, *n.; pl.* **pŏr·tă·men'tī,** [It., from *portare,* to carry; L. *portare.*] in music, a continuous gliding from one note to another, sounding all intervening tones; a glide.

pŏr'tănce, *n.* [Early Mod. Eng., from Fr. *portance,* from *porter,* to bear.] air; mein; carriage; port. [Archaic.]

pŏr'tass, *n.* [OFr. *porte-hors; porter,* to carry, and *hors,* out of doors; so called from being easily portable.] a breviary; a prayer book. [Obs.]

pŏr'tāte, *a.* [L. *portatus,* pp. of *portare,* to carry.] in heraldry, placed bendwise in an escutcheon; that is, lying as if carried on a person's shoulder, as a cross.

pŏr'tă·tive, *a.* [ME. and OFr. *portatif,* lit., that is carried, from L. *portatus,* pp. of *portare,* to carry, and OFr. *-if.*]
1. of or having the power of carrying a load, charge, etc.
2. that can be carried; portable. [Obs.]

CROSS PORTATE

pŏrt au·thor'i·ty, a governmental commission in charge of the traffic, regulations, etc. of a port.

pŏrt căp'tain (-tin), an official of a steamship company who assumes charge of vessels during their stay in port.

pŏrt chärğe, in commerce, a fee or duty charged for the privilege of keeping a ship or its cargo in a port.

pŏrt'çlúse, *n.* a portcullis. [Obs.]

pŏrt''crăy'ŏn, *n.* [Fr. *porte-crayon; porter,* to carry, and *crayon,* pencil.] a small metallic handle with a clasp for holding a crayon, etc. when used in drawing.

pŏrt'·cul'lis, *n.* [ME. *portcoles;* OFr. *porte coleice; porte,* a gate, and *coleice,* f. of *coleis,* sliding, from L. *colare,* to strain, filter.]
1. in fortification, a heavy grating or lattice-work of timber or iron with the lower ends pointed like the teeth of a harrow, suspended by chains over the gateway of a castle, fort, etc., to be let down to prevent the entrance of an enemy.
2. a coin used by the East India Company in the reign of Queen Elizabeth I: it had a design of a portcullis on one side. [Obs.]

PORTCULLIS

pŏrt·cul'lis, *v.t.* to shut; to bar. [Rare.]

Pŏrte, *n.* [the chief office of the Ottoman Empire was styled *Babi Ali,* lit., the High Gate, from the gate (*bāb*) of the palace at which justice was administered. The French translation of this term is *la Sublime Porte:* hence the use of this word.] the Ottoman Turkish government.

pŏrte'-çō'chere' (-shār'), *n.* [Fr. *porte,* gate, and *cochère,* coach.]
1. a large porch outside the entrance of a building, under which vehicles may be driven.
2. a large entrance gateway through which vehicles are driven into a square or courtyard.

pŏrt'ed, *a.* having gates. [Obs.]

pŏrte'feuille' (-fê'ye), *n.* [Fr., from *porter,* to carry, and *feuille,* L. *folium,* leaf.] a portfolio.

pŏr'tē·gūṣ, *n.* portague. [Obs.]

pŏrte'-lù·miere'' (-myār''), *n.* [Fr., from *porter,* to carry, and *lumière,* light.] a mirror that can be adjusted so as to cast rays of light in any required direction; a simple form of heliostat.

pŏrte'mŏn·nāie'' (-nā''), *n.* [Fr., from *porter* to carry, and *monnaie,* money.] a pocketbook for carrying money; a purse.

pŏr·tend', *v.t.;* portended, *pt., pp.;* portending, *ppr.* [L. *portendere, protendere; pro,* forth, and *tendere,* to stretch.]
1. to be an omen or warning of; to fore-

COMBINING FORMS PRESENTED IN *Vocabulary Expansion I*

The number after the meaning refers to the exercise in which the combining form is presented.

A. Without. 5
Able. Can do; able. 4
Agog. Leading; directing; inciting. 5
Agogue. Leading; directing; inciting. 5
Al. Relating to. 13
Ali. Other. 5
Ambi. Both. 13
An. Native of; belonging to. 18
Ance. Act of; state of; quality of. 13
Anima. Spirit; mind; soul. 15
Animus. Spirit; mind; soul. 15
Anni. Year. 1
Annu. Year. 1
Anthrop. Mankind; man; human. 6
Anthropo. Mankind; man; human. 6
Anti. Against. 9
Aqua. Water. 7
Aqui. Water. 7
Ar. One who; that which. 1
Arch. Rule; chief. 5
Archae. Ancient. 12
Archaeo. Ancient. 12
Astro. Star. 7
Aud. Hear. 9
Audi. Hear. 9
Aut. Self. 1
Auto. Self. 1
Belli. War. 13
Bello. War. 13
Bene. Good. 9
Bi. Two. 1
Biblio. Book. 10
Bio. Life. 1
Brevi. Short; brief. 12
Cap. Take; receive. 11
Capit. Head. 8
Cata. Down. 10
Cede. Go; give in; yield. 12

Ceed. Go; give in; yield. 12

Cent. Hundred; hundredth part. 4

Centi. Hundred; hundredth part. 4

Cep. Take; receive. 11

Chron. Time. 12

Chrono. Time. 12

Cide. Murder; kill. 8

Civ. Citizen. 13

Civis. Citizen. 13

Co. With. 7

Col. With. 7

Com. With 7

Con. With 7

Contra. Against; opposite. 3

Cor. With. 7

Corp. Body. 8

Corpor. Body. 8

Cred. Believe. 4

Crypt. Secret; hidden. 12

Crypto. Secret; hidden. 12

Cura. Care. 9

Cycl. Circle; wheel. 12

Cyclo. Circle; wheel. 12

De. Away; from; off; completely. 11

Dec. Ten. 4

Deca. Ten. 4

Deci. Tenth part. 4

Dem. People. 5

Demo. People. 5

Derm. Skin. 11

Dermo. Skin. 11

Di. Two. 17

Dia. Through. 10

Dic. Say; speak. 3

Dict. Say; speak. 3

Dis. Away from; apart; not. 12

Dorm. Sleep. 14

Duc. Lead. 12

E. Out of; from; lacking. 11

Ego. I; me; the self. 14

Em. In; into. 8

En. In; into. 8

Ence. Act of; state of; quality of. 13

Enni. Year. 1

Epi. Upon; beside; among. 10

Equi. Equal. 15

Er. One who; that which. 1

Err. Wander. 14

Ex. Out of; from; lacking; former. 11

Fac. Make; do. 9

Fect. Make; do. 9

Feder. Trust; faith. 15

Fer. Bring; bear; yield. 10

Fic. Make; do. 9

Fid. Trust; faith. 15

Fide. Trust; faith. 15

Fin. End. 10

Fort. Strong. 18

Frater. Brother. 8

Fratr. Brother. 8

Fy. Make; cause to be; change into; become. 18

Gamy. Marriage. 6

Gen. Kind; race; descent. 6

Geno. Kind; race; descent. 6

Geo. Earth. 2

Gnosi. Knowledge. 11

Gnosis. Knowledge. 11

Gram. Something written or drawn; a record. 3

Graph. Something written; machine. 1

Greg. Flock. 16

Gyn. Woman. 11

Gyno. Woman. 11

Hom. Same; man; human. 6

Homo. Same; man; human. 6

Hydr. Water. 18

Hydra. Water. 18

Hydro. Water. 18

Hyper. Over; above; excessive. 14

Hypn. Sleep. 15.

Hypno. Sleep. 15

Hypo. Under. 11

Ian. Native of; belonging to. 18

Ible. Can do; able. 4

Il. Not. 10

Im. Into; not. 10

In. Into; not. 10

Inter. Between; among. 14

Intra. Within; inside of. 14

Ion. State of; act of; result of. 3

Ir. Not. 10

Ist. One who. 6

Ize. To cause to be or become; to be like; to be formed into. 16

Juris. Law. 17

Jus. Law. 17

Kilo. Thousand. 4

Leg. Law. 6

Legis. Law. 6

Less. Without. 7

Lex. Law. 6

Loc. Place. 9

Loco. Place. 9

Log. Speech; word. 10

Logo. Speech; word. 10

Luc. Light; clear. 14

Lum. Light; clear. 14

Magna. Great; large. 15

Mal. Bad; ill; evil; wrong; not perfect. 15

Man. Hand. 9

Manu. Hand. 9

Matr. Mother. 17

Matri. Mother. 17

Matro. Mother. 17

Meter. Measure. 2

Micro. Very small. 2

Milli. Thousand; thousandth part. 4

Mis. Wrong; hate. 6

Miso. Wrong; hate. 6

Miss. Send. 15

Mitt. Send. 15

Mon. One. 5

Mono. One. 5

Mors. Death. 8

Mort. Death. 8

Nasc. Born. 15

Nat. Born. 15

Naut. Sailor. 7

Ness. Quality of; state of. 17

Nomin. Name. 9

Non. Not. 9

Nov. New. 14

Ology. Study of; science of. 1

Omni. All. 7

Onym. Name. 9

Or. One who; that which. 1
Ous. Full of; having. 16
Pac. Peace. 13
Pater. Father. 16
Pathy. Feeling; suffering. 8
Patri. Father. 16
Pax. Peace. 13
Ped. Foot; child. 1, 11
Pedo. Child. 11
Peri. Around. 14
Phil. Love. 16
Phile. Love. 16
Philo. Love. 16
Phob. Fear. 3
Phobo. Fear. 3
Phon. Sound. 2
Phono. Sound. 2
Pod. Foot. 1
Polis. City. 13
Poly. Many. 6
Pon. Place; set. 15
Pop. People. 15
Port. Carry. 4
Pos. Place; set. 15
Post. After. 13
Poten. Powerful. 7
Pre. Before. 8
Pro. Before; forward. 10
Pseudo. False. 9
Psych. Spirit; mind; soul. 16
Psyche. Spirit; mind; soul. 16
Psycho. Spirit; mind; soul. 16
Re. Again; back. 2
Ri. Laughter. 11
Ridi. Laughter. 11
Risi. Laughter. 11
Rog. Ask; beg. 17
Sci. Know. 7
Scio. Know. 7
Scope. A means for seeing; watching or viewing. 2
Scrib. Write. 2
Scrip. Write. 2
Se. Apart. 16

Semi. Half; not fully; partly; occurring twice in a period. 15

Sequi. Follow. 12

Sion. State of; act of; result of. 3

Sist. Stand. 14

Soph. Wise. 14

Spect. See; view; observe. 3

Sphere. Ball. 18

Sta. Stand. 14

Sub. Under; beneath; below; lower in rank. 12

Syl. Same; with; together; along with. 8

Sym. Same; with; together; along with. 8

Syn. Same; with; together; along with. 8

Tain. Hold. 12

Techno. Arts and crafts (especially industrial arts); method; system; skill. 18

Techni. Arts and crafts (especially industrial arts); method; system; skill. 18

Tele. From a distance. 2

Temp. Time. 11

Tempo. Time. 11

Tempor. Time. 11

Ten. Hold. 12

Tend. Stretch; strain. 13

Tens. Stretch; strain. 13

Tent. Hold; stretch; strain. 12, 13

Theo. God. 5

Therm. Heat. 18

Thermo. Heat. 18

Tion. Act of; state of; result of. 3

Tox. Poison. 11

Toxo. Poison. 11

Tract. Draw; pull. 18

Trans. Across; beyond; through; on the other side of; over. 10

Tude. Condition of; state of. 17

Un. Not. 8

Uni. One. 3

Ven. Come. 7

Veni. Come. 7

Vent. Come. 7

Vers. Turn. 17

Vert. Turn. 17

Vid. See. 7

Vis. See. 7

Voc. Voice; call. 13

Vox. Voice; call. 13

The number after the meaning refers to the exercise in which the vocabulary word is presented. If there is more than one number, it means the word has also appeared in "Extra Word Power."

Abbreviation. A shortened form of a word or phrase. 12

Abstract.[2] Thought of apart from any specific object; disassociated from any particular instance; difficult to understand; theoretical; not concrete; a short statement giving the main points of a book, article, or research paper. 18

Abstract.[2] To take away or remove; to withdraw; to take away secretly; slyly, or dishonestly; to divert; to make an abstraction. 18

Admission. Act of allowing to enter; entrance fee; a price charged or paid to be admitted; acknowledgment; a confession, as to a crime. 15

Adverse. Hostile; contrary to one's interest or welfare; unfavorable. 17

Advertise. To give public notice of in newspapers, radio, television, and so on; to praise the good qualities of a product, service, and so on; to call attention to; to notify, inform. 17

Affect. To act upon or to cause something; to influence; to produce an effect or change in. 9

Aggregate. A mass of separate things joined together; the whole sum or amount; formed by the collection of units or particles into a body, mass, or amount; total; to amount to; to come to; to total; to come together in a mass or group; to collect; to unite; accumulate. 16

Alias. Another name taken by a person, often a criminal. 5

Alien. A foreigner; a person from another country; foreign. 5

Alienate. To make others unfriendly to one; to estrange (to remove or keep at a distance). 5

Allocate. To set apart for a special purpose; to divide up something; to divide and distribute something. 9

Ambiguous. Having two or more meanings. 13

American. A native of America. 18

Americanize. To become an American. 16

Amoral. Without morals; without a sense of right or wrong. 5

Anarchist. One who believes that there should be no government. 6

Anarchy. The absence of government; no rule; a state of disorder; chaos. 5

Animosity. Hatred; resentment. 15

Anniversary. Yearly return of a date marking an event or an occurrence of some importance; returning or recurring each year. 1

Annual. Every year. 1, 13

Anonymous. Lacking a name; of unknown authorship. 9

---

[1] Additional Words are presented separately; see p. 333.

[2] *Abstract* and *abstract* are presented separately because they are pronounced differently.

Antacid. Something that acts against acid.   9

Anthropologist. One who is in the field of anthropology.   6

Anthropology. Study of mankind; study of the cultures and customs of people.   6

Antigambling. Against gambling.   9

Antilabor. Against labor.   9

Antimachine. Against machines.   9

Antimen. Against men.   9

Antiwar. Against war.   9

Antiwomen. Against women.   9

Antonym. A word opposite in meaning to some other word.   9

Apathy. Lack of feeling; indifference.   8

Apodal. Relating to being without feet.   13

Aquanaut. One who travels undersea; a person trained to work in an underwater chamber.   7

Aquarium. A pond, a glass bowl, a tank, or the like, in which aquatic animals and/or plants are kept; a place in which aquatic collections are shown.   7

Aquatic. Living or growing in or near water; performed on or in water.   7

Archaeology. The study of the life and culture of ancient people, as by the digging up of old settlements, ruins from the past, and old man-made or other objects.   12

Archaic. Belonging to an earlier period; ancient; old-fashioned; no longer used.   12

Arrogant. Full of pride and self-importance; overbearing; haughty.   17

Asian. A native of Asia.   18

Assist. To give help to; an act of helping.   14

Assistance. Act of helping.   13

Astrology. The art or practice that claims to tell the future and interpret the influence of the heavenly bodies on the fate of people; a reading of the stars.   7

Astronaut. One who travels in space; a person trained to travel in outer space.   7

Astronomy. The science that deals with stars, planets, and space.   7

Atheist. One who does not believe in the existence of God.   5

Atmosphere. The air that surrounds the earth; the mass of gases that surrounds the earth and is held to it by the force of gravity; the air in any given place; a mental or moral environment; surrounding influence; the feeling or coloring that surrounds a work of art.   18

Attention. Mental concentration; care; a position of readiness; acts of courtesy.   13

Audible. Capable of being heard.   9

Audience. An assembly of listeners or spectators at a concert, play, speech, and so on.   9

Audiovisual. Of, pertaining to, involving, or directed at both hearing and sight.   9

Audit. To examine or check such things as accounts; to attend class as a listener; an examination of accounts to report the financial state of a business. 9

Audition. A trial hearing, as of an actor or singer; the act of hearing; to try out for a part in an audition. 9

Auditorium. A building or hall for speeches, concerts, public meetings, and so on; the room in a building occupied by an audience. 9

Author. One who writes. 1

Autobiography. Lift story written by oneself. 1

Autocracy. A form of government in which one person rules absolutely. 5

Autocrat. A ruler who has absolute control of a country. 5

Autograph. Signature; written by a person's own hand: an *autograph* letter; containing autographs: an *autograph* album; to write one's name on or in. 1

Beautify. To make beautiful. 18

Beggar. One who begs. 1

Belligerent. Warlike; any nation, person, or group engaged in fighting war. 13

Benefactor. One who gives help or confers a benefit; a patron. 9

Beneficiary. One who receives benefits or advantages; the one to whom an insurance policy is payable. 9

Benefit. That which is helpful; advantage; a payment; a performance given to raise funds for a worthy cause; to aid. 9

Biannual. Twice a year; (loosely) occurring every two years. 1

Bibliography. A listing of books on a subject by an author (the description includes author's name, title, publisher, date of publication, and so on). 10

Bicentennial. Pertaining to or in honor of a two-hundredth anniversary; consisting of or lasting two hundred years; occurring once in two hundred years; a two-hundredth anniversary. 4

Bicycle. A vehicle having two wheels. 1

Biennial. Once every two years; lasting for two years. 1

Bigamist. One who is married to two spouses at the same time. 6

Bigamy. Marriage to two spouses at the same time. 6

Bimonthly. Every two months; twice a month. 1

Biographer. A person who writes biographies. 1

Biography. Person's life story. 1

Biologist. One who is in the field of biology. 6

Biology. Science of life. 1

Biped. Two-footed animal. 1

Biweekly. Every two weeks; twice a week. 1

Blameless. Without blame; without fault. 7

Capable. Able to be affected; able to understand; having ability; having qualities that are able to be developed. 11

Capital. City or town that is the official seat of government; money or wealth; first letter of a word at the beginning of a sentence; excellent. 8

Capitalism. The economic system in which all or most of the means of production, such as land, factories, and railroads, are privately owned and operated for profit. 8

Capital punishment. The death penalty. 8

Capsule. A small container made of gelatin (or other material that melts) that holds a dose of medicine; a special removable part of an airplane or rocket. 11

Captive. One who is taken prisoner; one who is dominated. 11

Captor. One who holds someone a prisoner. 1

Catalog. A listing of names, titles, and so on in some order; a book containing such a list; to make a catalog. 10

Centennial. Pertaining to a period of one hundred years; lasting one hundred years; a one-hundredth anniversary. 4

Century. Period of one hundred years. 4

Christian. Believing in the Christian religion. 18

Chronic. Continuing for a long time; prolonged; recurring. 12

Chronological. Arranged in time order (earlier things or events precede later ones). 12

Circumference. The distance around a circle; a boundary line of any rounded area. 10

Circumstance. Something connected with an act, event, or condition; (often pl.) the conditions, influences, and so on surrounding and influencing persons or actions; formal display, as in *pomp and circumstance.* 14

Civics. (Used in the singular.) The part of political science dealing with the study of civic affairs and the rights and responsibilities of citizenship. 13

Civil. Of a citizen or citizens; relating to citizens and their government; relating to ordinary community life as distinguished from military or church affairs; polite. 13

Civilian. One who is not in the military; of civilians; nonmilitary. 13

Civilization. A state of human society that has a high level of intellectual, social, and cultural development; the cultural development of a specific people, country, or region. 13

Collect. To gather together. 7

Combine. To join together; unite. 7

Concede. To give in; surrender; yield; grant; admit. 12

Conceive. To become pregnant with; to form in the mind; to understand; to think; to believe; to imagine; to develop mentally. 11

Conductor. One who guides or leads; a guide or director; one who has charge of a railroad train; the director of an orchestra or a chorus; any substance that conducts electricity, heat; and so on. 12

Conference. A discussion or meeting on some important matter. 10, 13

Confide. To tell in trust; to tell secrets trustingly. 15

Congregate. To come together into a group, crowd, or assembly; to come together or collect in a particular place or locality. 16

Consequence. That which follows from any act; a result; an effect. 12

Consist. To be made up of.   14

Contemporary. Belonging to the same age; living or occurring at the same time; current; one living in the same period as another or others; a person or thing of about the same age or date of origin.   11

Content.[3] Satisfied; not complaining; not desiring something else.   12

Content.[3] What something holds (usually plural in this sense); subject matter; the material that something is made up of; the main substance or meaning.   12

Contract.[4] A binding agreement between two or more parties; a covenant.   18

Contract.[4] To draw together; to make smaller; shrink; shorten; to shorten a word by omitting one or more sounds or letters; to bring on oneself as an obligation or debt; to get.   18

Contradiction. Something (such as a statement) consisting of opposing parts.   3

Contrary. Opposite.   3

Contrast. Difference between things; use of opposites for a certain result.   3

Controversy. A dispute, especially a lengthy and public one, between sides holding opposing views; a quarrel; debate; argument.   17

Convene. To come together; to assemble.   7

Convenient. Well suited to one's purpose, personal comfort, or ease.   7

Convention. A formal meeting of members for political or professional purposes; accepted custom, rule, or opinion.   7

Converse. A thing, especially a statement, that is turned around, usually producing a different idea or meaning; something that is opposite or contrary.   17.

Corporal punishment. Bodily punishment; a beating.   8

Corporation. A group of people who get a charter granting them as a body certain of the powers, rights, privileges, and liabilities (legal responsibilities) of an individual, separate from those of the individuals making up the group.   8

Corpse. Dead body.   8

Correspond. To be equivalent; to write letters to one another.   7

Co-workers. Someone working with you.   7

Credential. Something that entitles one to credit or confidence; something that makes others believe in a person; (pl.) testimonials entitling a person to credit or to exercise official power.   4

Credible. Believable.   4

Credit. Belief in something; trust; faith; good name; in an account, the balance in one's favor; a unit of academic study; to supply something on credit to.   4

Crypt. An underground vault.   12

Cryptic. Having a hidden or secret meaning; mysterious.   12

Cycle. A period that keeps coming back, in which certain events take place and

---

[3] *Content* and *content* are presented separately because they are pronounced differently.

[4] *Contract* and *contract* are presented separately because they are pronounced differently.

complete themselves in some definite order; a round of years or ages; a pattern of regularly occurring events; a series that repeats itself.   12

Cyclone. A system of violent and destructive whirlwinds.   12

Decade. Period of ten years.   4

Decapitate. To take off the head; to kill.   11

Deceive. To mislead by lying; to lead into error.   11

Decode. To change from code to simple language.   11

Decolor. To take color away.   11

Deduction. The act of drawing a conclusion by reasoning or reasoning that goes from the general to the particular; the taking away or subtraction of something; an inference or a conclusion.   12

Deflea. To take off fleas.   11

Dehydrate. To remove water from; to lose water or moisture; dry.   18

Delouse. To free from lice.   11

Demagogue. A person who stirs up the emotions of people in order to become a leader and achieve selfish ends.   5

Democracy. A form of government in which there is rule by the people either directly or through elected representatives.   5

Denude. To strip the covering from completely.   11

Dependence. Act of trusting; act of relying on someone for support.   13

Deport. To send someone away.   11

Deprive. To take something away from.   11

Dermatologist. A doctor who deals with skin disorders.   11

Derogatory. Tending to make less well regarded; tending to belittle someone or something; disparaging; belittling.   17

Description. An account that gives a picture of something in words.   2,3

Detract. To draw away or divert; to take away a part, as from quality, value, or reputation.   18

Detoxify. To take away poison; to destroy the poison.   11

Diagnose. To determine what is wrong with someone after an examination. 11

Diagram. An outline figure that shows the relationship between parts or places; a graph or chart.   10

Dialogue. A conversation in which two or more take part; the conversation in a play.   10

Diameter. A straight line passing through the center of a circle.   10

Dictation. The act of speaking or reading aloud to someone who takes down the words.   3

Dictator. A ruler who has absolute power.   3

Diction. Manner of speaking; choice of words.   3

Dictionary. A book for alphabetically listed words in a language, giving information about their meanings, pronunciations, and so forth.   3

Dilemma. Any situation that necessitates a choice between equally unfavorable or equally unpleasant alternatives; an argument that presents two equally unfavorable alternatives.   17

Disable. To make an object or someone not able to do something.   12

Disapprove. Not to approve of; not to regard as worthy. 12

Disband. To break up (a group). 12

Dishonest. Not honest; not to be trusted. 12

Disloyal. Not loyal. 12

Dismiss. To tell or allow to go; to discharge, as from a job; to get rid of; to have done with quickly; to reject. 15

Disrobe. To take off clothes. 12

Distant. Separated or apart by space and/or time; away from; far apart; not closely related. 14

Divert. To turn aside or from a path or course; to draw off to a different course, purpose, and so on. 17

Divide. To separate into parts. 17

Divorce. A legal dissolvement of a marriage relation usually by a court or other body having the authority; the legal ending of a marriage; to end legally a marriage; separate; disunite. 17

Dormant. Asleep or as if asleep; not active. 14

Dormitory. A large room in which many persons sleep; a building providing sleeping and living quarters, especially at a school, college, or resort (summer or winter hotel). 14

Effect. Something brought about by some cause; the result; consequence. 9

Effective. Producing or having the power to bring about an intended result; producing results with the least amount of wasted effort. 9

Egocentric. Self-centered; relating everything to oneself. 14

Empathy. The imaginative putting of oneself into another person's personality or skin; ability to understand how another feels because one has experienced it firsthand or otherwise. 8

Enjoyable. Able to be enjoyed. 4

Epilogue. A short section added at the end to a book, poem, and so on; a short speech added to a play and given at the end. 10

Equivalent. Equal in value, meaning, force, and so on. 15

Evidence. That which serves to prove or disprove something. 7

Evident. Obvious; clearly seen; plain. 7

Exactitude. The state of being exact. 17

Exception. The act of taking out; something or one that is taken out or left out; an objection. 11

Exclude. To keep from. 11

Excuse. To forgive. 11

Exhale. To breathe out. 11

Exit. To go out of. 11

Expect. To look out for. 11

Export. To carry away; to carry or send some product to some other country or place; something that is exported. 4

Ex-president. Former president. 11

Ex-wife. Former wife. 11

Factory. A building or buildings in which things are manufactured. 9

Fatherless. Without a father. 7

Federal. Of or formed by a compact; relating to or formed by an agreement between two or more states, groups, and so on; relating to a union of states, groups, and so on, in which central authority in common affairs is established by consent of its members. 15

Fertile. Able to produce a large crop; able to produce; capable of bearing offspring, seeds, fruit, and so on; productive in mental achievements; inventive; having abundant resources. 10

Fertilization. The act of making something able to produce; in biology, the union of a male and female germ cell; impregnation. 10

Final. Last; coming at the end; conclusive. 10

Finite. Having a limit or end; able to be measured. 10

Fortify. To strengthen against attack; to surround with defenses; to strengthen and secure (as a town) by forts; to give physical strength and courage to; to add mental and moral strength to. 18

Fortitude. Strength of mind that enables persons to bear pain or encounter danger with courage. 18

Fortress. A large place strengthened against attack; a fort or group of forts, often including a town; any place of security; a stronghold. 18

Fraternity. A group of men joined together by common interests for fellowship; a brotherhood; a Greek letter college organization. 8

General. Referring to all; in the U.S. Army and Air Force, an officer of the same rank as an admiral in the U.S. Navy. 6

Generic. Referring to all in a group or class. 6

Genocide. The systematic and deliberate killing of a whole group or a group of people bound together by customs, language, politics, and so on. 8

Geography. Study of the earth's surface and life. 2

Geologist. One who is in the field of geology. 6

Geology. Study of earth's physical history and makeup. 2

Geometry. Branch of mathematics dealing with the measurement of points, lines, planes, and so on. 2

Germicide. An agent that destroys germs. 8

Goodness. The state of being good. 17

Gratitude. The state of being grateful. 17

Gregarious. Tending to live in a flock, herd, or community rather than alone; marked by a fondness to be with others than alone; outgoing; sociable. 16

Gynecologist. A doctor dealing with women's diseases, especially in reference to reproductive organs. 11

Happiness. The state of being happy. 17

Harmless. Without harm; without hurting. 7

Hemisphere. A half sphere or globe; half the earth's surface (either the northern or southern half of the earth as divided by the equator or the eastern or western half as divided by a meridian). 18

Herbicide. An agent that destroys or holds in check plant growth. 8

Homicide. Any killing of one human being by another. 8

Homogeneous. Being the same throughout; being uniform. 6

Homograph. A word spelled the same way as another but having a different meaning. 6

Homonym. A word that agrees in pronunciation with some other word but differs in spelling and meaning. 9

Homosexual. Referring to the same sex or to sexual desire for those of the same sex; a homosexual individual. 6

Hydrant. An upright pipe or street fixture with a valve for drawing water directly from a water main; fireplug. 18

Hyperactive. Overactive. 14

Hyperproductive. Overproductive. 14

Hypersensitive. Oversensitive. 14

Hypertension. High blood pressure. 14

Hypnosis. A sleeplike trance that is artificially brought about. 15

Hypodermic. Referring to the area under the skin; used for injecting under the skin; a hypodermic injection; a hypodermic syringe or needle. 11

Hypothesis. An unproved scientific conclusion drawn from known facts; something assumed as a basis for argument; a possible answer to a problem that requires further investigation. 11

Illegal. Not legal; not lawful. 10

Immoral. Not moral; knows difference between right and wrong but chooses to do wrong. 5

Immortal. Referring to a being who never dies; undying; one who never dies. 8

Imperfect. Not perfect; having a fault. 10

Import. To carry in; bring in goods from another country; something that is imported. 4, 10

Important. Deserving of notice; of great value. 10

Impotent. Without power to act; physically weak; incapable of sexual intercourse (said of males). 7

Incorporate. To unite; combine. 8

Incredible. Not believable. 4

Ineffectual. Not being able to bring about results. 10

Infinite. Having no limit or end; not able to be measured. 10

Innate. Inborn; born with; not acquired from the environment; belonging to the fundamental nature of something. 15

Innovation. Something newly introduced; a new method, something new. 14

Insecticide. An agent that destroys insects. 8

Inspection. The act of looking into something. 10

Intense. Having great or extreme force; very strong; existing or occurring to a high or extreme degree. 13

Intention. Aim; goal; purpose. 13

Intercollegiate. Between colleges. 14

Interdepartmental. Between departments. 14

Interdependent. Dependent upon one another. 14

Intermission. Time between events; recess. 15

Interrogate. To ask questions of formally; to examine by questioning. 17

Interstate. Between states. 14

Intracollegiate. Within the college. 14

Intradepartmental. Within the department. 14

Intramural. Within a school or an institution. 14

Invisible. Not able to be seen. 7

Irregular. Not uniform; not the same. 10

Joyous. Full of joy. 16

Juror. One of a group of persons sworn to deliver a verdict in a case submitted to them; member of a jury. 17

Justice. The maintenance of what is reasonable and well founded; the assignment of deserved rewards or punishments; the quality or characteristic of being fair and impartial; rightfulness; fairness; correctness. 17

Justification. A reason, circumstance, explanation, or fact that justifies or defends; good reason. 17

Killer. One who kills. 1

Laughable. Able to be laughed at. 4

Legal. Referring to law; lawful. 6, 13

Legislature. Body of persons responsible for lawmaking. 6

Liquidize. To become liquid. 16

Local. Referring to a relatively small area, region, or neighborhood; limited. 9, 13

Location. A place or site; exact position or place occupied; a place used for filming a motion picture or a television program. 9

Logical. Relating to the science concerned with correct reasoning. 10

Lucid. Clear; easily understood; bright; shining. 14

Magnanimous. Forgiving of insults or injuries; high-minded; great of soul. 15

Magnificent. Splendid; beautiful; superb. 15

Magnify. To increase the size of; to make larger. 15

Maintain. To carry on or continue; to keep up; to keep in good condition. 12, 13

Maintenance. The act of keeping up. 13

Malformed. Abnormally formed. 15

Malfunction. To function badly. 15

Malnourished. Badly nourished. 15

Maltreated. Treated badly. 15

Manageable. Able to be managed. 4

Manicure. Care of the hands and fingernails; to care for the hands; to cut evenly. 9

Manual. Referring to the hand; made, done, or used by the hands; a handy book used as a guide or source of information. 9, 13

Manufacture. To make goods or articles by hand or by machinery; to make something from raw materials by hand or machinery; the act of manufacturing. 9

Manuscript. Written by hand or typed; not printed; a document written by hand; a book written by hand and usually sent in for publication; style of penmanship in which letters are not joined together.   9

Maternal. Motherly; having to do with a mother; inherited or derived from a mother; related on the mother's side of the family.   17

Maternity. The state of being a mother; motherhood; a hospital or a section of a hospital designated for the care of women immediately before and during childbirth and for the care of newborn babies.   17

Matrimony. The act or state of being married; the union of man and woman as husband and wife; marriage.   17

Metropolitan. Referring to a major city center and its surrounding area; a person who inhabits a metropolis or one who has the manners and tastes associated with a metropolis.   13

Microscope. Instrument used to make very small objects appear larger so that they can be seen.   2

Millennium. Period of one thousand years; a one-thousandth anniversary; a period of great happiness (the millennium).   4

Million. A thousand thousands (1,000,000); a very large or indefinitely large number; being one million in number.   4

Misanthrope. Hater of mankind.   6

Misnomer. A name wrongly applied to someone or something; an error in the naming of a person or place in a legal document.   9

Mission. Group or team of persons sent somewhere to perform some work; the task, business, or responsibility that a person is assigned; the place where missionaries carry out their work; a place where poor people may go for assistance.   15

Modify. To change slightly or make minor changes in character, form, and so on; to change or alter.   18

Mohammedan. Believing in the principles of Mohammed.   18

Monarchy. A government or state headed by a king, a queen, or an emperor: called absolute (or despotic) when there is no limitation on the monarch's power and constitutional (or limited) when there is such limitation.   5

Monogamist. One who believes in or practices monogamy.   6

Monogamous. Having to do with monogamy.   16

Monogamy. Marriage to one spouse at one time.   6

Morgue. Place where dead bodies (corpses) of accident victims and unknown persons found dead are kept; for reporters, it refers to the reference library of old newspaper articles, pictures, and so on.   8

Mortal. Referring to a being who must eventually die; causing death; ending in death; a human being.   8

Mortality. The state of having to die eventually; proportion of deaths to the population of the region; death rate; death on a large scale, as from disease or war.   8

Mortgage. The pledging of property to a creditor (one to whom a sum of money is owed) as security for payment; to pledge.   8

Mortician. A funeral director; undertaker.   8

326

Motherless. Without a mother. 7

Nature. The necessary quality or qualities of something; sort; kind; wild state of existence; uncivilized way of life; overall pattern or system; basic characteristic of a person; inborn quality; the sum total of all creation. 15

Nautical. Relating to sailing. (See Additional Words Glossary.) 13

Non-Arab. Not an Arab. 9

Nonbeliever. Not a believer. 9

Noncapitalist. One who is not a capitalist. 9

Non-Catholic. Not a Catholic. 9

Non-Communist. One who is not a Communist. 9

Noncriminal. Not criminal. 9

Nonefficient. Not efficient. 9

Non-English. Not English. 9

Novel. A work of fiction of some length; new; strange; unusual. 14

Obstacle. Something that stands in the way or opposes; an obstruction. 14

Omnipresent. Being present everywhere at all times. 7

Pacify. To bring peace to; to calm; to quiet. 13

Paternal. Of or like a father; fatherly; related on the father's side of the family; inherited or received from the father. 16

Paternalism. The principle or practice of managing the affairs of a country or group of employees as a father manages the affairs of children. 16

Paternity. Fatherhood; state of being a father; origin or descent from a father; provides for citizenship of the child born out of wedlock if fatherhood is established. 16

Patricide. The murder of one's own father. 16

Patriotic. Characteristic of a person who loves his or her country; loving one's country; showing support and loyalty of one's country. 16

Patron. A person who buys regularly at a given store or who goes regularly to a given restaurant, resort, and so on; a regular customer; a wealthy or influential supporter of an artist or writer; one who gives one's wealth or influence to aid an institution, an individual, or a cause; a guardian saint or god. 16

Pedestrian. One who goes on foot. 1

Pediatrician. A doctor who specializes in children's diseases. 11

Perception. The act of becoming aware of something through the senses of seeing, hearing, feeling, tasting, and/or smelling. 11

Period. A portion of time; a portion of time into which something is divided; a punctuation mark that signals a full stop at the end of a sentence; used after abbreviations. 14

Periodical. Referring to publications, such as magazines, that appear at fixed time intervals; a periodical publication. 14

Permission. Act of allowing the doing of something; a consent. 15

Persist. To continue in some course or action even though it is difficult. 14

Philanthropist. A person who shows love toward one's fellow human beings by active efforts to promote their welfare; one who shows goodwill toward others by practical kindness and helpfulness. 16

Philosophy. The study of human knowledge; the love of wisdom and the search for the general laws that give a reasonable explanation of something. 14, 16

Phobia. Extreme fear. 3

Player. One who plays. 1

Politician. A person engaged in politics; a person involved in the science or art of government; a person who seeks advancement or power within an organization by dubious (doubtful) means. 13

Politics. (Although plural, it is usually looked upon as singular.) The science or art of government or of the direction and management of public or state affairs. 13

Polygamist. One who is married to many spouses at the same time. 6

Polygamy. Marriage to many spouses at the same time. 6

Popular. Approved of; admired; liked by most people; referring to the common people or the general public. 15

Population. Total number of people living in a country, city, or any area. 15

Port. Place to or from which ships carry things; place where ships may wait. 4

Portable. Can be carried; easily or conveniently transported. 4

Porter. A person who carries things; one who is employed to carry baggage at a hotel or transportation terminal. 4

Position. An act of placing or arranging; the manner in which a thing is placed; the way the body is placed; the place occupied by a person or thing; the proper or appropriate place; job; a feeling or stand; social standing. 15

Positive. Being directly found to be so or true; real; actual; sure of something; definitely set; confident. 15

Post. A position or employment, usually in government service; an assigned beat; a piece of wood or other material to be used as a support; a place occupied by troops; to inform; to put up (as on a wall); to mail (as a letter). 15

Postnatal. Occurring after birth. 15

Postpone. To put off to a future time; to delay. 15

Postscript. Something added to a letter after the writer's signature; something added to written or printed legal papers. 13

Posture. The placing or carriage of the body or parts of the body; a mental position or frame of mind. 15

Potent. Physically powerful; having great authority; able to influence; strong in chemical effects. 7

Potential. The possible ability or power one may have; having force or power to develop. 7

Precede. To go or come before. 12

Pre-Christian. Referring to the time before there were Christians. 8

Predict. To say before; to foretell; to forecast; to tell what will happen. 8

Preference. The choosing of one person or thing over another; the valuing of one over another; a liking better. 10

Preheat. To heat before. 8

Prehistoric. Referring to the time before history was recorded. 8

328

Prejudge. To judge or decide before. 8

Prejudice. An opinion or judgment made beforehand. 8

Premature. Ripened before. 8

Prenatal. Being or taking place before birth. 15

Preparedness. The state of being prepared or ready. 17

Prerevolutionary. Referring to time before a revolution. 8

Preset. To set before. 8

Preunite. To join together before. 8

Prisoner. One who is kept in prison. 1

Proceed. To go on; to go forward; to carry on an action. 12

Prognosis. A prediction or conclusion regarding the course of a disease and the chances of recovery; a prediction. 11

Prologue. An introduction, often in verse (poetry), spoken or sung before a play or opera; any introductory or preceding event; a preface. 10

Proposal. An offer put forth to be accepted or adopted; an offer of marriage; a plan. 15

Provision. The act of being prepared beforehand; something made ready in advance; a part of an agreement referring to a specific thing. 7

Pseudonym. False name, used by an author to conceal his or her identity; pen name; false name. 9

Psychiatrist. A doctor who specializes in the treatment of persons with mental, emotional, or behavioral disorders. 16

Psychology. The science of the mind; the science that studies the behavior of humans and other animals; the mental or behavioral characteristics of a person or persons. 16

Psychotic. Having to do with or caused by serious mental disease; insane. 16

Question. The act of asking. 3

Reception. The act of receiving or being received; a formal social entertainment; the manner of receiving someone. 11

Recomb. To comb again. 2

Redo. To do again. 2

Reference. A referring or being referred; the giving of a problem to a person, committee, or authority for settlement; a note in a book that sends the reader for information to another book; the name of another person who can offer information or recommendation; the mark, or sign, as a number or letter, directing the reader to a footnote and so on; a written statement of character, qualification, or ability; testimonial. 10

Repay. To pay back. 2

Reporter. A person who gathers information and writes reports for newspapers, magazines, and so on. 4

Rerun. To run again. 2

Retract. To draw back; to take back; to withdraw. 18

Return. To go back. 2

Reversible. Capable of being opposite or contrary to a previous position; having two finished or usable sides (of a fabric, and so on). 17

Return. To go back. 2

Rework. To work again. 2

Rewrite. To write again. 2

Ridicule. Language or actions that make a person the object of mockery or cause one to be laughed at or scorned; to mock or view someone in a scornful way; to hold someone up as a laughingstock; to make fun of. 11

Ridiculous. Unworthy of consideration; absurd (senseless); preposterous. 11

Science. Any area of knowledge in which the facts have been investigated and presented in an orderly manner. 7

Script. Writing that is cursive, printed, or engraved; a piece of writing; a prepared copy of a play for the use of actors. 2

Scripture. Books of the Old and New Testaments; a text or passage from the Bible; the sacred writings of a religion. 2

Seclusion. The act of keeping apart from others; the act of confining in a place hard to find; the act of segregating or hiding; the act of isolating oneself; isolation. 16

Sedition. Conduct consisting of speaking, writing, or acting against an established government or seeking to overthrow it by unlawful means; incitement to rebellion or discontent. 16

Seduce. To tempt to wrongdoing; to persuade into disobedience; to persuade or entice (lead on by exciting desire) into partnership in sexual intercourse. 16

Segregate. To set apart from others; to separate. 16

Semiannual. Twice in a year; every half year. 15

Semiblind. Partly blind. 15

Semicircle. Half circle. 15

Semistarved. Partly starved. 15

Semiwild. Partly wild. 15

Sequence. The following of one thing after another; order; a continuous or related series, with one thing following another. 12, 13

Simplify. To make easier. 18

Solitude. The state of being alone. 17

Sophisticated. Not in a simple, natural, or pure state; worldly-wise, not naive; cultured; highly complicated; complex; experienced. 14

Sophomore. A second-year student in American high schools or colleges; an immature person; one who thinks he or she knows more than he or she does. 14

Spectacle. Something showy that is seen by many (the public); an unwelcome or sad sight. 3

Spectacles. Eyeglasses. 3

Spectacular. Relating to something unusual, impressive, exciting, or unexpected. 3

Spectator. An onlooker; one who views something. 3

Sphere. A round geometrical body whose surface is equally distant at all points from the center; any rounded body; a globe; a ball. 18

Subcommittee. A committee under the original committee.   12

Subfloor. Floor beneath.   12

Submarine. Ship that sails under the sea.   12

Submit. To give in to another; to surrender; to concede; to present for consideration or approval; to present as one's opinion.   15

Subsequent. Following soon after; following in time, place, or order; resulting.   12

Subset. Something that is under the larger set.   12

Substitute. To put in place of another person or thing; one who takes the place of another person; something that is put in place of something else or is available for use instead of something else.   14

Subtraction. The act of taking something away.   12

Succeed. To accomplish what is attempted; to come next in order; to come next after or replace another in an office or position.   12

Suffer. To feel pain or distress.   10

Suicide. Killing of oneself.   8

Sympathy. Sameness of feeling with another; ability to feel pity for another.   8

Synonym. A word having the same or nearly the same meaning as some other word.   9

Technical. Having to do with an art, science, discipline, or profession; having to do with industrial arts, applied sciences, mechanical trades, or crafts; marked by specialization; meaningful or of interest to persons of specialized knowledge rather than to laypersons; marked by a strict legal interpretation.   18.

Technician. A specialist in the details of a subject or skill, especially a mechanical one; any artist, musician, and so on with skilled technique.   18

Technique. The manner in which a scientific or complex task is accomplished; the degree of skill or command of fundamentals shown in any performance.   18

Technology. Applied science; a technical method of achieving a practical purpose; the totality of the means employed to provide objects necessary for human existence and comfort.   18

Telegram. Message sent from a distance.   3

Telegraph. Instrument for sending a message in code at a distance; to send a message from a distance.   2

Telephone. Instrument that sends and receives sound, such as the spoken word, over distance; to send a message by telephone.   2

Telescope. Instrument used to view distant objects.   2

Television. An electronic system for the transmission of visual images from a distance; a television receiving set.   7

Temporary. Lasting for a short period of time.   11

Tenant. A person who holds property; one who lives on property belonging to another; one who rents or leases from a landlord; one who lives in a place.   12

Tension. The act of stretching or the condition of being stretched tight; mental strain.   13

Theocracy. A form of government in which there is rule by a religious group. 5

Theologist. One who is in the field of theology. 6

Theology. The study of religion. 5

Thermal. Pertaining to, using, or causing heat. 18

Thermometer. An instrument for measuring the temperature of a body or of space, especially one consisting of a graduated glass tube with a bulb, usually mercury, that expands and rises in the tube as the temperature increases. 18

Thermostat. An automatic device for regulating temperature; any device that automatically responds to temperature changes and activates switches controlling equipment such as furnaces, refrigerators, and air conditioners. 18

Toxic. Relating to poison. 11

Traction. The act of drawing; the state of being drawn; the force exerted in drawing; friction; in medicine, a pulling or drawing of a muscle, organ, and so on for healing a fracture, dislocation, and so on. 18

Transatlantic. Across the Atlantic Ocean. 10

Transfer. To carry or send from one person or place to another; to cause to pass from one person or place to another; an act of transferring or being transferred. 10

Transhuman. Beyond human limits. 10

Translucent. Permitting light to go through but not permitting a clear view of any object. 14

Transmit. To send from one place to another; to pass on by heredity; to transfer; to pass or communicate news, information, and so on. 15

Transparent. Able to be seen through. 10

Transport. To carry from one place to another. 10

Unable. Not able. 8

Unaided. Not helped. 8

Uncarpeted. Not carpeted. 8

Uncaught. Not caught. 8

Unclaimed. Not claimed. 8

Uncooked. Not cooked. 8

Uniform. Being always the same; a special form of clothing. 3

Union. A joining; a putting together. 3

Unionize. To form into a union. 16

Unique. Being the only one of its kind. 3

Unison. A harmonious agreement; a saying of something together. 3

Universal. Applying to all. 3, 13

Universe. Everything that exists. 3

Unloved. Not loved. 8

Unwed. Not married. 8

Verify. To affirm. 18

Versatile. Capable of turning from one subject, task, or occupation to another; able to do many things well; many-sided; changeable; variable. 17

Visible. Able to be seen; evident; apparent; on hand. 7

Vision. The sense of sight. 7

Vocabulary. A list of words and phrases, usually arranged alphabetically, that are defined or translated from another language; a stock of words possessed by an individual or group.   13

Vocal. Referring to the voice; having voice; oral; freely expressing oneself in speech, usually with force; speaking out.   13

Vocation. A calling; a person's work or profession.   13

Wondrous. Full of wonder.   16

ADDITIONAL WORDS PRESENTED IN *Vocabulary Expansion I*

The number after the meaning refers to the exercise in which the vocabulary word is presented.

Abrogate. To abolish a law, custom, and so on by an authoritative act; to repeal; to do away with; to invalidate.   17

Accreditation.   Act of bringing into favor; a vouching for; a giving authority to.   4

Acrophobia. An abnormal fear of high places.   3

Adversity. A condition marked by unhappiness, misfortune, or distress; a stroke of misfortune; an unfavorable or harmful event; a hardship.   17

Affinity. Close relationship; attraction to another.   10

Agnostic. Professing uncertainty; one who is not for or against; one who doubts that the ultimate cause (God) and the essential nature of things are knowable.   11

Ambidextrous. Able to use both hands equally well.   13

Amortize. The gradual extinction of a debt such as a mortgage or a bond issue by payment of a part of the principal at the time of each periodic interest payment.   8

Anachronism. Something out of time order; an error in chronology in which a person, an object, or an event is assigned an incorrect date or period.   12

Animate. To make alive; to move to action.   15

Annuity. An investment yielding a fixed sum of money, payable yearly.   1

Anthropoid. A person resembling an ape either in stature, walk, or intellect; resembling man, used especially of apes such as the gorilla, chimpanzee, and orangutan; resembling an ape.   6

Anthropomorphic. Giving human shape or characteristics to gods, objects, animals, and so on.   6

Antipathy. A dislike for someone.   9

Antitoxin. Something used against bacterial poison; a substance formed in the body that counteracts a specific toxin; the antibody formed in immunization with a given toxin, used in treating certain infectious diseases or in immunizing against them.   11

Apodal. Having no feet.   5

Archetype. The original pattern or model of a work from which something is made or developed.   5

Audiology. The study of hearing. 9

Audiometer. An instrument used to measure hearing. 9

Automatic. Moving by itself; performed without thinking about it. 1

Automaton. A person or an animal acting in an automatic or mechanical way. 1

Autonomous. Self-governing; functioning independently of other parts. 1

Aversion. A strong dislike; a fixed dislike; a feeling of distaste toward something with a desire to avoid it or turn from it. 17

Avocation. Something a person does in addition to his or her regular work, usually for enjoyment; a hobby. 13

Benediction. A blessing; the expression of good wishes. 9

Bibliophile. A lover of books; a book collector. 16

Bifocals. Pair of glasses with two-part lenses. 1

Bilateral. Involving two sides. 1

Bilingual. Able to use two languages equally well; a bilingual person. 1

Binary. Made up of two parts; twofold; relating to base two. 1

Biopsy. In medicine, the cutting out of a piece of living tissue for examination. 1

Bisexual. Of both sexes; having both male and female organs, as is true of some plants and animals; a person who is sexually attracted by both sexes. 6

Capitulate. To give up; surrender. 8

Caption. The heading of a chapter, section, or page in a book; the title or subtitle of a picture. 8

Centimeter. In the metric system, a unit of measure equal to 1/100 meter (.3937 inch). 4

Centipede. Wormlike animal with many legs. 4

Chronometer. A very accurate clock or watch; an instrument used to measure time. 12

Claustrophobia. An abnormal fear of being confined, as in a room or a small place. 3

Concession. An act of giving in; a right granted by the government or other authority for a specific purpose. 12

Convocation. A group of people called together; an assembly. 13

Corpulent. Fat; fleshy; obese. 8

Creditor. One to whom a sum of money or other thing is due. 4

Creed. A statement of religious belief; a statement of belief; principles. 4

Curator. Head of a department of a museum; one in charge. 9

Decameter. In the metric system, a measure of length containing ten meters, equal to 393.70 inches or 32.81 feet. 4

Decimal. Numbered by tens; based on ten; pertaining to tenths or the number 10; a decimal fraction. 4

Decimate. To take or destroy a tenth part of; to destroy but not completely; to destroy a great number or proportion of. 4

Decimeter. In the metric system, a unit of length equal to 1/10 meter. 4

Defer. To leave to another's opinion or judgment; to delay; to postpone. 10

Deference. Respect; a giving in to another's opinion or judgment. 10

Definitive. Conclusive; final; most nearly complete or accurate. 10

Demography. The statistical study of human populations, including births, deaths, marriages, population movements, and so on. 5

Deportment. Manner of conducting or carrying oneself; behavior; conduct. 4

Depose. To remove from a throne or other high position; to let fall. 15

Derisive. Mocking; jeering. 11

Detain. To stop; to hold; to keep from proceeding; to delay. 12

Detente. Easing of strained relations, especially between nations. 13

Detention. A keeping or holding back; confinement. 13

Dialect. A variety of speech; a regional form of a standard language. 10

Dichotomy. Division into two parts, especially mutually exclusive or contradictory parts; division into two parts, kinds, and so on; a schism. 17

Dictaphone. A machine for recording and reproducing words spoken into its mouthpiece (differs from a tape recorder because it has controls that fit it to use in transcription). 3

Dictum. An authoritative statement; a saying. 3

Disposition. One's usual frame of mind or one's usual way of reacting; a natural tendency. 15

Egotistic. Conceited; very concerned with oneself; selfish; vain. 14

Egregious. Remarkably bad; conspicuously bad; outrageous; flagrant. 16

Emancipate. To set free from servitude or slavery; to set free. 9

Emissary. A person or agent sent on a specific mission. 15

Envision. To imagine something; to picture in the mind. 7

Epidermis. Outermost layer of skin. 11

Equivocate. To use ambiguous language on purpose. 15

Erratic. Wandering; not regular; not stable. 14

Expatriate. To banish; exile; to withdraw oneself from one's native country; to renounce one's citizenship; (as a noun) an exile; (as an adjective) an expatriated person. 16

Expound. To state in detail; to set forth; to explain. 15

Extemporaneous. Done or spoken without special preparation; makeshift. 11

Facsimile. An exact copy; to make an exact copy of. 9

Faction. A number of persons in an organization, group, government, party, and so on, having a common goal, often self-seeking. 9

Finale. The last part; end; the concluding movement of a musical composition; the last scene of an entertainment. 10

Forte. Something a person does very well; a strong point. 18

Forte. (for′ tā). Loud; strong; in a loud and foreceful manner; loudly; strongly. 18

Fratricide. Killing of a brother; may also refer to the killing of a sister. 8

Genealogy. The science or study of one's descent; a tracing of one's ancestors. 6

Generate. To produce; to cause to be; to bring into existence. 6

Genus. A class, kind, or group marked by shared characteristics or by one shared characteristic. 6

Geocentric. Relating to the earth as the center. 2

Grammar. That part of the study of language that deals with the construction of words and word parts (morphology) and the way in which words are arranged relative to each other in utterances (syntax); the study or description of the way language is used. 3

Graphic. Marked by realistic and vivid detail. 1

Graphology. The study of handwriting. 1

Hydraulics. The science dealing with water and other liquids in motion, their uses in engineering, the laws of their actions, and so on. 18

Hydrophobia. An abnormal fear of water; an inability to swallow water when rabies is present. 3

Hydrotherapy. The treatment of disease by the use of water. 18

Hyperbole. Great exaggeration; an overstatement. 14

Illuminate. To give light to; make clear. 14

Indictment. A charge; an accusation. 3

Inference. Something derived by reasoning; something that is not directly stated but suggested in the statement; a logical conclusion that is drawn from statements; deduction. 10

Infidelity. Breach of trust; lack of faith in a religion; unfaithfulness of a marriage partner; adultery. 15

Infinitesimal. Too small to be measured; very minute. 10

Inscription. Something written or engraved on a surface; a brief or informal dedication in a book to a friend. 2

Intercede. To come between; to come between as an influencing force; to intervene. 15

Intercept. To stop or interrupt the course of. 11

Intermittent. Starting or stopping again at intervals; not continuous; coming and going at intervals. 15

Intervene. To come between; to act as an influencing force; to intercede. 15

Introvert. A person who directs his or her thoughts inward; a person who is more interested in his or her own thoughts than what is going on around him or her; *informal*: a shy person. 17

Irrevocable. Not to be recalled, withdrawn, or annulled; irreversible; not able to be changed. 13

Jurisdiction. The right or power of administering justice or law; authority; power; control; the extent of authority; the territory over which such authority extends; the limits in which authority may be exercised. 17

Jurisprudence. A system or body of law; the course of court decisions; the science or philosophy of law; a branch of law. 17

Kilometer. In the metric system, a unit of length equal to one thousand meters. 4

Magnate. A very important or influential person. 15

Malediction. A speaking badly of someone; slander; a curse. 15

Malefactor. Someone who does something bad; a criminal. 15

Manipulation. The act of handling or operating; the act of managing or controlling skillfully or by shrewd use of influence; the act of changing or falsification for one's own purposes or profit. 9

Matriarch. A mother who is the ruler of a family or of a tribe; a woman who is ruler of a family, group, or state. 17

Matricide. The murder of a mother by her son or daughter. 17

Magalopolis. One very large city made up of a number of cities; a vast, populous, continuously urban area. 13

Meter. In the metric system, a unit of length equal to approximately 39.37 inches; an instrument for measuring the amount of something (as water, gas, electricity); an instrument for measuring distance, time, weight, speed, and so forth; a measure of verse. 2

Microbe. A very small living thing; a microorganism. 2

Microfilm. Film on which documents are photographed in a reduced size for storage convenience. 2

Micrometer. An instrument used to measure accurately very small distances, angles, and diameters. 2

Microorganism. An organism so small that it can be seen only under a microscope. 2

Microphone. A device that magnifies weak sounds (non technical definition used as shorthand for the entire sound amplification system); a device to convert sound waves to electrical waves (technical definition). 2

Millimeter. In the metric system, a unit of length equal to 1/1,000 meter (.03937 inch). 4

Misogamist. Hater of marriage. 6

Misogynist. Hater of women. 11

Missile. An object, especially a weapon, intended to be thrown or discharged, as a bullet, arrow, stone, and so on. 15

Monoglot. Person who knows, speaks, or writes only one language; speaking and writing only one language. 5

Monologue. A long speech by one person; a dramatic sketch performed by one actor. 10

Monophobia. Abnormal fear of being alone. 5

Monopoly. Exclusive control of a commodity or service in a given market; control that makes possible the fixing of prices and the elimination of free competition. 5

Monorail. A single rail serving as a track for trucks or cars suspended from it or balanced on it. 5

Monosyllable. A word consisting of one syllable. 8

Monotone. Speech not having any change in pitch; to speak in an unvaried tone. 5

Monotonous. Changeless; dull; uniform; having no variety. 5

Mortify. To cause to feel shame; to punish (one's body) or control (one's physical desires or passions) by self-denial, fasting, and the like, as a means of religious or ascetic (severe) discipline. 8

Nautical. Pertaining to sailors, ships, or navigation. 7

Novice. Someone new at something; a rookie; a beginner. 14

Obstinate. Stubborn; tenacious. 14

Oligarchy. A form of government in which there is rule by a few (usually a privileged few). 5

Omnibus. A large bus; an *omnibus* bill is a legislative bill that carries a mixture of provisions. 7

Omnipotent. All-powerful. 7

Omniscient. All-knowing. 7

Orthography. The part of language study that deals with correct spelling. 1

Pacifist. One who is against war. 13

Pedagogue. A teacher. 11

Pedestal. A base or bottom support. 1

Pedicure. Care of the feet, toes, and nails. 9

Perceptive. Being aware; having insight, understanding, or intuition, as a *perceptive* analysis of the problems involved. 11

Perfidious. Violating good trust; treacherous; deceitful; deliberately faithless. 15

Perimeter. A measure of the outer part or boundary of a closed plane figure; boundary line of a closed plane figure. 14

Periodic. Taking place, occurring, or appearing at regular intervals. 14

Periphery. The outer part or boundary of something. 14

Periscope. An instrument used by a submarine to see all around. 14

Personification. A figure of speech in which a nonliving thing or idea is made to appear as having the qualities of a person. 9

Pervert. To lead astray; to turn or lead from the right way; to corrupt; (as a noun) a person who has been led astray; a person who practices sexual perversion, that is, one who deviates from the normal in sexual habits. 17

Philanderer. A person who makes love without serious intentions; a person who flirts; a person who has many love affairs; a person who has many love affairs without intentions of marriage. 16

Philanthrope. A lover of mankind; a philanthropist; a humanitarian. 16

Phonetics. A study dealing with speech sounds and their production. 2

Phonics. Study of the relationship between letter symbols of a written language and the sounds they represent; a method used in teaching word recognition in reading. 2

Podiatrist. Foot doctor. 6

Podium. A raised platform for the conductor of an orchestra; a dais. 1

Polyglot. A person who knows, speaks, or writes many languages; speaking or writing many languages. 6

Polygon. A closed plane figure with several angles and sides. 6

Posterior. In the rear; later; following after; coming after in order; succeeding; located behind; the buttocks. 13

Posterity. Future generations; all of one's descendants (offspring). 13

Posthumously. After death. 13

Postmortem. Happening or performed after death; referring to an examination of a human body after death; autopsy. 13

Potentate. A person possessing great power: a ruler; a monarch. 7

Prerogative. The right or privilege that no one else has; special superiority or privilege that one may get from an official position, office, and so on. 17

Prescription. A doctor's written directions for the preparation and use of medicine; an order; direction; rule. 2

Procession. A parade, as a funeral *procession*; any continuous course. 12

Proficient. Knowing something very well; able to do something very well. 10

Protract. To draw out; to lengthen in time; to extend forward or outward; to prolong in time. 18

Proposition. A plan or something put forth for consideration or acceptance. 15

Provoke. To stir up anger or resentment; to irritate. 13

Pseudopodium. False foot. 9

Pseudoscience. A false science. 9

Psychic. A person sensitive to nonphysical forces; a medium; lying outside the sphere of physical science or knowledge; immaterial or spiritual in origin or force; marked by extraordinary or mysterious sensitivity, perception, or understanding. 16

Psychopath. A person suffering from mental disease. 16

Psychosis. Any severe form of mental disturbance or disease, which has far-reaching and deep disorders of behavior; mental derangement by defective or lost contact with reality. 16

Recession. The act of going back; in economics, the decline of business activity. 12

Remission. A temporary stopping or lessening of a disease; a pardon. 15

Retentive. Having the ability to retain or keep in things; tenacious, as a *retentive* memory; having a good memory. 12

Scribe. A writer, author; a public writer or secretary; in Scripture and Jewish history, a man of learning. 2

Secede. To withdraw from. 12

Sophistry. Faulty reasoning; unsound or misleading but clever and plausible (appearing real) argument or reasoning. 14

Speculate. To think about something by viewing it from all sides; to take part in any risky business venture. 3

Stamina. Staying power; resistance to fatigue, illness, and the like. 14

Stethoscope. A hearing instrument used in examining the heart, lungs, and so on. 2

Subscription. An agreement; a promise in writing to pay some money; an agreement to receive something and pay for it. 12

Subversion. A systematic attempt to overthrow or undermine a government or political system by persons working secretly within the country involved; anything that tends to overthrow. 17

Surrogate. A substitute; a deputy; a person appointed to act in the place of another; something that serves as a substitute. 17

Susceptible. Easily influenced by or affected with; especially liable to. 11

Syllable. A vowel or a group of letters with one vowel sound. 8

Symbol. Something that stands for or represents another thing; an object used to represent something abstract. 8

Symmetry. Balanced form or arrangement; balance on both sides. 8

Symphony. Harmony of sound; harmony of any kind. 8

Symptom. In medicine, a condition that results from a disease and serves as an aid in diagnosis; a sign or token that indicates the existence of something else. 8

Synchronize. To cause to agree in rate or speed; to occur at the same time. 12

Synthesis. A putting together of two or more things to form a whole. 8

Technocracy. Government by technical experts. 18

Telemeter. An instrument that measures distance; instrument that sends information to a distant point. 2

Tempo. The rate of speed at which a musical composition is supposed to be played; rate of activity. 11

Tenacious. Stubborn; tough; holding or tending to hold strongly to one's views, opinions, rights, and so on; retentive, as a *tenacious* memory. 12

Thermography. A process of writing or printing involving the use of heat; a technique for detecting and measuring variations of heat emitted by various regions of the body and transforming them into signals that can be recorded photographically—used to diagnose abnormal or diseased underlying conditions. 18

Thermophilic. Growing at a high temperature; requiring high temperature for development. 18

Toxicologist. One who specializes in the study of poisons. 11

Tractable. Easily managed or controlled; easy to deal with; obedient. 18

Transcript. A written or typewritten copy of an original; a copy or reproduction of any kind. 2

Unify. To make or form into one. 3

Unilateral. Occurring on one side only; done by one only; one-sided. 3

Untenable. Not able to be held or defended. 12

Venture. A risky or dangerous undertaking. 7

Visa. Something stamped or written on a passport that grants an individual entry to a country. 7

Visage. The face; the appearance of the face or its expression. 7

Visionary. A person who sees visions. 7

Visor. The projecting front brim of a cap for shading the eyes. 7

Vociferous. Of forceful, aggressive, and loud speech; clamorous. 13